Use in

She

p. 170

p 176 interp. of The Law

p. 183 Torah

p. 184 eternal Torah

p. 199

p. 210

p. 214

p. 221

* p. 225

repentance p. 226

interpreting O.T. - pp. 226-227

p. 51 - Total obedience - whole heart.

FROM THE EXILE TO CHRIST

FROM THE EXILE TO CHRIST

A Historical Introduction to Palestinian Judaism

WERNER FOERSTER

Translated by

GORDON E. HARRIS

FORTRESS PRESS
PHILADELPHIA

This is a translation of *Neutestamentliche Zeitgeschichte I: Das Judentum Palästinas zur Zeit Jesu und der Apostel,* 3rd revised edn., published in 1959 by Furche Verlag, Hamburg.

Library of Congress Catalog Card Number 64-18151

ISBN 0-8006-0978-6

First American Edition 1964

Sixth Printing 1981

9096A81 Printed in the United States of America 1-978

FROM THE PREFACE TO THE FIRST GERMAN EDITION

THE New Testament does not speak about an idea such as that of love, or even of the Fatherhood of God; it testifies rather to an event—it proclaims "history." Thus it is essential (as in all genuine history) that even though the testimonies relating to this history—for instance in the Gospels—do not portray the event in every detail, they should portray its fundamental and decisive features accurately and credibly. If the Gospels were merely the poetic form of some idea, they might for that reason be more widely read and treasured by many people, but they would no longer be capable of making any Christian community come together. But even if everything depends in this way on the actual historicity of the events recorded, this, strange though it may and must sound, is not the decisive thing. A man can study the Gospels, the historical event known as "Jesus," at length and in depth, without grasping what really "happened" at that time. The historical event, "Jesus," is a supra-historical event, not as something *alongside* its historical actuality but precisely *within* it. A man can be gripped by this special quality in it, even though his knowledge of the historical event "Jesus," is defective.

So it is that both these things, which we shall call, for short, the historical and the supra-historical, are inextricably bound up with each other; and in such a way that every representation of the historical event involves the risk of missing its actual significance and content while, on the other hand, a proper grasp of the latter provides points of departure for a true understanding of the historical process. For example, it is certainly not immaterial for the correct interpretation of the Gospels whether the Pharisees were aiming at merely an externalised, dead righteousness of works or whether Jesus' attack upon them went to a deeper level; on the other hand a true conception of Jesus' mission can help us to see the profundities in His dispute with Pharisaism.

Because this is so, a "History of New Testament Times" can render a service and offer help to the Church and to the Bible reader. . . .

In conclusion I wish to thank all those who have helped me in the investigation of sources and subject, and especially Professor Gerhard Kittel who gave the manuscript his kindly perusal.

W. FOERSTER

Münster/W., January 1940

FROM THE PREFACE TO THE SECOND GERMAN EDITION

The second edition has been completely revised. The first compendious, general section has been abridged and rendered more concise (especially at the beginning); I did not, however, feel able to drop the Babylonian exile as the point of departure for the narrative, partly in regard to the handling of the material, and partly because the recollection of some of my lectures in captivity showed me how necessary it is to bridge the gap between the Old and New Testaments. I greet any of my former listeners in camps Jabbeke and Zedelghem into whose hands this book might fall.

At the end of the preface to the first edition I thanked "all those who have helped me in the investigation of sources and subject." At that time I was unable to mention, without jeopardising the publication of the book, the man to whom I owed special thanks, the former Chief Rabbi of the Jewish community in Münster, Dr. Steinthal. In selfless fashion he gave me access to the Talmud in weekly meetings over many years; I should like to think that his exertions will not have been without fruit. . . .

W. FOERSTER

Münster/W., 4th December 1954

FROM THE PREFACE TO THE THIRD GERMAN EDITION

In this edition, following from the publication of the finds in Cave I at Qumran, and from the fact that further publications of texts will only ensue gradually, an attempt has been made to place in the context of Jewish history the movement on which the finds give information. Chapter IV has been entirely, and chapters V and XIV almost entirely, revised.

W. FOERSTER

Münster/W., 7th May 1959

TRANSLATOR'S ACKNOWLEDGEMENTS

THE translator wishes to thank the author, Dr. Werner Foerster, for his help with the documentation of this English edition. He is also indebted to the Rev. Dr. J. Y. Campbell of Cambridge for checking many of the more difficult references, and to Rabbi Dr. I. Lerner of Jesmond, Newcastle-upon-Tyne and W. Lishman, Esq., of Hexham for translating some of the Hebrew and Greek passages which were not otherwise available in English.

GORDON E. HARRIS

List of Abbreviations

Ab.	= Pirqe Aboth
Ass. Mos.	= Assumption of Moses
A. Zar.	= Abodah Zarah
B.B.	= Baba Bathra
Ber.	= Berakhoth
B.K.	= Baba Kamma
B.M.	= Baba Metzia
B.T.	= Babylonian Talmud
Hag.	= Hagigah
Hor.	= Horayoth
Hull.	= Hullin
J.B.L.	= *Journal of Biblical Literature and Exegesis*
J.T.	= Jerusalem Talmud
Jub.	= Book of Jubilees
Ker.	= Kerithoth
Kidd.	= Kiddushin
M.	= Mishnah
Makk.	= Makkoth
Meg.	= Megillah
Men.	= Menahoth
Midr.	= Midrash
M.Kat.	= Moed Katan
Naz.	= Nazir
Ned.	= Nedarim
Pes.	= Pesahim
Pes. K.	= Pesikta Kahana
Ps. Sol.	= Psalms of Solomon
R.	= Midrash Rabbah
R.G.G.	= *Die Religion in Geschichte und Gegenwart*
R. Sh.	= Rosh ha-Shanah
Sanh.	= Sanhedrin
Shab.	= Shabbath
Sot.	= Sotah
Strack-Billerbeck	= H. L. Strack and P. Billerbeck *Kommentar zum Neuen Testament aus Talmud und Midrasch*, 4 vols. in 5, München 1922–28.
Sukk.	= Sukkah
Sybill.	= Sybilline Oracles
Taan.	= Taanith

Tanh. B.	= Tanhuma, ed. S. Buber
Test.	= Testaments of the Twelve Patriarchs
Th. L. Z.	= *Theologische Literaturzeitung*
Th.R., N.F.	= *Theologische Rundschau, Neue Folge*
Th. W.	= *Theologisches Wörterbuch zum Neuen Testament*, edd. G. Kittel and G. Friedrich, Stuttgart 1933, *et seq.*
Tos.	= Tosefta
Yom.	= Yoma
Z.N.W.	= *Zeitschrift für die Neutestamentliche Wissenschaft*
Z.D.P.V.	= *Zeitschrift des Deutschen Palästina-Vereins*
Z.Th.K.	= *Zeitschrift für Theologie und Kirche*

CONTENTS

Part I

THE HISTORICAL SITUATION

INTRODUCTION

Israel and Judaism

An alert reader of the Bible may well be struck by the fact that among a variety of important concepts lacking in the Old Testament, but to be found in the New, is that of the "Jew." In the Old Testament we find reference only to Haman, "the enemy of the Jews," (Esther VIII.1 and IX.10), but the New Testament speaks repeatedly of the "Jews." This arises from the fact that those who survived Nebuchadnezzar's destruction of Jerusalem and maintained the historical continuity of the people of Israel were for the most part members of the tribe of Judah. But the emergence of the name "Jew" also indicates that with the Babylonian captivity (the "Exile") a new factor had come into the history of the children of Israel. The terms "children of Israel" and "the Jews" denote two different stages in the history of the same people.[1]

It is fundamental to this history at every period that the people of Israel not only saw itself as guided by a living, personal Power, but also as owing its existence as a people to this power, that is, to God. It sees itself as chosen out of all nations by an unconditioned act of the divine will. The goal of this election is salvation for all humanity; "in you all the families of the earth will be blessed." (Gen. XII.3 mg.)

In the course of a lengthy history beginning with the "patriarchs" *Israel* had been welded together into a people and led into an independent existence as a state. It expresses its awareness of this guidance with jubilant thanksgiving: "Happy are you, O Israel! Who is like you, a people saved by the Lord, the shield of your help, and the sword of your triumph!" (Deut. XXXIII.29). The prophet solemnly proclaims the responsibility that goes along with election: "You only have

[1] On the linguistic usage "Israelite," "Hebrew," "Jew," see G. Kittel and G. Friedrich, *Theologisches Wörterbuch zum Neuen Testament*, henceforth cited as *Th.W.*, Stuttgart 1933 *et seq.*, VOL. III, pp. 356–394; see also the literature listed there on p. 356.

I known of all the families of the earth; therefore I will punish you for all your iniquities." (Amos III.2). Outwardly there was nothing to distinguish this people from the other peoples and nations of its time. But God had made His covenant with them; He led them through many dangers; He claimed their obedience. Their whole life, the struggles against their enemies, the administration of justice, the performance of the cult and the life of the individual stood under the claim of God. This claim found a certain embodiment in a series of laws, headed by the ten commandments. These laws took account of the private, public, legal, ceremonial and political life of the people. God's claim was, however, especially voiced in the preaching of the prophets. They were concerned with moral and religious matters, with justice and righteousness in society, with trust in God in the making of political decisions, with God or idols in questions of religion and worship. The history of Israel was one of constant falling and rising again, of constant failure and reorientation. The prophets' struggle for the obedience of the people was carried even into prophetic circles; there the "prophets of doom" and the "prophets of salvation" stood in mutual antithesis. The former proclaimed the living and the zealous God, who even over the chosen people can and will exercise His rights as a sovereign to bring judgment and evil upon them, but who also can and will work out His saving purposes through the darkness of judgment. The latter, however, viewed God's relationship to His people rather in the same light as did the pagan peoples; they regarded the God of Israel as the One who, come what may, was there for His people's benefit.

The judgment proclaimed by the "prophets of doom" came about. The kingdom that David had welded together split under his grandson Rehoboam into two parts, the northern and the southern kingdom, the "kingdom of Israel," and the "kingdom of Judah." In 722 B.C. Samaria, the capital of the northern kingdom, was conquered by the Assyrians and the ruling circles were taken into exile, where they eventually merged with the surrounding population. In line with the Assyrian custom foreign tribes were settled in their place; these intermarried with the remnants of the people of Israel and blended veneration of the God of Israel with that of their own gods (II Kings XVII.24–41). In 587 the Babylonian king Nebuchadnezzar was responsible for bringing the kingdom of Judah to an end. A section of the people, comprising the chief officials, soldiers and artisans, had already been deported ten years previously; now Jerusalem itself was captured, the temple destroyed and the remainder of the population, with the exception of the peasants, transplanted to Babylon (II Kings XXIV.8–16; XXV.1–22).

That the history of the children of Israel continued at all after this is due, historically speaking, to the fact that the Babylonians permitted the deportees from Judea to live in enclosed settlements on the banks of the Euphrates. Thus they were able to preserve their tribal ties and their national individuality. They were therefore still, in a certain sense, a "people" when in 537 B.C. the Persian king Cyrus, who had conquered Babylon, gave permission for the reconstruction of the temple, and the deportees were able, some little time later, to return once more to their own country.

It was during this Babylonian captivity that *Judaism* arose. Prior to the destruction of Jerusalem most Jews had given no credence to the preaching of the "prophets of doom." Heathen ways had been widely adopted in Jerusalem. The fall of the city, however, set the seal to the message of the "prophets of doom." Impressed by this judgment, the Babylonian exiles turned from their own and their fathers' ways, acknowledged with an earnest repentance the judgment of God, and resolved to break with all godlessness and paganism. They collected the sayings of the "prophets of doom," the traditions regarding the history of their people and the laws pertaining to political, private, public and ceremonial life, and thus preserved the guiding principles by which they henceforth intended to walk. Thus they created the bond which, from then on, was to keep the "children of Israel" together. They did not relinquish the hope of renewed national independence; but the "prophets of doom" had declared that salvation lay not in independent political activity, but in waiting upon God's help; so the exiles took upon themselves the downfall of Judah and affirmed it as God's judgment. Their earnest hopes for a change in this respect were now pinned upon the day of salvation which God Himself would bring to pass. Thus the lack of national independence is not only an historic fact of Judaism but, at the same time, one of its essential features. This is clear for several reasons: after the Exile not all the deportees seized the opportunity to return to Palestine; in the Maccabean period the setting up of an independent Jewish state resulted in no greater flow of Jews back to the promised land; and even at the present time not all Jews aspire to return to the state of Israel. Ever since the Babylonian captivity Judaism has been "on the move," on the move between judgment and grace. "Judaism" is therefore comprised of the children of Israel, who know themselves to be on the move, driven from normal independent existence as a people, driven from the land of their fathers because of their sins, on the move towards a time of salvation, which God Himself will bring to pass, when He will gather the dispersed of His people out of the nations and turn the captivity of Israel, on the move under the cloud of God's judgment and God's grace. Life in exile is thus an essential feature of Judaism.

A second characteristic feature of Judaism, bound up closely with being "on the move," is the irrational fact that prophecy gradually died out. Judaism itself was sensible of this: "There is no longer any prophet, and there is none among us who knows how long" (Ps. LXXIV.9).

I Maccabees IX.27 declares: "Thus there was great distress in all Israel, such as had not been since the time that the prophets ceased to appear among them"; a definite and specifiable interval had elapsed, therefore, since the time the prophets ceased to appear. Similar statements are made in I Maccabees IV.46, XIV.41 and The Prayer of Azariah vs. 15.[2] The Church Father, Origen (3rd century A.D.),[3] mentions as

[2] *Tos. Sot.* XIII.2 quoted H. L. Strack and P. Billerbeck, *Kommentar zum Neuen Testament aus Talmud und Midrasch*, henceforth cited as *Strack-Billerbeck*, 4 vols. in 5, München 1922–28, VOL. I, p. 127 under b: "When Haggai, Zechariah and Malachi, the last of the prophets, died, the Holy Spirit disappeared from Israel"; further references in *Strack-Billerbeck ibid.* Cf. II Baruch LXXXV.3.

[3] *Contra Celsum* VII.8; A. Schlatter, *Geschichte Israels von Alexander dem Grossen bis Hadrian*, henceforth cited as *Geschichte Israels*, 3rd edn. Stuttgart 1925, note 239. Origen's pronouncement reproduces the opinion of the Pharisees who became dominant after 70 A.D. Before this date, however, mention was frequently made of men with prophetic gifts or in possession of the Holy Spirit: (1) Josephus calls the Hasmonean, John Hyrcanus, happy because God had esteemed him worthy of the three greatest privileges, the government of his nation, the dignity of the high priesthood, and prophecy, *Jewish Antiquities*, henceforth cited as *Antiquities*,

a generally held conviction the rabbinic precept that the Spirit had been taken from the Jewish community. The work of the rabbis cannot be understood apart from this conviction.

God was silent, and instead of the God whose guiding hand could be traced in Israel's history, instead of the prophets who caused the divine summons to resound again and again in relation to public and private life, there now stood the Law, i.e. the account of Israel's special history in the past, and the provisions established once and for all in relation to political, legal, ceremonial and private life. The former introduced a retrospective feature into the piety of Judaism, the latter led to a tension: for the Law reckoned with a political independence which now no longer existed. The Jews considered themselves bound to this Law in its entirety, and yet, for its execution, they were bound to the foreign "occupying power," whose standpoint and interests were necessarily different from those of the Law.

Two things delineate the movement of repentance from which Judaism developed, and these two things also constitute its difficulties. The rejection of the syncretism of the pre-Exilic period during the Exile culminated in the fact that the Jews in Babylon did not transfer their allegiance to the gods of their captors, as subject peoples otherwise easily did, but held to the God of their fathers. Positively, this is particularly evident from their observance of the customs which set them apart from the pagan peoples: *circumcision*, which the Babylonians did not practise, *the Sabbath* and *the commandments regarding purity and impurity*. Insofar as these things received the status of confessional acts, the danger of degeneration into purely external piety was a growing menace. And this danger has gone along with Judaism ever since. It was rendered even greater by the

---

xiii.10,7 (§§ 299f.); cf. in this connexion Jn. xi.49–51. (2) Josephus ascribes prophetic gifts (in the sense of foretelling the future) to members of the Essene sect, *Antiquities*, xiii.11,2 (§ 311); xv.10,5 (§§ 373–379); xvii.13,3 (§ 346); *Jewish War*, henceforth cited as *War*, ii.8,12 (§ 159). This agrees with the fact that the writer of the Qumran "Hymns" is conscious of being endowed with the Holy Spirit, see Ch. iv. The refusal to acknowledge the inspiration of the "Teacher of Righteousness" is probably one of the points at which Pharisaism was divorced from the Essene movement. (3) The various messianic movements of the Zealots are inconceivable unless their instigators had regarded themselves as inspired, see Ch. vi pp. 88ff. See also E. Fascher, *Prophetes*, Giessen 1927, pp. 161–164.

fact that the movement for repentance was directed at the whole people. Any popular movement runs the risk of placing the greatest emphasis upon what is visible and therefore can be controlled, to the neglect of weightier matters which are hidden from human gaze. In Judaism, therefore, the things that can be established by means of laws and decrees receive, almost automatically, a dangerous importance. Indicative of this are the points named in Nehemiah x.30ff. as those to which the people under Nehemiah solemnly bound themselves by oath. The scribes in Jesus' day and after directed most of their energies to such outwardly ascertainable things as the tithing of "mint and dill and cummin" while the "weightier matters of the law, justice and mercy and faith," although certainly not forgotten, did not receive the attention which they deserved; the more so because, in the collection of laws contained in the Pentateuch legal matters, questions of custom, etc., stood without any distinction alongside the command to love God and one's neighbour. Only a prophet would have been able to give new directions in this respect; but with the destruction of Jerusalem God let the Jewish people go their own way, and thus demonstrated to all what results when man, with the best will in the world, of himself, seeks to repent. We shall repeatedly encounter this struggle for a right understanding of what the Law requires, and the sheer overwhelming might of external piety.

The other factor which moulded the movement of repentance during the Exile was the *belief in election.* For the "prophets of doom" the election of Israel was an unmotivated operation of God's love (Deut. vii.7f.) upon which man could stake no claim (Am. iii.2), but for the "prophets of salvation," on the contrary, God was indissolubly bound up with His people, who had a claim upon His help. The catastrophe which befell Jerusalem gave the lie to this expectation, and so the captives in Babylon cut themselves loose from it: "Your prophets have seen for you false and deceptive visions; they have not exposed your iniquity . . ." (Lam. ii.14; cf. iv.13 and Zech. i.6). The comparison with other peoples was given up: "For the iniquity of the daughter of my people has been greater than the sin of Sodom" (Lam. iv.6 mg.); the lament, "Alas, for we have sinned," runs through the history of Judaism. And in answer Deutero-Isaiah[4] declares the divine comfort: "Comfort, comfort my people, says your God." (Is. XL.1.) But this prophet was of relatively slight significance for developing Judaism. The view that the chosen people were essentially different from the peoples round about, that it required *only* repentance to compel God to bring about the day of salvation, became a powerful determinant of Jewish history. Political sanctions to force the whole nation to repent and turn away from paganism were not at the disposal of the Babylonian captives, nor indeed of the later Jews. Repentance had to proceed from the people itself. Thus right into the New Testament period the history of Judaism was marked by a series of ever recurring movements for repentance, which sought by means of an ever more precise understanding of the "Law" to unite the whole nation in perfect obedience, so that the day of salvation proclaimed by the prophets might come about. The struggle for the inclusion of the whole nation then created the split between those who desired to keep the Law and the "ungodly." The more the Law was viewed as the sum of specifiable obligations, the fulfilment of which required only a good will, the deeper this split within the nation grew, and the more did election become for the pious a ground for pride and glory.

In time of political independence the drawing of a line of demarcation to exclude members of other nations presents no problem. Because the Jews in Babylon were united around the Law, the *preservation of racial purity* by avoidance of heathen ways became a duty. Blood-relationship to the patriarchs became important, as we see by the lists in Ezra II and Nehemiah VII as well as by the genealogies in the source P[5] and in Chronicles. It was, however, this very rallying round the Law which then opened up the possibility of admitting as proselytes members of other races, who desired to keep the Law.

The story of Judaism is therefore the story of the children of Israel who, after the destruction of Jerusalem, feeling themselves to be labouring under the silence and the judgment of God, bind themselves to strive earnestly never to depart from the God of their fathers, as revealed by the history of their

[4] Is. XL–LV. This prophet wrote during the Babylonian Captivity.
[5] On P see p. 21.

people, nor from His will, as declared to them by the traditional laws of their people.

From this there arose in consequence three expedients or, as it were, *three pillars*, which were intended to and did uphold Judaism in this altered situation.

First, *the Canon*. In Ezekiel xx the prophet gives a review of Israel's history as a key to understanding what has happened; the so-called deuteronomic history[6] presents the whole history of the people from the standpoint of showing how God's guidance has been manifest in disobedience and judgment, in obedience and grace; Deutero-Isaiah alludes again and again to the manner in which the "former things," i.e. God's judgment, have come about (Is. XLII.9; XLVIII.3; cf. Zech. I.6); Psalm LXXVIII is a meditation upon this very history; the solemn engagement under Nehemiah to keep the Law mentions some important points from the Law: all of which indicates the lively necessity continually to recall to mind the sacred Law and history. In this necessity lies the inner motive for the formation of the Canon.

Secondly, the deportees in Babylon could no longer participate in the temple-cult. Their gatherings in a foreign land served them as a substitute; in these the history of their people was brought to remembrance and the Law recollected. Thus the basis was provided for the rise of the *Synagogue*.

This presupposes a third fact: namely, that there were men available to expound the Scriptures. In the time of Israel's political independence they were the priests. We shall see, however, that the movements for repentance originated in increasing measure not from the priests, but from laymen, who meditated on God's Law day and night (Ps. I.1). Thus arose a class of *Rabbis*.

The canon, the synagogue and rabbinic learning are the three pillars of Judaism which supported it at a time when all other props collapsed.

[6] Joshua, Judges, I and II Samuel, I and II Kings.

Part I

THE HISTORICAL SITUATION

In the New Testament, and particularly in the Gospels, we find a series of historical phenomena which are new in relation to the Old Testament: Herod, the king and tetrarch, Pharisees and tax-collectors, Galileans and Samaritans, God-fearers and proselytes. We also encounter important concepts which are missing in the Old Testament, e.g. the antithesis between "this world" and "the world to come." It is the task of this section to bridge the gap between the Old and New Testaments, and to sketch the historical and spiritual developments which Judaism underwent in the period from the Babylonian exile to the time of Jesus and the apostles. This historical survey will end and focus at the point where, after a period of ferment and self-questioning, Judaism entered as a matter of history and of deliberate choice upon the course which it was to follow through the centuries. That point will be the final destruction of Jerusalem in A.D. 135, after which the Jews were forbidden access to Jerusalem, and the last glimmer of political independence was extinguished. In the decades before and after this event the foundations of the Talmud were laid.

CHAPTER I

FROM THE BABYLONIAN EXILE TO NEHEMIAH

The Children of Israel at the Beginning of the Exile

WHERE at all do we find "Children of Israel" in the period immediately after the destruction of Jerusalem? First of all, in *Judea*. The little country of Judea was not completely depopulated as a result of the two deportations. The total number left behind would by no means have been small. A fair proportion of them fled to Egypt after the assassination of Gedaliah, who had been appointed governor by the conquerors (II Kings XXV.22–26; Jer. XL–XLIV). Of those left behind there would certainly have been many who paid homage to their conquerors' gods, or worshipped the Canaanite Baal; but there were not lacking those who remained faithful to the God of their fathers (Jer. XLI.4ff.).

At the time *Galilee* and the area around *Samaria* were inhabited by the remaining population of the kingdom of Israel. But nothing creative was forthcoming either from the latter, who had intermarried with the new colonial settlers, or from those left behind in Judea.

The above-mentioned flight into Egypt gave rise to an Egyptian Jewish community in *Lower and Upper Egypt* (Jer. XLIV.1), who, according to Jeremiah XLIV.15ff., were determined to carry on the worship of pagan gods.

According to Deuteronomy XVII.16 it had been the practice for Jewish kings to sell their subjects to Egypt. From a series of papyri discovered at Aswan on the *southern border of Egypt*[1]

[1] A. H. Sayce and A. E. Cowley, *Aramaic Papyri discovered at Assuan*, London 1906; E. Sachau, *Aramäische Papyri und Ostraka aus einer jüdischen Militärkolonie in Elephantine*, Leipzig 1911; E. G. Kraeling, *The Brooklyn Museum Aramaic Papyri*, New Haven 1953. Cf. A. Vincent, *La religion des judéo-araméens d'Elephantine*, Paris 1937.

we know of the existence in about 400 B.C. of a Jewish military colony charged with keeping watch upon the border. This colony imported and extended the syncretism which had been the rule in Judea before the days of Josiah. After the year 400 it disappears from our view; there was no possibility of anything creative coming from that direction either.

The historically decisive element in the situation was the body of people deported to *Babylon.*[2] They were settled in the area around Nippur and enjoyed a sort of conditional liberty, the majority of them probably as tenant-farmers. They could acquire property, hold meetings and even correspond with people left in Judea. Family and tribal ties, along with their native social structure, were preserved.

According to their personal outlook many would even have gone over to their captors' gods; others, taking their cue from the "prophets of salvation," would have regarded the destruction of Jerusalem as merely a passing episode. The historical books of the Old Testament (with the exception of Chronicles, which came later!) impress firmly upon the idol-worshippers that idolatory had always been the cause of Israel's downfall; Deutero-Isaiah likewise attacks them (Is. XL.17ff.; XLIV.9ff; XLVI.1ff.). In his letter to the exiles (Jer. XXIX.8ff.) Jeremiah directs his attack against the "prophets of salvation." For the seventy years for which, in his view, the Exile will last, signify that the present generation will not experience the return, the day of salvation. But Deutero-Isaiah, Jeremiah and Ezekiel all direct the exiles' gaze towards the salvation to come (Ezek. XXXVII).

[2] It used to be assumed that a minority remained in Palestine, while the majority were deported to Babylon; R. Kittel in his *Geschichte des Volkes Israel*, Stuttgart 1927–29, VOL. III, pp. 61f., estimates 15–20,000 in Palestine, 50–70,000 deported; E. Sellin in *Geschichte des israelitisch-jüdischen Volkes*, henceforth cited as *Geschichte*, Lepizig 1932, VOL. II gives even higher figures. Now, however, the number of "exiles" together with women and children is estimated at approximately 30–45,000; thus K. Galling in *Zeitschrift des Deutschen Palästina Vereins*, henceforth cited as *Z.D.P.V.*, LXX (1954), p. 22; L. Ehrlich, *Geschichte Israels*, Berlin 1958, p. 74; E. Janssen, *Juda in der Exilszeit*, henceforth cited as *Juda*, Göttingen 1956, p. 121. Accordingly the importance for the new outlook of the Jewish people of those who remained behind is valued more highly than has, in consequence of the account by the Chronicler, been the case hitherto; thus M. Noth, *The History of Israel*, 2nd edn., revised translation by P. R. Ackroyd, London 1960, pp. 292ff.; Janssen, *Juda, passim.* But the pre-eminent rôle of the Babylonian exiles remains unchallenged.

Thus with the exiles in Babylon there began a new chapter in the history of Israel. "It is the greatest example in all history of the rebirth of a nation from within."[3] In exile Israel was delivered from the evil impulse to idolatry, says a later rabbinic pronouncement.[4] Zechariah I.6 looks back upon the great movement for repentance during the Babylonian captivity in these words: "But my words and my statutes, which I commanded my servants the prophets, did they not overtake your fathers? So they repented and said, as the Lord of hosts purposed to deal with us for our ways and deeds, so has he dealt with us." Thus the brilliance of Babylonian culture and religion faded, the deceitful words of the "prophets of salvation" were silenced; the "Gola," as the deportees called themselves in Hebrew, took the destruction of Jerusalem as the merited judgment of God upon themselves (Lam. I.18 and *seriatim*; Ezra V.12) and separated themselves from heathen ways. The fact that Ezekiel XX surprisingly often stresses that neglect of the Sabbath, along with idolatry, was *the* sin of the fathers, indicates a point which made plain among the exiles who had "repented" and who had not.

Not only the far-flung exiles, but also many of those left in Palestine, learnt to surrender their hopes of an imminent salvation, in order to submit wholeheartedly to divine guidance and separate themselves from heathen ways.

The Return under Cyrus and Reconstruction of the Temple

In 538 B.C. the Babylonian kingdom, which had captured and destroyed Jerusalem, fell into the hands of Cyrus, king of Persia. The latter gave permission a year later for the reconstruction of the Temple and, to that end, made restitution of the temple-vessels pillaged by Nebuchadnezzar. Judea did not thereby have its political independence restored; rather was Jerusalem to be a temple-city, situated in a strategically important place, subject to and under the direct control of the Persian king. By ancient custom the surrounding countryside belonged to this temple-city, but not the whole of the former kingdom of Judah. Hebron, the city in which David was

[3] R. Kittel, *Gestalten und Gedanken in Israel*, Leipzig 1925, p. 395

[4] Midr. Song of Sol. VII.8 quoted *Strack-Billerbeck* VOL. III, p. 112; see in general the passages there cited and Judith VIII.18ff.

anointed king (II Sam. II.1–4), had become Edomite territory; the limits of "greater Jerusalem" could be reached by a day's march in any direction. Some time later, probably shortly before 520 B.C., a large number of exiles, according to Ezra II about 50,000, returned to Jerusalem.[5] These were resolved to make a fresh start on the basis of their repentance. They possessed the necessary spiritual authority (cf. also Jer. XXIV).

At first progress was difficult, as obstacles of many kinds stood in their path. We gain some idea of these from Trito-Isaiah (Isaiah LVI-LXVI), which probably stems from this period, and also from Zechariah VIII.10. An altar was doubtless erected first, and the foundation-stone of the new Temple laid, but the building still remained uncompleted.

In 520, however, as the result of an internal crisis which convulsed the Persian kingdom, it appeared as if the day of salvation, the messianic age, was about to dawn. The prophets Haggai and Zechariah arose at this time. Haggai spoke of an imminent shaking of the world to its foundations (Hag. II.6). Zechariah saw in his nocturnal visions the coming of the "Branch" (Zech. III.8), the cleansing of the land from sin (Zech. V.1–11), and Jerusalem as a city without walls, in whose midst God Himself dwelt (Zech. II.5–9). Messianic hopes were attached to Zerubbabel, the governor appointed by the Persian king, a member of David's line and grandson of king Jehoiachin. The appearance of Haggai and Zechariah doubtless led to the completion of the Temple, which was solemnly dedicated on 1st April, 515 (Ezra V and VI). But the messianic age did not dawn; Zerubbabel disappeared, for reasons now no longer apparent; at all events, everything remained as before, in the poverty-stricken conditions prevailing at the start.

Ezra and Nehemiah

Of the period 515 to about 460 B.C. we know just a little from the short book of Malachi. We might summarise this period under the heading "The Decay of the New Community."[6]

[5] Ezra I links together the permission to rebuild the temple and the permission to return. Cyrus's decree as recorded in Ezra VI.3–5 makes no mention of a return, although some priests will probably have returned immediately to Jerusalem with the temple vessels. Sheshbazzar (Ezra I.11) is named as their leader, while the 50,000 or so who returned according to Ezra II were led by Zerubbabel.

[6] Sellin, *Geschichte*, VOL. II, p. 127.

The messianic hopes receded; Judaism threatened to sink back slowly into idolatry and to be swallowed up by the neighbouring peoples. There was a general slackening of religious zeal among the returned exiles; numerous mixed marriages with members of neighbouring races occurred in defiance of the law (Mal. II.11ff.; Ezra IX.1–2).

Babylonian Jewry again came to the rescue. Ezra the priest had an official post in the Persian administration as the person responsible for Jewish affairs.[7] He had collected the old records of the history of his people and the laws given to them, and received authority from the Persian king Artaxerxes I (465–424 B.C.) to proceed to Jerusalem with as many Jews as wished to come and "to make inquiries about Judah and Jerusalem according to the law of your God, which is in your hand" (Ezra VII.14). About 5,000 souls returned with him carrying a rich votive offering from the Persian king and the Babylonian Jews (Ezra VIII.25f.). After more than a decade[8] Ezra's activity, which had as its aim a fresh vindication of and adherence to the Law, was reinforced by Nehemiah, the Persian king's Jewish cup-bearer. The latter, on his appointment as governor of Judea, succeeded in pledging the returned exiles from Babylon and their posterity, together with the Jews who had remained in the country, solemnly and in writing "to walk in God's law which was given by Moses the servant of God, and to observe and do all the commandments of the Lord our God, and his ordinances and statutes" (Neh. x.29). The main articles of the covenant are listed as follows: avoidance of mixed marriages and dissolution of existing ones, avoidance of trade with Gentiles on the Sabbath, the observance of the sabbatical year, and the prompt payment of all taxes and dues to the Temple (Neh. x.30–39).

Summary

While we can only infer the "repentance" of the exiles in Babylon, there is clear historical evidence for the solemn

[7] H. H. Schäder, *Esra der Schreiber*, Tübingen 1930.

[8] The chronological relationship of Ezra and Nehemiah is a matter for dispute; it is now generally stated that Ezra followed Nehemiah; W. Rudolph, *Esra und Nehemia*, Handbuch zum Alten Testament, Series I, VOL. 20, Tübingen 1949, pp. 65ff.; Noth, *The History of Israel*, pp. 318–337; Ehrlich, *Geschichte Israels*, p. 79, Note 107 with bibliography.

covenant made by the Jews in Jerusalem under Nehemiah. This covenant was in fact constitutive of "Judaism" as such. Some considerations by way of a summary would therefore be appropriate at this point.

Some of the Jews in Babylon had sent very considerable contributions of money and goods to Jerusalem (Ezra II.68f.; VIII.24–27; Zech. VI.9–11). From this fact as well as from documents in cuneiform script belonging to a banking house by the name of "Muraschu,"[9] we can infer that the Jews there, whose limited freedom had probably been turned by the Persians into complete freedom, possessed a certain wealth. It is therefore understandable that not all of the deportees took advantage of the permission to return to Jerusalem. Those who did—and this applies especially to the 5,000 who returned with Ezra—made a real sacrifice in so doing, for they were venturing into the wretched living conditions and manifold difficulties of life in Judea. Those therefore who took this step would have been primarily the ones caught up in the movement for repentance. But many of these had also remained in Babylon. The spiritual, political and material reins were held in those days by the Babylonian Jews.

Amongst the obligations assumed, according to Nehemiah X, matters of cult, of course, stand well to the forefront. But they do not stand alone. General reference is made first of all to the "commandments of the Lord our Lord and his ordinances and his statutes." In Trito-Isaiah (Isaiah LVI–LXVI), Haggai, Zechariah and Malachi the purely "legal" points do not stand alone either. A fast "only to quarrel and to fight and to hit with wicked fist" is not acceptable to the Lord (Is. LVIII.4). The only matters of cult which are mentioned are the points at which confession of the God of the fathers becomes manifest. But there is no mistaking the danger inherent in this. Even in Isaiah LVI.2 the keeping of the Sabbath is mentioned as an especially important point *before* the avoidance of evil; Haggai attributes the misery in the land not to the struggle of every man against his fellow (cf. Zech. VIII.10) but to the neglect to rebuild the Temple. Malachi may well condemn sorcery, adultery,

[9] Kittel, *Geschichte des Volkes Israel*, VOL. III, pp. 116f., 518f. The votive offering described in Ezra VIII.25–27 was worth £400,000, thus Sellin, *Geschichte*, VOL. II, p. 138.

perjury, the withholding of a man's wages and disregard of a foreigner's rights (Mal. III.5), but the central point, as he sees it, is nevertheless something else: namely, that cult obligations are not taken seriously.

We must not fail to recognise that the Jews under Nehemiah bound themselves to great sacrifices in order to maintain a great cult in circumstances of poverty. The keeping of the Sabbath, the observance of the sabbatical year, the splitting up of mixed marriages, the trek back from the country to the town all meant further sacrifices, and showed that the Jews were in bitter earnest where the Law of the Lord was concerned. But the chief stress was still laid upon what were not the "weightier matters of the law."

Special mention must be made of the attitude to the *Samaritans.* Right at the start of the erection of the Temple the remaining population of the northern kingdom of Israel living around Samaria wished to participate in the building and were rebuffed (Ezra IV.1ff.). Whereupon they sought to place difficulties in the way of building the Temple and, particularly, the wall of Jerusalem, though finally without success. The attitude of the returning deportees was understandable. If they did not hold the tiller in their hands the work of renewal was threatened with shipwreck. Their fears that their spiritual task would be endangered were not unjustified. Another consideration that certainly played a part was that the Samaritans had entered into blood-ties with foreign peoples. The purity of the race was endangered.[10]

Finally, one more danger became clear under Nehemiah: that of the *secularisation of the priesthood.* Next to the governor, Zerubbabel, the high-priest had a commanding position. In chapter IV.14 Zechariah sees the two "anointed ones", prince and high-priest, standing by the Lord. When, with Zerubbabel's departure, the office of governor remained vacant for a lengthy period, the high-priest gained in power. For the person with the power, however, political points of view have a part to play and these counselled keeping on good terms with the governor in Samaria and departing somewhat from the strict principles of those returning home. Under Nehemiah

[10] Other points of view in A. Alt, *Die Rolle Samarias bei der Entstehung des Judentums,* in the *Festchrift für O. Procksch,* Leipzig 1934, pp. 5–28.

one of the high-priest's sons married a foreign woman (Neh. xiii.28).

Thus in those early days the basic structure of Judaism was already clearly discernible; already too the problems with which it was subsequently to come to grips were beginning to take shape.

Chapter 2

FROM NEHEMIAH TO SYRIAN RULE

A hundred years or so after Ezra and Nehemiah the whole Jewish community changed its overlord. In an unprecedented victory march the Macedonian king, Alexander the Great (334–323), drove through Asia Minor, Syria, Palestine and Egypt to Babylon and across the Indus. In the process the total Jewish community from the southern border of Egypt as far as Babylon received a new overlord. After his premature death, Alexander's mighty kingdom disintegrated under the impact of protracted battles into several separate kingdoms, in which the political and intellectual leadership fell into the hands of the conquerors and, with them, the Greeks. Until 200 B.C. Palestine was subject to the Ptolemies, who ruled over Egypt; Babylon, along with Syria, was subject to the rule of the Seleucids. The whole oriental world was thus drawn into another cultural province, whose power and influence they had no capacity to resist. Hellenistic culture plunged all countries of the east into a great crisis, just as the culture of the white man has done with the coloured peoples today. Judaism also experienced this crisis, although only after 200 B.C. did it enter upon its acute stage; we shall leave consideration of it, therefore, to the next chapter. The period which we are now reviewing is divided into the Persian period up till 330 and the Greek period from 330 to 200.

Judaism in the last Century of Persian Rule

What we know of *external events* is due to a large extent to the papyri from Aswan (Elephantine Papyri) mentioned in the previous chapter (page 11). We learn from them that, besides the governor of the temple-city Jerusalem, there existed, for domestic affairs, a kind of elders' council consisting of representatives of the leading families, at whose head a member of the Davidic line is named. It constituted a first step towards the "Sanhedrin" of the New Testament.

From Josephus[1] we further learn that in about 400 the high priest Jochanan slew his brother Jeshua (=Jesus) in the temple.[2] This reveals very glaringly to what little depth the solemn obligation to the Law went even on the part of the leading priests.

Apart from this, the book of Judith probably refers to an event in the Persian period; the Holofernes there mentioned is probably a general of Artaxerxes III (358–338) by the name of Orofernes. This king is said to have deported Jews to Hyrcania and the Caspian Sea;[3] this meant an extension of the Jewish Diaspora.

The most important event that can be mentioned in association with Alexander's march, though it cannot be more precisely dated, is *the erection of a Samaritan temple* on Mount Gerizim near Shechem. We have hardly any information about the precise circumstances. The antithesis between Jews and Samaritans was, as we saw, immediately determined by the attitude of the returned exiles. It then became further heightened, even though the Samaritans took over the Pentateuch (and only the Pentateuch!) from the Jews as their sacred writings.[4] The breach became absolute through the building of the Samaritan temple on the basis of Deuteronomy XXVII.4 where the Samaritans read "Mount Gerizim" instead of "Mount Ebal"; it was never healed and during New Testament times it could hardly have been wider. For a Jew, as we see from John VIII.48, "Samaritan" was a strong term of abuse. Josephus and the Talmud merely call the Samaritans "Cuthaeans" after II Kings XVII.24. Racial interbreeding was accordingly the main argument on the Jewish side; the fact, however, that the Samaritans adopted the Pentateuch indicates

[1] On Josephus, see pp. 112f.

[2] *Antiquities* XI.7,1 (§§ 297–301).

[3] References in E. Schürer, *Geschichte des jüdischen Volkes im Zeitalter Jesu Christi*, henceforth cited as *Geschichte des jüdischen Volkes*, 3 vols. and index, Leipzig 1900–11, VOL. III, p. 7, note 11.

[4] In connexion with this and the following cf. the Introductions to the Old Testament cited in the Bibliography under C.3.

that they had put away the idolatry of which II Kings XVII speaks. They also show themselves to have been influenced in other directions by the spiritual movements of Judaism.

Regarding *the internal development* and the ideas which stirred the Jewish community in the Persian period, we learn something from the writings of the Old Testament which arose after the Babylonian captivity.

In this respect, mention must first be made of the so-called *Priestly Code* (P).[5] The Pentateuch was not written in one piece but edited into a unity from several writings, the latest of which was the *Priestly Code*. It begins with the story of the creation in six days and the founding of the Sabbath. Next to the legal matters the genealogies have a great part to play; they reflect the struggle for the preservation of racial purity. At the centre, however, stand the cult, the sacrificial legislation and the purity-regulations. Peculiar to P is the great day of atonement, which reflects the repentant mood of the post-exilic community.

Later than the Priestly Code are the *books of the Chronicles*, a re-editing of the books of Samuel and Kings with a lengthy genealogical introduction. An extensive account is given of David and Solomon, and the blemishes in their portraits erased. David is said to have prepared and organised the construction of the temple and the musical and vocal part of the cult down to the last detail. The divine retribution is depicted in the story in an exact correspondence of guilt and punishment. An unqualified belief in the miraculous power of God apparent in an almost grotesque heightening of the old accounts runs through the writing (cf. II Chron. XX.21–24). The history of the northern kingdom is passed over; it is merely a story of apostasy. This is the consequence of the attitude towards the Samaritans, the heirs of the northern kingdom!

The Persian period gave rise to many *Psalms*. A great deal is said in Chronicles about the temple-music, for which the Levites were responsible, and in the Psalter we have several of their hymns, of the sons of Korah, Asaph, Teman, etc. Less emphasis is laid upon the sacrificial cult itself (cf. Ps. XL.6; L.8ff.; LI.18f.), though the congregation's participation in it

[5] For the theology of the Chronicler see Rudolph, *Esra und Nehemia* chs. XXVII–XXX and the bibliography listed there; also O. Procksch, *Theologie des Alten Testamentes*, Gütersloh 1950, pp. 367–371.

through hymns, thanksgiving, praises and petitions certainly is emphasised. The temple itself is the sign of God's presence (Ps. v.7, etc.). The history of God's dealings with His people and the promises made to the fathers, along with the Creator's power over nature, are the foundations of confident prayers and keep alive the hope that God will one day restore Israel and be king over the whole earth.

One difficult problem running through many a psalm is the question of the sufferings of the pious. We saw how quickly secular ways became widespread in priestly circles; the Psalms indicate that in the long run the solemn obligation assumed by the whole people under Nehemiah had lost its hold upon many. The antithesis of the pious and the ungodly became linked, as is readily understandable, with that of the poor and the powerful and rich. In these circumstances it seemed to many of the pious a duty to separate themselves clearly from the ungodly and to despise them: Psalm xv.4: (who shall sojourn in thy tent?) ". . . in whose eyes a reprobate is despised."

We must not overlook the fact that many Psalms which the New Testament Church prays "in Christ" are prayers from the first centuries of "Judaism."

The so widely contrasted writings *Jonah*, *Ruth* and *Esther* also stem from the Persian period, the first two with their broad outlook upon the Gentiles, the book of Esther with its hatred of them engendered by anti-semitism.

Palestine under Ptolemaic Rule

The external events. Alexander the Great's victory march appears to have by-passed Jerusalem without endangering it. In the battles of his successors, the so-called Diadochoi, the first of the Ptolemies to whose rule Palestine was subject until 200 B.C. captured Jerusalem and exported Jewish slaves to Egypt as captives. After the conquest of Cyrenaica he also settled a Jewish colony there.[6] The Diaspora was spreading out still further.

In the countries of the near east the Macedonians, together with the Greeks, formed only a thin ruling crust who created

[6] Josephus, *Against Apion*, II.4 (§ 44).

for themselves in the towns, centres of Greek culture and Greek life. Thus around Jerusalem the temple-city there arose a great number of towns in which Greek, and therefore pagan, culture was cultivated. Jerusalem was actually hemmed in by them on all sides. On the other hand, the need arose for the Jewish community in Palestine to extend at this time, and probably even earlier, beyond the narrow frontiers of its little country. Some districts north of Jerusalem consequently became so strongly Judaised that in the Maccabean period they were annexed to Jerusalem; at the same time we also find Jews in Galilee and in the so-called Perea, the country east of the Jordan. The Samaritan territory was by-passed.

But then eyes were also being turned towards the wider world which had been opened up to the east by Greek hegemony. The situation of economic depression in Jerusalem had, at least for many families, been ameliorated; long journeys could now be undertaken (Prov. VII.19). Above all the great enterprises of the Diadochoi in founding cities attracted the Jews. This is understandable, for Judaism had lost its political independence and was dependent no less in Babylon than in Palestine and Egypt on the ruling classes, who for their part were seeking those upon whom they could rely. Thus the information that Jews in Alexandria, the capital of Ptolemaic Egypt, and in Antioch had obtained a more privileged status than the natives is certainly no fabrication.[7] So the horizon of Judaism in the Greek period became enlarged. But in one essential point Jerusalem remained distinct from the other cities: in these the indigenous religious heritage was immediately swamped by Hellenism; this did not happen in Jerusalem until the beginnings of the Syrian period.

The internal development. We gain a special acquaintance with this in the so-called *Wisdom Literature*, to which belong Proverbs, Jesus ben Sirach (Ecclesiasticus) and the book of Tobit. The form of this literature is Egyptian, and has a long history in that

[7] It is disputed whether the Jews in the Hellenistic towns like Alexandria and Antioch had full civil parity, "isopolity," as Josephus frequently maintains (references in Schürer, *Geschichte des jüdischen Volkes*, VOL. III, pp. 121ff.), but, at any rate, they did enjoy certain special privileges in these towns. Cf. H. I. Bell, *Juden und Griechen im römischen Alexandrien*, Lepizig 1926; A. Segré, *The Status of the Jews in Ptolemaic and Roman Egypt*, Jewish Social Studies, VOL. 6, 1944, pp. 375–400.

country. In the individual writings the Greek influence is notably manifest in the relative absence of the link with history.[8] (This is particularly striking in Proverbs). It is in many respects a this-worldly morality, often set forth in homely rules of prudence. Wisdom, as introduced in the Proverbs of Solomon partly in the first person and appearing, in Greek fashion, as a power standing beside God—an "hypostasis"—consists in knowing that goods acquired through ungodliness are transient. But good deeds have lasting worth.

The most comprehensive work of this kind is the *book of ben Sirach*,[9] written about 200 B.C. and translated two generations later into Greek. "Whereas many great teachings have been given to us through the law and the prophets and the others that followed them, on account of which we should praise Israel for instruction and wisdom; and since it is necessary not only that the readers themselves (i.e. those who can read it in the original language) should acquire understanding but also that those who love learning should be able to help the outsiders (i.e. those who can no longer understand the original language of the Old Testament) by both speaking and writing, my grandfather Jesus, after devoting himself especially to the reading of the law and the prophets and the other books of our fathers, and after acquiring considerable proficiency in them, was himself also led to write something pertaining to instruction and wisdom." with these words the grandson prefaces the translation of his grandfather's work. The Law is the source of wisdom. Wisdom sought a resting-place where she could abide upon the earth; then God directed her to Israel for a dwelling (Sirach XXIV.1ff.); and with reference to this wisdom we read (Sirach XXIV.23–27): "All this is the book of the covenant of the Most High God, the law which Moses commanded us as an inheritance for the congregations of Jacob. It fills men with wisdom, like the Pishon, and like the Tigris at the time of the first fruits. It makes them full of understanding, like the Euphrates, and like the Jordan at

[8] J. Fichtner, "Zum Problem Glaube und Geschichte in der israelitisch-jüdischen Weisheitsliteratur" in *Theologische Literaturzeitung*, henceforth cited as *Th. L.Z.*, LXXVI (1951), pp. 145–150.

[9] J. Koeberle, *Sünde und Gnade im religiösen Leben des Volkes Israel bis auf Jesus Christus*, München 1905, pp. 451–458. It should be noted that 'Ecclesiasticus' is the usual English name for ben Sirach's book.

harvest time. It makes instruction shine forth like light." The wisdom is little different in content from that in Proverbs, namely, a solid worldly wisdom. The basic outlook of Sirach is also that, at any rate in the long run, it fares well with the pious but badly with the ungodly. Contemplation of the omnipotent Creator, whom nothing escapes and who sees that His will is done, gives the writer the confidence for this expectation that only the genuine and the good is of lasting duration. Indeed Sirach knows even more: he knows of sin and its forgiveness (Sirach II.9; XIV.1f.; XXI.1). He draws his confidence in God's forgiveness of sins from the contemplation of history. But man need not sin; he who has chosen wisdom holds the (evil) "impulse" in check. "A mind settled on an intelligent thought is like the stucco decoration on the wall of a colonnade." (Sirach XXII.17).

In contrast to Proverbs, however, Sirach betrays more interest in history. This is shown particularly by the "praise of the fathers" that comes in part VII of the book after the praise of God (chs. XLIVff.). The section on Aaron is particularly full. The whole book concludes with the praise of the reigning high-priest, Simon; his measures on behalf of Jerusalem are enumerated, and then special praise is bestowed upon his dignified and brilliant appearance at the temple services.

The *book of Tobit* has an even more typically Israelite flavour: the piety of Tobit is apparent in the offering of first-fruits, the first and second tithes, and the observance of food-commandments. Tobit feeds the hungry and buries the dead, for whom no one cares. Chapter IV indicates that this book also belongs to the wisdom literature. But its problem is different: it is precisely in doing a good deed that Tobit becomes blind; how can this be? In the end he is healed again, and a long life sets the seal to his piety.

This review of the earlier wisdom literature shows us, therefore, that the broadening of outlook that the new period of Alexander brought, can be linked with the currents that we have so far seen in Judaism, i.e. with currents legal and ceremonial; but that the Greek spirit could also lead to a neglect of the historical and thus of the foundations of Judaism generally.

The three "Pillars" of Judaism

The Canon, as it was fixed by the Jewish community after the destruction of Jerusalem in A.D. 70, consists of three parts: the Pentateuch, the "Prophets" (comprising the historical and the actual prophetic writings, but without Daniel; the book belongs in the Hebrew Old Testament to the third group), and the "Writings." Sirach mentions these three groups in the preface quoted above (see page 19), although he has no definite title as yet for the third.

Of greatest importance is the fact that at the onset of the Greek period a start was made on the *translation of the Old Testament* into the Greek language. The Pentateuch, the so-called "Law," was translated first. This translation is known by the Latin title "Septuagint" (written LXX) because, according to tradition, six representatives of the twelve tribes respectively, thus, to be precise, seventy-two men, are supposed to have prepared it in Alexandria in the time of Ptolemy II (285–247 B.C.). Although the LXX, because of its connexion with the original text, sounded very strange to Greek ears, its significance cannot be overestimated; even Luther's translation can hardly vie with it in importance. For here men were confronted for the first time with the task of translating the Scriptures of the Biblical revelation into a pagan language. Words had thus to be found for concepts which paganism completely lacked, such as "Gentile," and "create" (with reference to God's activity); an attempt had also to be made to avoid the manifold hazards concealed in certain words belonging to Greek language, religion and culture, when they were intended to be used as vessels for a Biblical content; one need only think of the word for "love," where the LXX avoids the tainted word "eros." The LXX was also the Bible of the growing Gentile-Christian Church.[10]

[10] For earlier literature on the LXX see Schürer, *Geschichte des jüdischen Volkes*, VOL. III, pp. 424ff.; further literature cited by G. Bertram in *Theologische Rundschau, Neue Folge*, henceforth cited as *Th.R., N.F.*, III (1931), pp. 283–296; V (1933), pp. 173–186; X (1938), pp. 133–159. See also J. W. Wevers, *Th.R., N.F.*, XXII (1954), pp. 85–138, 171–190. The edition of the LXX by A. Rahlfs, 3rd. edn., Stuttgart 1949 offers a brief introduction; noteworthy also is the contribution to LXX studies by W. S. van Leeuwen in the collective work edited by J. H. Waszink, W. C. van Unnik and Ch. de Beus, *Het oudste Christendom en de antieke cultuur*, VOL. I, Haarlem 1951, pp. 561–582; further information in E. Würthwein, *Der Text des Alten Testamentes*, Stuttgart 1952, pp. 40–61

The LXX came gradually into existence. It included a series of writings which the Jewish community in Palestine did not accept as canonical, namely those which the Reformers separated from the Bible as the "Apocrypha," while the Catholic Church, following the LXX, retained them as canonical. These writings are of the greatest value to us historically.[11]

The Synagogue. For the temple congregation[12] around Jerusalem there existed no necessity for a special house in which the community could assemble for prayer and the reading of the Scriptures. The first trace we have of a synagogue—from the middle of the third century B.C.—takes us to Egypt. In the following centuries synagogues arose in all the towns and villages of Palestine and even in Jerusalem itself.[13]

The Rabbis. As wider circles of the Jewish community in Palestine became more and more secularised, beginning with the priests and the rich, so much the more isolated did those who desired to adhere earnestly to the Law of the fathers become. The teachers of wisdom were no longer priests but laymen who meditated on the Law day and night. Sirach himself recognises a class of rabbis (or scribes), whom he contrasts with the artisan class:

"The wisdom of the scribe depends on the opportunity of leisure; and he who has little business may become wise.

[11] The order of the separate writings differs in the LXX from that of the Hebrew Old Testament: the Pentateuch is followed by all the historical writings in approximately their historical order: Joshua, Judges, Ruth, Samuel and Kings (entitled I–IV Kings), Chronicles, the apocryphal book of Esdras, Ezra and Nehemiah (entitled II Esdras), Esther, Judith, Tobit and the books of Maccabees; these are followed by Psalms, Proverbs, Ecclesiastes, the Song of Songs, Job, the Wisdom of Solomon and Jesus Sirach (Ecclesiasticus), then by the twelve minor prophets, followed by Isaiah, Jeremiah, including Baruch and the Letter of Jeremiah, and concluding with Daniel and its additions.

Luther, like the EVV, placed the major prophets before the minor and included the "Writings" under the heading "Doctrinal Writings" (*Lehrschriften*). The LXX concludes with the book of Daniel and its prophecy of the 1,290 days which meant so much to the Jews (Dan. XII.11); Luther and the EVV, on the other hand, conclude with Malachi and its prophecy of Elijah's return which Jesus applied to John the Baptist; thus in Luther's version the last book of the Old Testament points forward to the first books of the New.

[12] Throughout the book the German word "Gemeinde" is rendered variously as "congregation" or "community" (Tr.).

[13] The way was paved for the rise of the synagogue and synagogue worship as far back as the Persian period or even the period of the Babylonian Captivity; see Ehrlich, *Geschichte Israels*, p. 75; Noth, *The History of Israel*, pp. 339ff.

How can he become wise who handles the plow . . . ? He sets his heart on plowing furrows . . . . So too is every craftsman and master workman . . . . Without them a city cannot be established . . . . Yet they are not sought out for the council of the people, nor do they attain eminence in the public assembly. They do not sit in the judge's seat, nor do they understand the sentence of judgment; they cannot expound discipline or judgment . . . . On the other hand he who devotes himself to the study of the law of the Most High will seek out the wisdom of all the ancients, and will be concerned with prophecies . . . . He will set his heart to rise early to seek the Lord who made him, and will make supplication before the Most High; he will open his mouth in prayer and make supplication for his sins. If the great Lord is willing, he will be filled with the spirit of understanding; he will pour forth words of wisdom and give thanks to the Lord in prayer." (Sirach XXXVIII.24–XXXIX.6 *passim.*)

Greek influence is at work in this contempt for a trade; the rabbis in Jesus' day were different in this respect.

The Problem of Theodicy[14]

The Old Testament history books, particularly the books of Chronicles, depict in the history of the people of Israel how national disaster results when the people abandon God, and how they become master of their enemies when they return to Him. The writings of the wisdom literature are buoyed up by the confidence that, at least in the long run, it fares well with the pious and ill with the ungodly. But at the end of the Persian and the beginning of the Greek period the powerful and rich members of the Jewish community became ever more indifferent to the Law, so that there arose an ever more agonising problem: Is it then always the case, as in the Book of Tobit, that at least in the end it will become clear, even in a man's outward fate, who is pious and who is ungodly? It is a testimony to the realism of their faith that the pious did not merely accept the contradiction between their faith and life but that it became a cause of deep vexation to them. Had

[14] Problem of theodicy: the problem of how misery, sin and death, but especially the prosperity of those who deny God and the suffering of the pious can be reconciled with God's omnipotence, omniscience, holiness and love.

their faith been less genuine, glib comfort would have sufficed for it. Instead it led to a deep spiritual struggle of which Psalm LXXIII, the Book of Job and also, in its way, Ecclesiastes, give us some idea.

The anonymous writer of *Ecclesiastes* does not put his ideas into the mouth of a rich idler, whose idleness has led to boredom with life, but into the mouth of a king who has "made great works" (Ecclesiastes II.4) and who doubtless could have surveyed his life's work with satisfaction. Nietzsche once said that "all desire requires eternity, deep, deep eternity." But not only desire, even fulfilment requires eternity. And the Preacher has no knowledge of this eternity. So everything on earth, however beautiful, is nonetheless "vanity." All the paths that a man can follow, in order to make his life worth living in this situation, are followed, only to be unmasked as false—even the plunging of oneself into life's enjoyments. Thus a most important problem is raised, and a great symphony of complaint echoes forth. *One* note in it is again that of the undeserved suffering of the righteous: "Again I saw all the oppressions that are practised under the sun. And behold, the tears of the oppressed, and they had no one to comfort them! On the side of the oppressors there was power, and there was no one to comfort them." (Ecclesiastes IV.1.) The lament finds no consolation, the question no answer, even though as the "end of the matter" we read: "Fear God and keep his commandments" (Ecclesiastes XII.13).

"I was envious of the arrogant, when I saw the prosperity of the wicked . . . . All in vain have I kept my heart clean," says Psalm LXXIII. Even though the Psalmist answers that the ungodly are "destroyed in a moment," in the final verses he rises above the whole question of his outward fortunes: "My flesh and my heart may fail, but God is the strength of my heart and my portion for ever."

The "answer" thus given is also the solution offered by the book of *Job*. Job is righteous and is hit by unimaginable suffering and trouble. With unwavering perseverance Job rejects the friends who, according to the old belief, desired to see in his suffering a punishment for his sins. The question whether Job is sinless does not arise; instead the poet desires to prove that it can fare badly with the pious upon earth, and that man cannot remonstrate with God on that account. Again the question is here left unanswered, but the unanswered question is rendered tolerable: in face of God's greatness, might and wisdom it becomes possible for Job to realise that the unsolved question is hidden and answered in God. Thus the "answer" of the book of Job runs: "I know that thou canst do all things, and that no purpose of thine can be thwarted . . . . Therefore I have uttered what I did not understand, things too wonderful for me, which I did not know . . . . I had heard of thee by the hearing of the ear, but now my eye sees thee; therefore I despise myself, and repent in dust and ashes." (Job XLII.2–5; the omitted sentences do not belong in this context.)

One answer does not appear in these writings: the answer that only in a judgment after death will the pious and the ungodly reap the harvest of their deeds upon this earth. For this answer was not as yet available to the pious. The belief in a life after death is only touched upon in the Old Testament;[15] it has not yet become a determining factor. The situation altered when, at a time of desperate crisis for Judaism, the pious had to expect a martyr's death for the sake of their faith. Vistas of a life after death were then opened up to them.

[15] Ezek. XXXVII.1ff.; Ps. XVI.10(?); Is. XXV. 8. Job XIX.25f. runs: "For I know that my Redeemer lives, and at last he will stand upon the earth; and after my skin has been thus destroyed, then without my flesh I shall see God." On Dan. XII.2f. see pp. 42f.

Chapter 3

THE SYRIAN RULE. THE MACCABEAN WAR

Events leading up to the Maccabean War

After a number of indecisive battles Palestine eventually transferred at the battle of Paneas in 198 B.C. from the dominion of the Egyptian Ptolemies to that of the Syrian Seleucids. This transition was accomplished in the first instance without friction; in fact, it is recorded that the Jews assisted the Syrian king Antiochus III (the Great) (223–187 B.C.) in the expulsion of the Egyptian garrison; thereupon, not only did he grant the elders, priests and Levites a generous tax-relief and establish endowments for sacrifices and temple-construction, but, above all, he permitted the Jews to live in accordance with the laws of their fathers.[1] Thus the Jewish Law received government sanction, as it had also done under the Persians. An uprising in Lydia and Phrygia occasioned the same king to settle 2,000 Jewish families there from Babylon and Mesopotamia as a reliable garrison.[2]

Thus the Diaspora grew: In the first third of the second century B.C. we find Jews in Babylon, around Jerusalem, in Joppa, in Galilee and various parts of the country beyond the Jordan, in Phrygia and Lydia, in Hyrcania, in Egypt, particularly in Alexandria, and also in Cyrenaica. Because of Palestine's transfer to Syrian rule the Egyptian and Palestinian Jewish communities now became separated politically. This to prove fateful.

Jewish Hellenism. We have already discovered a certain influence of Greek thought upon the wisdom literature. But the infiltration of Greek thought into Judaism went to unparalleled

[1] Josephus, *Antiquities* XII.3, 3 (§§ 129ff.).
[2] Josephus, *Antiquities* XII.3, 4 (§§ 147–153).

lengths. There existed a current in the Greek spirit which acted as a solvent of all religion, both its own and that of foreign peoples, in that it declared the gods to be personifications of natural forces and the myths about the gods to be accounts of the deeds of ancient kings, and which interpreted the meaning of sacrifices and cult-regulations as external indications of an inward spiritual disposition. Thus, the religion might well be preserved in its external form, and the husk remain, but the kernel disappeared. Indeed, the "husk," the myths and the cult, were still highly treasured. For behind the ancient myths, behind the exotic images of the gods, the Greek conjectured deep wisdom. The older and the more exotic other religions appeared to him the greater was the awe with which he suspected secret wisdom to lie behind them. As the history of their own people and of their own culture appeared to be so recent to the Greeks of this period, the so-called Hellenists, they sought after the oldest religions, which were held to conceal within them the original wisdom of mankind. But this original wisdom was in its turn their own, i.e. Greek, thought.

The first to allow themselves to be caught up in this spiritual current was a section of the Egyptian Jewish community, who learned to view their own history through the eyes of these Greeks. The sacred book of the Bible had now to be the oldest book in the world and contain the profoundest wisdom of the Greeks; it had to be men of the biblical story to whom the Egyptians, to whom mankind were indebted for culture and civilisation. So Abraham, Joseph and Moses were turned into heroes who had produced the Egyptian culture admired by the Hellenists, and indeed had taught the Egyptian religion, with its animal worship. What the Egyptians traced back to their gods, what according to the Hellenists they owed rather to deified kings, was now held in reality to have been invented and introduced by the patriarchs and Moses. This whole outlook, which is expressed in a series of fragmentarily preserved Jewish writings,[3] meant nothing but the surrender of the very substance of the religion of Israel although the outer husk was retained.

[3] It mainly concerns fragments transmitted by Eusebius of such writers as Aristobulus, Artapan, Demetrius, Eupolemos, Ezekiel, Cleodemos and Malchas. Texts in W. N. Stearns, *Fragments from Graeco-Jewish Writers*, Chicago 1908.

We learn what these ideas meant in practice from the *History of the Tobiads*, preserved for us in novelettish form by Josephus.[4] It begins about the middle of the third century B.C. in the Egyptian period. Joseph, son of a certain Tobiad, acquires, by means of bribery with borrowed money and an audacious appearance at the royal court, the lucrative right to farm taxes throughout Syria, Phoenicia, Judea and Samaria. He is skilled in collecting taxes, even by cruelty, and thereby grows rich. He has seven sons, but then falls in love with an Egyptian dancer and desires to marry her. His brother secretly substitutes his own daughter, in order that Joseph should not infringe the Law, which forbids the marriage of a Jewish male with a non-Jewish female. This mixture of unscrupulousness and legalism is typical of the rootlessness of Hellenistic Judaism. The marriage with his niece results in a son, Hyrcanus, for whom his father has a special love and who is very like him in character. Tension arises between this son and the elder brothers which involves Jerusalem itself; Hyrcanus is forced to flee beyond the Jordan, where he builds himself a castle, the remains of which are still preserved today.[5] Meanwhile Jerusalem had fallen into Syrian hands.

The Hellenisation of Judea.[6] In the first decades of the Syrian period the superior Greek culture and education penetrated forcibly even into the temple-city, Jerusalem. The priesthood was divided; the reigning high-priest Onias III was averse to the new spirit, and the elder Tobiad brothers had at first sided with him in the dispute with Hyrcanus. Under Antiochus the Great's successor, however, they sought to extend their power, and, when Onias frustrated the attempt, one of their number, Simon, induced the Syrian king to march against the temple, as is described somewhat fantastically in II Maccabees 3. This pushed Onias in an anti-Syrian direction, resulting in an inclination towards Egypt and an alliance with Hyrcanus beyond the Jordan. Thus a political element entered into a personal struggle for power. The leader of the "Reform Jews"

[4] Josephus, *Antiquities* XII.2f. (§§ 160ff.).

[5] C. C. McCown, "*The Araq el-Emir and the Tobiads,*" in *The Biblical Archaeologist*, XX,3 (1957), pp. 63–76.

[6] For what follows see, besides the historical works listed in Bibliography under C.4, E. Bickermann, *Der Gott der Makkabäer*, Berlin 1937 and his short account in *Die Makkabäer*, Berlin 1935.

was the brother of the high priest, Jesus (Jason) by name. I Maccabees characterises his attitude in the words: "Let us go and make a covenant with the Gentiles round about us, for since we separated from them many evils have come upon us." (I Maccabees I.11.) Jason went to king Antiochus IV (Epiphanes) (175–164 B.C.), secured permission to transform Jerusalem into a Greek city, and offered the king a large sum of money if he made him high-priest. The king agreed; Onias III was arrested in Antioch, where he happened to be at the time, and Jason was appointed high-priest. Even this sale of the high-priestly office was a Greco-pagan custom and an infringement of the Jewish practice. But besides this the Jewish Law confirmed by Antiochus III was abrogated, Jerusalem became a city with Greek law, and Greek culture was introduced into it; a gymnasium was built, i.e. a place for physical and mental education of the young in the Hellenistic, and therefore Gentile, sense. Jews, even priests, exercised there naked, and many abandoned circumcision, the sacred token of the covenant that God made with Abraham.

The Greeks recognised no priestly class; anyone could become a priest. This foreign outlook was now imported into Jerusalem: one of the Tobiads, Menelaus, purchased the high-priesthood for an even larger sum, and thus the office was taken over by one who was not an Aaronite. A more blatant transgression of the Law was hardly conceivable: it no longer had any validity. Jerusalem had entered upon a crisis. But its climax was yet to come.

The dispossessed high priest, Jason, had fled beyond the Jordan, where Hyrcanus himself, of course, no longer lived. Onias III had been murdered in Antioch at the instigation of Menelaus. His son fled to Egypt and, with the help of the Ptolemies, erected a temple in Leontopolis,[7] for which Isaiah XIX.19 offered a certain pretext. Thus the political opposition between Syria and Egypt again became linked with the struggle for the Law in Jerusalem.

After a rather unsuccessful campaign against Egypt, Antiochus IV again marched against this land in 168 B.C. Here the Roman emissary, Popillius Laenas met him and categorically

[7] This temple in Leontopolis, directed by an undoubtedly legitimate high priest, survived until A.D. 73.

demanded his withdrawal. Antiochus had to comply, and retired gnashing his teeth. Rumour had it that he had died. Jason then, believing that his hour had come for winning back the high-priestly office, set upon Jerusalem with a thousand men and besieged Menelaus. But at the news of Antiochus' approach he was forced to retreat. For Antiochus this surprise attack represented open rebellion on the part of the "orthodox party"; he regarded them and the Egyptian party as one and the same, punished Jerusalem bloodily and published a decree forbidding the Jews to live according to their law. The sabbath could now no longer be celebrated, and possession of the sacred books, together with the circumcision of newborn boys, was forbidden. A royal commission travelled up and down the country to supervise the carrying out of the decree. The temple in Jerusalem became a temple of the god of heaven under the Greek name of the Olympian Zeus; the Samaritan temple was likewise dedicated to Zeus; a smaller altar was set upon the great altar in Jerusalem and swine's flesh sacrificed upon it. This was the "abomination that makes desolate" mentioned in Daniel XI.31, XII.11. Temple-prostitution now found its way even into Jerusalem. All over the country altars were erected and incense burned at the doors of the houses. The king's birthday-festival took place every month with a sacrificial banquet, in which the Jews had to participate; Dionysian festivals were celebrated. But the death-penalty was attached to the practice of the Jewish religion.

The king's measures stand out as unique in his day. They were grounded in the fact that the "Reform party" leaned upon the Syrian court while the "orthodox," at least to all appearances, had connexions with Egypt. Accordingly the persecution was, as far as we know, restricted to Palestine. Moreover there was the fact that Antiochus IV needed peace and unity in his country for the pursuit of his far-ranging aims. The Jews, who clung obstinately to their Law and cut themselves off so cleanly from their Gentile neighbours, must have appeared as disturbers of imperial unity and imperial order. It seemed that their obstinacy could only be met by a prohibition of their Law.

The Hasidim. After what has been said so far it must appear as if the end at least of Palestinian Judaism had come. That this was not so is due to a movement of which we know little more than the name from I Maccabees but of whose growth and aims we are informed by some extra-canonical Jewish writings.[8] This was the movement of the Hasidim, mentioned in I Maccabees II.42, VII.13, II Maccabees XVI.6. The first-named passage reads: "Then there united with them a company of Hasideans, mighty warriors of Israel, every one who offered himself willingly for the law." Who were this "company of Hasideans?"

We saw that at the solemn covenant to keep the Law under Ezra and Nehemiah the destruction of Jerusalem and the wretched state of Judea were viewed as a sign of God's ever-present anger, and that the above-mentioned covenant would bring about the day of salvation. But it had still not yet come. Religious apathy became widespread and laid the foundation for the invasion of heathen ways of which we have already spoken. This situation stirred a group of men in about 200 B.C. to take serious stock of themselves. They arrived at the conviction that amongst the people the will of God was not being done as God had laid down in the Law of Moses. They delved into the Law, "meditated upon it day and night," and came to the conclusion that the cult was not being performed in the Jerusalem temple as the Law, according to its exact meaning, intended. These men were "scribes" in a new sense. They did not view it as their first task to teach the Law or apply it practically to every-day life, as the teachers of wisdom had done, but asked first what in fact was the will of God as laid down in the Law. They now arrived at a new exposition of the Law not only in relation to the temple cult but also to the many other commandments.

The attempt to convince the leading men of the people and in the temple of the correctness of their exposition failed. Thereupon they formed a covenant and pledged themselves to treat the Law with all seriousness according to their new interpretation. One of their principles was: "Make a fence around the Law."[9] In the process they compared the Law

[8] Cf. my essay, "Der Ursprung des Pharisäismus" in *Zeitschrift für die Neutestamentliche Wissenschaft*, henceforth cited as *Z.N.W.*, XXXIV (1935), pp. 34–41, which the Qumran discoveries have modified to the extent that it is a question not of the origin of Pharisaism, but of the Hasidim, who subsequently separated into Essenes and Pharisees.

[9] M. Ab. I.1.

with a precious flower-bed that under no circumstances could be trodden upon; at a certain distance from it a fence was placed so that whoever broke it down, possibly unintentionally, had not yet walked upon the flower bed. The Law was thus hedged around by a number of supplementary conditions: for example, it was laid down regarding the sabbath that it began not merely at sunset but somewhat earlier. Whoever overstepped this time inadvertently had not yet thereby transgressed the actual sabbath commandment. This "fence" around the Law was the basis of what the New Testament calls the "tradition of the elders." (Mark VII.3.)

The aim of this covenant of the Hasidim was again to imbue the whole nation with their ideas in order to prepare for the coming of the day of salvation. It was a new movement of repentance which, like that under Ezra and Nehemiah, related mainly, though not exclusively, to ritual and cult matters. The names of the men who called this movement into life are unknown to us, although the book of Daniel refers to them when, in XI.33, it mentions "those among the people who are wise," who "make many understand" (cf. Dan. XII.3). They kindled a movement whose supporters were filled with resolute zeal for obedience to the Law, ready to maintain this zeal to the death. Thus simultaneously with the crisis for Judaism those forces which were summoned to overcome it gathered strength.

The Maccabean War

The edict of Antiochus IV forbidding the practice of the Jewish religion led to martyrdoms. A deep impression was made upon posterity by the martyrdom of the seven sons of one mother, recounted in II Maccabees VII and greatly enlarged upon in IV Maccabees. Many fled to hiding-places in the highlands of Judea. I Maccabees II.29–38 recounts how on one occasion, when the king's myrmidons nosed out one group of about a thousand of the "pious" on the sabbath day, they made no move to defend themselves, as their sharpened interpretation of the sabbath-commandment forbade all manual work on this day, even to the carrying of arms; they died loyal to the Law.

Besides the Hasidim there remained many others in Judea who stood by the Law without having participated in the

Hasidic movement for repentance and renewal. To these belonged a priest Mattathias with his sons in the village of Modein, north-west of Jerusalem. The king's commission arrived there, and ordered Mattathias as the chief man in the village to be the first to make the required pagan sacrifice. He refused. Then another Jew stepped forward and made to offer sacrifice. What happened then can be told in the words of I Maccabees: "When Mattathias saw it, he burned with zeal, and his heart was stirred. He gave vent to righteous anger; he ran and killed him upon the altar. At the same time he killed the king's officer, as Phinehas did against Zimri the son of Salu. Then Mattathias cried out in the city with a loud voice, saying: 'Let every one who is zealous for the law and supports the covenant come out with me!' And he and his sons fled to the hills and left all that they had in the city." (I Maccabees II.24–28.)

All the Jews faithful to the Law banded together around Mattathias and his sons, and the Hasidim joined them too. Under the impact of the massacre described above, they resolved to *defend* themselves against an attack on the sabbath. This led to a series of skirmishes between the rebels and smaller units of the Syrian troops, in which Mattathias and his men were victorious. After the quickly ensuing death of Mattathias, his sons assumed the leadership, first *Judas Maccabeus*, i.e. the "Hammerer" (d. 160), then *Jonathan* (d. 143) and *Simon* (d. 135).

The Maccabean War lasted almost two generations until, after the death in 129 B.C. of the last energetic Syrian king, Antiochus VII (Sidetes), *John Hyrcanus* (135–104), the son and successor of Simon, managed to reign unmolested over an independent Jewish kingdom. The changing fortunes of war are recounted in I Maccabees up to the death of Simon, in II Maccabees up to the death of Judas. Only a few dates and landmarks in their long struggle will be mentioned here. After three and a half years Judas was able to enter Jerusalem and rededicate the desecrated temple (165 B.C.);[10] the period of greatest distress, during which the temple lay defiled in pagan hands, is indicated in Daniel XII.7 by the cryptic expression

[10] The day of dedication was subsequently celebrated annually with great pomp (I Macc. IV.59); the feast is mentioned in Jn. X.22.

"a time, two times and half a time," and plays a part in the Book of Revelation as the symbolic period of the final oppression.[11] An armistice concluded after the capture of Jerusalem broke down on account of the anti-semitism prevailing in the Greek towns, and Judas had to undertake various campaigns in order to rescue his hard-pressed countrymen and take vengeance on his enemies. When the Syrians appointed an Aaronite Alcimus as high priest in place of Menelaus, the Hasidim withdrew from the struggle; not long afterwards, in 160 B.C., Judas fell in battle. His successor Jonathan had subsequently to remain in hiding for a period. Finally struggles developed for the Syrian crown, and the pretenders hastened to woo Jonathan for his support as an ally. He made the most of this opportunity to establish and then to extend his power. In 152 B.C. he donned the high-priestly mantle. Under his brother and successor Simon the Jews began subsequently to date documents according to the years of his reign; that is, to feel themselves free (1 Maccabees XIII.42). Simon was murdered by his son-in-law, but the latter's attempt to seize control miscarried. Simon's son, John Hyrcanus, succeeded his father as ruler but during the war he was besieged in Jerusalem by the Syrian king Antiochus VII (Sidetes) and was forced to surrender. Then the Syrian command once more considered resuming the policy of Antiochus IV and suppressing Judaism by force. But the king rejected this course, as other tasks awaited him, and the attempt to suppress Judaism now that the Maccabees had in the meantime disposed of the "Reform Party" he regarded as hopeless. He therefore recognised the Jewish religion and John Hyrcanus as high priest, but demanded political subjection. When, however, Sidetes fell a few years later during a campaign in the eastern part of the kingdom, Hyrcanus reasserted his independence, and the Syrian kingdom had now no longer the power to suppress him.

In the course of the wars the Jews developed *three objectives*. The first concerned the simple possibility of living unmolested according to the Law. The Hasidim had no other goal. But already in the early years of the war the Maccabees conceived a further aim. We are told how Judas even then hunted out the

[11] Rev. XI.2, 11; XII.6, 14; XIII.5. 3½ years = 42 months = 1,260 days. 3½ days also refers to the same period.

"ungodly" and persecuted them. Whereas the Hasidim sought to vindicate the sovereignty of the Law by precept and example, the Maccabees reached for the sword. So we read of Jonathan: "He destroyed the ungodly out of Israel." (1 Maccabees ix.73.) The third objective was to allow only believers in the one God of Israel to dwell anywhere in the "promised land," i.e. in the land promised to Israel according to the Old Testament (cf. Josh. xiiiff.).[12] Accordingly the inhabitants of Idumea[13] and the region east of the Jordan were presented, as far as the power of the Maccabees permitted, it, with the choice either of circumcision, and thus of accepting the Jewish Law, or of death. So Idumea and Perea, the land "beyond" (Gk. "peran") the Jordan, became "Jewish," if not by race then certainly by religion, which, however, also involved a process of racial integration. Galilee was likewise at this time incorporated into the Jewish kingdom. Only the Samaritans were treated differently. They were already circumcised, possessed the Law and yet stood in irreconcilable opposition to the Jews. Thus their temple on Mount Gerizim was probably destroyed in 128 B.C., but they were not recognised as Jews. Even the towns which had a Hellenistic population were treated in the same manner as Idumea and Perea. They, however, preserved the consciousness of their individuality and a few generations later were freed once more of the Jewish yoke. But in the period of its greatest power, the "Hasmoneans," as the dynasty to which Judas and his brothers belonged was called, reached once again approximately to the borders of David's kingdom.

[12] Regarding the borders of the "promised land," see *Sifre Deut.* § 51 on Deut. xi.24 and the observations of G. Kittel upon this question in his translation, *Sifre zu Deuteronomium*, I Lieferung, Stuttgart o.J., pp. 135ff. Cf. Josephus, *Antiquities* xiii ff.

[13] The territory around Hebron and further to the south.

Chapter 4

THE RISE OF THE PARTIES

At the beginning of the Maccabean period stood the alliance of the Hasidim with the Maccabees, in which the Maccabees accepted the new Hasidic interpretation of the Law.[1] But already during the reign of Jonathan we hear, through Josephus,[2] of three parties, the Sadducees, the Pharisees and the Essenes. They differed, in the first place, in their interpretation of the Law, in that the Sadducees did not recognise the "fence around the law," the "tradition of the elders," while both the other parties further developed it in various ways; in the second place, however, they differed in material aspects of their climates of thought and faith, again to the extent that the Sadducees represented the older standpoint, whereas the two other groups developed out of the Hasidic movement for repentance new ideas and new dogmas. These may be summed up by the term "transcendentalism," i.e. "that world," "the world to come," a "transcendental" world beyond, stands in antithesis to "this world." In the process decisive presuppositions were created for New Testament thinking. In first considering the beginnings of this new climate of ideas among the Hasidim and so showing the aims they were pursuing, we shall later be able to fit the Essene and Pharisaic outlooks into this development.

[1] Josephus, *Antiquities* XIII.10, 6 (§ 296) says that Hyrcanus abrogated the regulations which the Pharisees established for the people; he uses a similar phrase in respect of the reintroduction of the pharisaic regulations under Alexandra, *Antiquities* XIII.16, 2 (§ 408). It is hard to conceive of any other time for the initial introduction of these regulations than that of the alliance of the Maccabees with the Hasidim, of whose distinction from the Pharisees Josephus was no longer aware.

[2] *Antiquities* XIII.V, 9 (§§ 171–173).

The Beginnings of New Ideas among the Hasidim

As sources in this respect we have at our disposal the book of Daniel, II Maccabees, and the oldest portion of the Ethiopic Book of Enoch (see p. 76), the so-called "Vision of the Seventy Shepherds."[3]

The *Book of Daniel* was written during the period of trial under Antiochus IV. Although the Maccabean struggle had already begun, the writer regards it as only "a little help" (Daniel XI.34). He anticipates a victorious campaign on the part of the Syrian king against Egypt and a crushing oppression of Palestine since the pagan prince would encamp there in the height of his fury and with all the power of a conquering field-marshal. But his end will then come, with none to help him (Dan. XI.45). In reality, however, Antiochus had to return from Egypt with his mission unaccomplished, and later fell in the eastern part of his kingdom. We can gather from these facts when Daniel was written.

The Book of Daniel has only one object: to summon the Jews in the distressing time of religious persecution to loyalty and belief to the very end. It consists in part of ancient stories about Daniel and shows by means of them that God can rescue His own, when they hold fast to Him, even from the jaws of lions, and from the fiery furnace, and can humble to the dust the proudest ruler who rears himself against Him. The reply that Shadrach, Meshach and Abednego made to king Nebuchadnezzar must be the reply of all righteous people to Antiochus IV and his commands: "If it be so, our God whom we serve is able to deliver us from the burning, fiery furnace; and he will deliver us out of your hand, O king. But if not, be it known to you, O king, that we will not serve your gods or worship the golden image." (Dan. III.17f.)

The *Vision of the Seventy Shepherds* portrays the history of humanity from Adam to the coming of the Messiah in terms of a history of animals and derives its name from its portrayal of the fate of Israel since the destruction of Jerusalem as the story of a flock of sheep given over to be pastured by seventy shepherds, i.e. the seventy angels of the nations.

Both these writings have in common the fact that they view

[3] I *Enoch* LXXXV–XC.

world-history as a unified event, in which the nations of the world exist, inhuman and opposed to God, in a state of war with the people of God. The various nations of the Old Testament at enmity with Israel, their predatory character symbolised in Daniel VII by the image of beasts of prey, are contrasted with the "saints of the Most High," seen under the aspect of a man. In similar fashion the birds of prey in the "Vision of the Seventy Shepherds" stand in opposition to the sheep, the people of Israel. In Daniel II.31ff. the unity of the world-empires is even more clearly indicated by the single statue. Behind this might of the nations of the world viewed as such a unity Daniel already sees supernatural, "transcendental" powers: the "prince" of the kingdom of Persia (Dan. x.13, 20), the "prince" Michael, Israel's guardian angel (Dan. x.21; XII.1, 5f.). By the seventy shepherds in the book of Enoch are also meant the guardian angels of the Gentile nations. Moreover, mention is made there, in connexion with Genesis VI.1ff., of a fall of angelic powers. In the end, just as the world-powers at enmity with God were viewed as a unitary whole, so the spiritual powers ranged behind them received a single head; the Old Testament figure of Satan, the "Divine Attorney-General,"[4] became the head of the spiritual and human world inimical to God.

If the eyes of the Hasidim were thus opened to the prospect of a world beyond, this had necessary consequences for the conception of the time of salvation. This is described in the Old Testament as a period of peace and plenty under a king of David's line. Now men gradually became freer to contemplate a time of salvation which burst the conditions of the present earth. The clearest expression of this in the period after the New Testament is that the world will at some time return to "primeval silence" and then the new world, "which is not yet awake" will be roused.[5] This meant that the Messiah also received supra-mundane characteristics; these were gathered up in the figure of a pre-existent "Son of Man" abiding with God, and appointed to be judge of the world.

If we survey this whole development from its beginnings to

[4] Cf. W. O. E. Oesterley and T. H. Robinson, *An Introduction to the Old Testament*, London 1934, p. 167.

[5] IV Ezra VII.30f.

Summary its final elaboration we see that it concerns two things: a world beyond and a schism between God and Satan, good and evil, that reaches right into the invisible world, and will only be ended in a new world. The motives and starting-points for this development are clear: the conflict between the righteous and the ungodly, in the home-land and in the world, which attained epoch-making proportions in the Maccabean Wars, and the Old Testament consciousness of God's "otherness" and transcendence of the world; finally, the problem of theodicy which became an increasingly heavy burden, especially in the Maccabean period. For at that time many of the pious had to suffer a martyr's death for their faith, and we can see how it was the belief in God's omnipotence which enabled them to grasp the hope of resurrection of the dead. So the mother says to the youngest of her seven sons, who were martyred for the sake of their fidelity to the Law: "I beseech you, my child, to look at the heaven and the earth and see everything that is in them, and recognise that God made them out of things that did not exist. Thus also mankind comes into being. . . . Accept death, so that in God's mercy I may get you back again with your brothers." And he goes to his death with the words: "For your brothers after enduring a brief suffering have drunk of everflowing life under God's covenant" (II Maccabees VII.28, 29, 36; cf. XIV.46).

But it cannot be denied that the formulation of these new ideas resulted from the influence of an exotic and Gentile climate of thought, namely Iranian Zoroastrianism, with which the Jews became acquainted in Babylon during the Persian period. A clear indication of the Iranian influence is the name of the demon Asmodeus in Tobit III.8 who corresponded to the Iranian "devil of lust," Aeshma Daéva;[6] it is also of significance that the remembrance was preserved in Judaism that the angelic names had come from the east.[7] The Iranian religion of Zoroaster recognised a primeval dualism between good and evil, light and darkness, truth and falsehood, between which every man had at one time made his choice; it also recognised a conflict running through the world between the good god

[6] E. Lehmann in A. Bertholet and E. Lehmann, *Lehrbuch der Religionsgeschichte*, 4th edn. Tübingen 1925, VOL. II, p. 225; H. Lommel, *Die Religion Zarathustras*, Tübingen 1930, p. 78.

[7] *J.T.R.Sh.* 1.56 d, quoted Strack-Billerbeck VOL. II, p. 90.

Ahura Mazda and the wicked god Ahriman; again it recognised a multiplicity of good and evil spirits and expected a final destruction of Ahriman and a cosmic judgment.[8]

The Dead Sea Discoveries

A few years after the Maccabeans and the Hasidim had resolved to make common cause, tensions became apparent between them. The two books of the Maccabees are already highly suggestive in this respect. The first gives us on the whole a very reliable account of the Maccabean wars up till the death of Simon; its author censures the attitude of the Hasidim (I Maccabees VII.12f.) and there is no trace in him of the resurrection hope developed in Hasidic circles. The second book of Maccabees, which only describes Judas' career, does represent on the other hand the belief in the resurrection of the dead, but is less reliable in many historical data.[9]

Ever since 1947 when two Bedouin discovered in a cave at the north-west corner of the Dead Sea some jars containing manuscripts wrapped in linen, there has been an unbroken chain of discoveries and investigations in that area, which has yielded a literature which now defies mastery.[10] It concerns three things:—

a) The manuscript finds in the caves. In that area over two hundred caves, most of them very difficult of access, have been

[8] On the religio-historical aspects of Judaism see E. Meyer, *Ursprung und Anfänge des Christentums*, Stuttgart 1925, VOL. II, chs. II–IV; W. Bousset, *Die Religion des Judentums im späthellenistischen Zeitalter*, henceforth cited as *Die Religion des Judentums*, 3rd edn. edited by H. Gressmann, Tübingen 1926, ch. XXV; W. F. Albright, *From the Stone Age to Christianity*, 2nd edn. Baltimore 1946, pp. 356ff.; W. O. E. Oesterley, *The Jews and Judaism during the Greek Period*, London 1941, pp. 85ff. For further literature see footnote 65 of this chapter.

[9] III Maccabees, so-called, is a legendary account of an unsuccessful attempt on the part of the Egyptian king Ptolemy IV Philopater (221–214 B.C.) to annihilate the Jews in Egypt, and of his change of heart. IV Maccabees is a freely elaborated legendary narrative of the martyrdom related in II Macc. 7, and is intended to show that reason allied to the Law is supreme over sufferings and passions; the writer attempts to combine stoic ideas with Judaism.

[10] Complete bibliography up till 1955: Chr. Burchard, *Bibliographie zu den Handschriften vom Toten Meer*, Berlin 1957; continuation in *Revue de Qumran*, Paris October 1958 *et seq.* Extensive account of the discussion with full bibliography in M. Burrows, *The Dead Sea Scrolls*, London 1956; sequel by the same author in *More Light on the Dead Sea Scrolls*, henceforth cited as *More Light*, London 1958. Short summaries: J. M. Allegro, *The Dead Sea Scrolls and the origins of Christianity*, Harmondsworth 1956; F. F. Bruce, *Second Thoughts on the Dead Sea Scrolls*, London

examined in systematic searches; in thirty-seven of them pottery has been found, and in eleven of them manuscripts or fragments of manuscripts down to the tiniest shreds. The finds in Cave I[11] and some important fragments from Cave IV[12] have been published. Tens of thousands of small and minute shreds of manuscripts from Cave IV and the even richer discoveries from Cave XI, together with the texts from the other caves still await editing and publication.[13]

As radio-active tests have shown, the linen in which the texts from Cave I were wrapped dates from the period *circa* 170 B.C. to A.D. 230; the texts are accordingly not a modern forgery, nor did they originate only in the Middle Ages.

b) Since 1949 the site (already long known) of a ruin in that area called Khirbet Qumran has been excavated in several sections. This has yielded a network of buildings covering an area approximately 260 feet square, which an aqueduct fed with water to fourteen cisterns. While surprisingly no coins were found in any of the caves, the building-complex did yield some from the time of John Hyrcanus to the beginning of the Jewish war; only the period of Herod the Great was quite unrepresented in this respect. Besides a large room approximately 15 by 72 feet and, adjacent to it, another containing a remarkable amount of table crockery (over 1,000 pieces!) it is significant that the existence has also been established there of a pottery, a bakery, a flour-mill and a writing-room, complete with writing desks and ink-wells. It is moreover noteworthy that in many places there had been stored in earthenware vessels carefully selected bones from animals which according to Jewish ideas were "pure."

1956; J. T. Milik, *Dix ans de découvertes dans le Désert de Juda*, Paris 1957; K. Schubert, *Die Gemeinde vom Toten Meer*, München 1958; F. M. Cross, *The Ancient Library of Qumran*, New York 1958; H. Bardtke, *Die Handschriften vom Toten Meer*, VOL. I, Berlin 1952, VOL. II, Berlin 1958; G. Vermès, *The Dead Sea Scrolls in English*, London 1962.

[11] With the exception of some severely damaged pages of the Genesis Apocryphon.

[12] Published by J. M. Allegro in *Journal of Biblical Literature and Exegesis*, henceforth cited as *J.B.L.*, LXXV (1956), pp. 89–95, 174–187. Translation by Burrows, *More Light*, pp. 401ff. (see note 10).

[13] I omit at this point the discoveries at Wadi Murabba' at which yielded, *inter alia*, letters written by the leader of the war of A.D. 132–135.

c) East of the ruin and adjoining it a great cemetery was discovered whose graves, over 1,000 of them, had all been laid out in rows running from north to south, and made identifiable by uniform layers of stone. Only males had been interred in them, and the interiors of the graves, which were identical in every case, yielded no supplementary items of any kinds. In the surrounding area, still further graveyards were found, which, however, were not orientated so uniformly; women and children had been buried in them, and some here and there yielded a few supplementary items.

These three things, the caves with their manuscripts, the site of the ruin at Khirbet Qumran and the cemetery or cemeteries, belong together and give us information about the quasi-monastic community of the Essenes about which we knew something before the finds, principally through Pliny, Josephus and Philo of Alexandria.

Pliny, the Roman, who died in A.D. 79 during the eruption of Vesuvius, writes that the Essenes lived on the west side of the Dead Sea: ". . . a solitary tribe . . . which is remarkable above all other tribes in the whole world, as it has no women, and has renounced all sexual desire, has no money and has only palm-trees for company. Day by day the throng of refugees is recruited to an equal number by numerous acessions of persons tired of life and driven thither by the waves of fortune to adopt their manners. Thus through thousands of ages (incredible to relate) a race in which no one is born lives on for ever: so prolific for their advantage is other men's weariness of life!"[14]

Josephus' extensive account of the Essenes must be discussed later (vide pp. 164ff.); here we need only stress the fact that according to Josephus the Essenes formed in its main branch a purely male order, which demanded of its members on initiation the surrender of personal property, and bound them to live with the utmost simplicity and not to outdo each other in their dress.[15] This fits in with the absence of coins in the caves and the simplicity and uniformity of the male cemetery.

[14] Pliny, *Natural History*, v.15 trans. H. Rackham, Loeb Classical Library, 9 vols., London 1938 *et seq.*, VOL. II, p. 277.

[15] *War* II.8, 7 (§ 140). Strictly speaking, this refers only to the case of an Essene acquiring an office, but it must then have applied all the more to the whole community.

And what we hear elsewhere from Josephus is confirmed by the writings found in the caves to the extent that we can connect the caves containing manuscripts, Khirbet Qumran and the cemetery with the Essenes. As Josephus speaks of several branches of the Essenes, one of which was not celibate, and as the cave texts do not agree on every point (e.g. in the matter of the sharing of goods), it would be better to speak of an Essene movement rather than "the Essenes."[16]

The manuscripts and fragments found in the caves can be divided into three groups; firstly they yielded copies of Old Testament books, including *inter alia* two of the book of Isaiah, but mainly only fragments from all parts of the Old Testament except the book of Esther; these finds are of utmost significance for the textual history of the Old Testament. In addition there are a few fragments from the Apocryphal books of Jesus Sirach and Tobit.

Secondly, some writings were found, hitherto completely unknown to us, which throw light upon the ideas and also upon something of the history of the Essenes, especially the so-called "Sectarian Document" or, better, "Manual of Discipline," a "Book of Hymns" or "Psalms of Thanksgiving" and a document called "The War of the Sons of Light and the Sons of Darkness" (the "War Scroll"); with these goes a document already known to us earlier from a Cairo synagogue, the so-called "Damascus Document,"[17] of which a few fragments were also found in the caves. With these belong, moreover, commentaries on some of the prophets and the Psalms, especially the comparatively well-preserved Habakkuk Commentary; in these writings the Old Testament prophecies are applied to the present and immediate future situation of the Essenes.

Thirdly, a series of writings was discovered in the caves—unfortunately only in fragments—with which we were already familiar earlier, since Christian Churches, mostly in outlying areas, had preserved them. These include the Book of Jubilees,

[16] Josephus makes no mention of *one* centre, that might be Khirbet Qumran; according to him the Essenes live in several towns, but the Qumran documents also presuppose this fact.

[17] Henceforth cited as the "*Zadokite Document*," the title used by T. H. Gaster in *The Scriptures of the Dead Sea Sect*, London 1957, from which translation the passages quoted in this chapter are taken, except where otherwise indicated (Tr.).

the Ethiopic Book of Enoch and the Testaments of the Twelve Patriarchs, to which we must return later (vide p. 76). For, of all these texts, the Commentaries, the Manual of Discipline, the Hymns and the Zadokite Document give us testimonies from the first period of the Essene Movement, while the other writings cannot automatically be fitted into the history of the Essenes. Even in the writings mentioned it is difficult to gain a more detailed picture of the events and their dating, as the key characters are almost exclusively referred to by cryptic titles such as "Teacher of Righteousness," "Wicked Priest," "House of Absalom," *inter alia*. Yet we can gain from them some impression, at least, of the decisive events.

The First Period of the Essene Movement

The decisive events lie between two points: the beginning of the Maccabean Wars and the warlike dispute between Alexander Jannaeus and the Pharisees (88 B.C.);[18] they took place therefore principally in the second half of the second century B.C. In this period, which was regarded by the Essenes as an age of the dominion of Belial,[19] "three snares" were sent by the latter upon Israel: whoredom, lucre and pollution.[20] By "whoredom" was meant polygamy, which was treated by the Pharisees of the Temple as entirely and unhesitatingly permissible,[21] but which the Zadokite Document, in its exegesis of Genesis I.27 and VII.9, regards as forbidden of God. It is explicitly said at this point that this prohibition of polygamy applies also to the "prince," i.e. to one of the reigning Hasmoneans; it therefore concerns a concrete instance. By "pollution of the Temple" is meant, amongst other things, the marriage of uncle and niece. In Leviticus XVIII.13 the Old Testament forbade marriage between aunt and nephew; but

[18] The Pharisaic writings pass over the Essenes in silence and no specifically pharisaic document has been discovered amongst the finds at Qumran; only the book of Daniel has been found in Caves I and IV at Qumran, where it was not yet regarded as canonical, although the Pharisees had taken it up into their canon. On the other hand, the *Commentary on Nahum* (*J.B.L.* LXXV (1956) pp. 90f.) alludes to the struggle between Jannaeus and the Pharisees in such a way as to make clear that the Essenes had already by that time separated from the Pharisees.

[19] Belial is the title for Satan that was preferred at Qumran; cf. II Cor. VI.15 "Beliar" (R.S.V. mg.).

[20] *Zadokite Document*, IV.13ff.

[21] Strack-Billerbeck, VOL. III, pp. 647–650.

some Hasidim were of the opinion that marriage between uncle and niece was thereby also forbidden. Here again Pharisaism did not concur with this exegesis. By "lucre" is meant all wealth which stems from "sinners." Thus the "wicked priest" is accused of amassing the wealth of the "criminals" and also the wealth of the (Gentile) peoples: according to a fresh interpretation of the Law on the part of some Hasidim the prince was forbidden (especially if he was high priest at the same time) to enrich himself at the expense of the godless and the Gentiles.[22] The unprecedented nature of this demand becomes clear when one considers that it had to do here with what according to the ancient Law were completely legitimate spoils of war; we see how earnestly in other respects the Essene order took the avoidance of unrighteous wealth in the fact that it forbade its members to accept anything from non-members, who were regarded as ungodly, other than in return for cash. In each of the three points mentioned there arose sharp opposition to the ruling high priest and prince, whose conduct in these matters was condemned as ungodly. Thereby the whole temple worship appeared to be defiled. Other things that we can no longer exactly recognise ensued: unrighteous judgment, questions of the calendar, etc. Thus at a time that cannot be fixed with any precision Hasidic priests resolved no longer to go "into the sanctuary to keep the flame alive on the altar"[23] and broke away from both it and the "men of ill-repute" in general. Laymen also joined up with them.

With this separation from the temple, not only did the alliance of Hasidim and Hasmoneans break up, but it led to a split among the Hasidim themselves: some did not break with the temple and the reigning Hasmonean; these were the "Pharisees." But those who did split away joined the order of the Essenes.

The Superior of this order was a man whom we know by the title "Teacher of Righteousness." The Damascus Document, which is rich generally in allusions to the history of the Essene community, describes the beginning of the movement in the following words:

[22] *Commentary on Habakkuk*, VIII.8ff. on Hab. II.5–6.
[23] *Zadokite Document*, VI.11ff.

"[God] brought to blossom alike out of the priesthood and out of the laity that root which had been planted of old. . . . Then they realised their iniquity and knew that they had been at fault. For twenty years, however, they remained like blind men groping their way, until at last God took note of their deeds, how that they were seeking Him sincerely, and He raised up for them one who would teach the Law correctly (i.e. a Teacher of Righteousness), to guide them in the way of His heart and to demonstrate to future ages what He does to a generation that incurs His anger, that is, to the congregation of those that betray Him, and turn aside from His way."[24]

The activity of the "Teacher" is described here as lying in two directions: to guide along God's way and to convey a message regarding God's dealings at the end of time.

The first God-given task of the Teacher is, therefore, *to teach the will of God*. The texts make clear what that means. His prophetic message can be summed up in the phrase: total obedience to the total will of God. Total obedience means, as the texts frequently declare, to do His will with the whole  heart and the whole soul,[25] to "walk blamelessly."[26] It concerns something all-embracing, and the expression "circumcision of the heart," known from the Old Testament and from Paul (Romans II.25ff.), is also found in the Essene texts.[27] This striving after radical obedience is especially apparent in that these writings know only an "either-or"; either love God, or rebel against Him, either cleave to Him, or reject Him, either walk in His path, or stray from it, either do His will, or follow one's own inclinations and walk in the "stubbornness of the heart." Outside the covenant of the Essenes there are only the ungodly, who fail to surrender themselves wholly to what is the whole will of God. And whatever Levitical purifications are practised outside the Order these are ineffective as long

[24] *Zadokite Document* I.7–12. Instead of "generation that incurs His anger" (literally "generation of anger") the MS. reads, erroneously, "final generation" (a difference of one letter).

[25] *Zadokite Document*, I.10; XV.12; *Manual of Discipline*, V.9; *Hymns*, XV.10, etc.

[26] *Zadokite Document*, I.20f.; II.15; XX.2, 5, 7; *Manual of Discipline*, I.8; II.2; III.3, 9; IV.22; VIII.10, 20f., 25; IX.2, 5, 8f., 19, etc.

[27] *Manual of Discipline*, V.5; *Commentary on Habakkuk*, XI.13.

as one "rejects the government of God and refuses the discipline of communion with Him."[28]

That which must be done with the whole heart is the total will of God. It is a matter of not "turning aside from the ordinances of God's truth," of not "turning either to the right or to the left."[29] This involves "carrying out explicitly the Law," as the Damascus Document formulates it.[30] The "Teacher" has given no new Law, although certainly a new exposition of the old. That was already clear from the "three snares of Belial," commented on above (see p. 49), but is also perceptible in the fact that frequently the Old Testament is quoted as the basis of a precept.[31] In places the calendar plays a great rôle, being so ordered that the same feasts fall annually on the same day of the week.[32] Apart from this, however, rules are laid down covering the whole gamut of matters regulated by the Old Testament Law: the administration of justice, the giving of testimony, lost property, clean and unclean animals, etc.[33]

In the Damascus Document the stipulations regarding the Sabbath are particularly detailed. In all, twenty-eight regulations, all of them prohibitions, are laid down in relation to this day. Most of these precepts are to be found scattered throughout the Pharisaic writings,[34] a sign of the common origin of Essenism and Pharisaism. But one thing cannot be gainsaid, although it is not clear in the rabbinic writings: the aim of these stipulations about the Sabbath is to keep it holy, not merely outwardly through avoidance of certain actions, but also in thought and in word.

After the fundamental rule that the Sabbath already commences some time before sundown (see p. 37), it goes on to say:

[28] *Manual of Discipline*, III.5f.; cf. IX.3–5.

[29] *Manual of Discipline*, I.15; III.10.

[30] *Zadokite Document*, IV.8 and *passim*.

[31] *Zadokite Document*, IX.2–8; XI.19–21; XVI.14f.

[32] *Zadokite Document*, III.13–15: God made good His everlasting Covenant, i.e. allowed the Essene movement to arise, "revealing to them the hidden things concerning which Israel in general had gone astray—even His holy sabbaths and glorious festivals . . . ." Further information in, e.g. Burrows, *The Dead Sea Scrolls*, pp. 238–242.

[33] The *Halakhah* of the movement has been preserved only in the *Zadokite Document*; it is not expounded in the *Manual of Discipline*.

[34] H. Braun, *Spätjüdisch-häretischer und frühchristlicher Radikalismus*, Tübingen 1957, VOL. I, pp. 116ff.

"On the Sabbath day, no one is to indulge in ribald or empty talk. . . . No one is to talk about labour or work to be done the next day. No one is to go out into the field while it is still Sabbath with the intention of resuming his work immediately the Sabbath ends. . . . No one is to put pressure on his male or female servant or on his hired help on the Sabbath."[35]

Indicative of the spirit that was alive in the Order are some brief summary admonitions:—

> "To pay their required dues in conformity with the detailed rules thereof; to love each man his neighbour like himself; to grasp the hand of the poor, the needy and the stranger; to seek each man the welfare of his fellow, to cheat not his own kin; to abstain from whoredom, as is meet; to bring no charge against his neighbour except by due process, and not to nurse grudges from day to day."[36]

and

> "to seek God; to do what is good and upright in His sight, in accordance with what He has commanded through Moses and through His servants the prophets; to love all that He has chosen and hate all that He has rejected; to keep far from all evil and to cling to all good works; to act truthfully and righteously and justly on earth and to walk no more in the stubbornness of a guilty heart and of lustful eyes, doing all manner of evil."[37]

To love one's brother was a matter of serious concern within the Order, and many separate precepts are devoted to it. How far the "Teacher" himself developed this new deepened understanding of the Law in detail we cannot tell, but that it derives from him in the first place is certain.[38] Of course, the moral, casuistic and legal aspects are also interwoven here, but

[35] *Zadokite Document*, X.17–22, 35.

[36] *Zadokite Document*, VI.20–VII.3.

[37] *Manual of Discipline*, I.1–7.

[38] *Zadokite Document*, VI.10f. appears to suggest that none of the Teacher's regulations could be altered until another man, also called the "Teacher of Righteousness," arose at the end of the days. It is hard to imagine, however, that no development in the understanding of the Law occurred in a community to which each member contributed his intellectual powers and in which the Law was pondered upon unceasingly, a community also where justice was administered among themselves and where members exercised the care of each other's souls. Yet the "Halakhah" is not developed to the same extent as in Pharisaism.

with the clear intention that the moral aspects should penetrate the legal.

The second task of the Teacher, of which the Damascus Document speaks, relates to *a new understanding of the prophetic predictions of the Old Testament.* In the Habakkuk Commentary we read: "God told Habakkuk to write down the things that were to come upon the latter age, but He did not inform him when the moment would come to fulfilment."

But "God has made (the Teacher) *au courant* with all the deeper implications of the words of His servants the prophets."[39]

Although none of the Qumran commentaries, which are preserved mainly in fragmentary form, may be ascribed to the "Teacher" himself, nevertheless the basic presupposition that the hour which the prophets had predicted has now actually come in his, i.e. the Teacher's, time may be traced back to him. The prophecy of Habakkuk I about the coming of the "Chaldeans" refers, according to the interpretation of the Commentary introduced by the Teacher, not to the ancient people of the Chaldeans now long extinct, but to a people who, at the time of the Teacher, loomed large on the Jewish horizon as the invincible nation. The text alludes to them only by the cryptic name of "Kittim," meaning by that the Romans;[40] the woes of the second chapter of Habakkuk are referred to the antagonist of the "Teacher," the "wicked priest;" the well-known passage in Habakkuk II.4, upon which Paul based Romans I.17, "the righteous shall live by his faith," is interpreted in the Habakkuk Commentary as referring "to all in Jewry who carry out the Law (*Torah*). On account of their labour and of their faith in him who expounded the Law aright (i.e. the Teacher of Righteousness), God will deliver them from the house of judgment."[41]

So the Teacher believes himself to be living with his movement in the final age predicted by the prophets, the final age which is in a special sense a time of distress and of the rule of the wicked one, Belial, a time which is moving quickly towards a final mighty struggle between the "Sons of Light" and the

[39] *Commentary on Habakkuk*, VII.1-5, on Hab. II.1–2.

[40] On the debate as to whether by the Kittim are meant the Syrians or the Romans see Burrows, *The Dead Sea Scrolls*, pp. 123-142. The whole tenor of the statements about the Kittim accords, in my opinion, only with the Romans.

[41] *Commentary on Habakkuk*, VIII.1–3.

"Sons of Darkness," which is likewise a conclusive struggle between God and His angels on the one hand, and Belial and his hosts on the other. This struggle leads to the destruction of Belial and the rout of all evil and of all wicked men upon the earth and brings a time of salvation, of eternal peace and blessing for the "Sons of Light," a communion with the angels and a restoration of all things. These three factors are probably looked on as together signifying the return of the day of Paradise, the day when men, in fellowship with God and the heavenly hosts, live on a renewed earth and under a renewed heaven.[42] Only a few statements can be made out regarding the final judgment. Besides a judgment upon the ungodly in fire and brimstone mention is made of their eternal destruction. Of the Gentiles it is not only said that they will be destroyed but that "all peoples" shall one day know God's "glory."[43] Only a few hints are given about the resurrection of the righteous.[44]

Already in the great final struggle of the "Sons of Light and the Sons of Darkness," which is the theme of the "War Scroll," reference is made to the two "Messiahs," i.e. the two anointed ones,[45] the "Anointed of Aaron," the high priest of the final age, and the "Anointed of Israel," the "Prince of the whole Community" in the final age. There the high priest of the final age is superior to the "prince." In the final struggle he does not, it is true, take up arms, as he is priest, but he blesses and encourages the warriors. At the messianic meal he has precedence. This surprising duplication of the Messiah has its starting-point in Zechariah IV.1–14, its historical occasion in the fusion on the part of the Maccabees of the princely and high priestly offices, which led to a secularising of their whole function.

The task of the anointed high priest of the final age is, as the anointed of the Spirit, to direct the people spiritually; the

[42] *Hymns*, VII.14f.; XI.25f.; XV.16; *Manual of Discipline* IV.25; *Hymns*, III.21f.; VI.13; XI.11f.; XIII.11f. Is the stress laid in *Manual of Discipline*, III.17f. upon the fact that God has destined man to rule the world connected perhaps with the fact that it will only achieve total fulfilment in the time of salvation?

[43] *Hymns*, VI.12f. This hope is already apparent in the *Vision of the Seventy Shepherds*, I Enoch, XC.37f. For the destruction of the ungodly see *Hymns*, IV.20, 26, etc.

[44] *Hymns*, VI.34; XI.10–14; *Manual of Discipline*, IV.7f., 23. *Zadokite Document*, VII.6 speaks of life "preserved for a thousand generations."

[45] The titles "Messiah" and "Christ" both mean "Anointed."

anointed prince of the whole community is his secular arm. He will "maintain the sovereignty of [God's] people for ever . . . and judge the needy in righteousness and . . . walk blamelessly in all the ways of [His truth]."[46]

Neither of the "anointed" is a Saviour-figure, neither has any significance for the salvation of the individual, and this is true all the more of the "Teacher." There is no sign of the transcendentalising of the messianic conceptions.

The existence of the Essene Community is of significance for the coming of the time of salvation in that it sees itself as the community of the final age. By its complete commitment to total obedience to the law it creates "atonement for the earth."[47] This is not to be understood in the sense of a treasury of merits but in the sense that the obedience demanded of the community by God so purifies the land of Israel that God can bring about the time of salvation.

The significance of the "Teacher" extends, however, beyond what has been observed hitherto. This follows from the two most important documents, the Manual of Discipline and the Hymns. Neither of the writings mentions the "Teacher," and it is a very probable assumption that this is connected with the fact that they were written by him. Even if that should not be the case, they give us the profoundest insight into the religious life and the theological thinking of the man who moulded the Essene movement in its first period.

The first and at the same time decisively important characteristic of the speaker in the "Hymns" is that he knows himself to be endowed with the Holy Spirit: it is, indeed, a spirit of knowledge that is given to him: ". . . through the spirit Thou hast placed within me, [I have] come to know Thee, my God."[48]

As such, as one endowed with a spirit, he is the leader of the Qumran movement.

"They that walked in the way Thou desirest have hearkened unto me . . . ."[49] "Thou hast . . . hidden Thy teaching

[46] D. Barthélemy and J. T. Milik, *Qumran Cave I*, henceforth cited as *Cave I*, pp. 127f. (I QSb v.20–29) [Translation by H. Gaster, *The Scriptures of the Dead Sea Sect*, p. 101]. A. S. van der Woude, *Die messianischen Vorstellungen der Gemeinde von Qumrân*, Assen u. Neukirchen 1957.

[47] *Manual of Discipline*, v.6; VIII.6, 10; IX.4.

[48] *Hymns*, XII.11f.

[49] *Hymns*, IV.24.

[within me], until it be shown unto me that the hour of Thy triumph is come."[50] "Thou hast [chosen me] and set me as a father to them Thou holdest dear, and as a nurse unto them whom Thou hast made exemplars of men."[51] "Yet didst Thou, O my God, set in my mouth rain at all seasons."[52] "Albeit unto transgressors I am but a symbol of weakness, yet unto them that repent I am a source of healing (cf. II Cor. II.15f.); prudence to the unwary, temperance to the rash. Thou hast made me a reproach and a derision to them that live by deceit, but a symbol of truth and understanding to all whose way is straight."[53]

The insights which the speaker, presumably the Teacher, believes he has been given, are not exhausted by the things with which we have already become acquainted, namely, the new understanding of the Law which throws into prominence as especially important aspects of it the requirement of monogamy, the radical putting away of ill-gotten wealth, and the demands of love towards God and the neighbour; neither are they exhausted by perceiving that the predictions of the prophets are being fulfilled in his, the Teacher's, time. What he has recognised over and above this is God's majesty and man's insignificance and sinfulness. When we have in our mind's eye the traditional picture of the Pharisee as the self-satisfied, self-righteous man, proud of his works, we are amazed here to detect other tones:

"Verily I know that righteousness lies not with man, nor perfection of conduct with mortals. Only with God on High are all works of righteousness; and ne'er can the way of man be stablished save by the spirit which God has fashioned for him, to bring unto perfection the life of mortal man."[54] [I am] shapen of clay and kneaded with water, a bedrock of shame and a source of pollution, a cauldron of iniquity and a fabric of sin, a spirit errant, wayward and witless, distraught by every just judgment. . . . Thine, O God of all knowledge, are all works of righteousness and the secret of truth; while man's is but thraldom to wrongdoing, and works of deceit."[55] "Without Thee nothing is wrought, and without Thy will can

[50] *Hymns*, V.11f.
[51] *Hymns*, VII.20f.
[52] *Hymns*, VIII.16.
[53] *Hymns*, II.8–10.
[54] *Hymns*, IV.30–32.
[55] *Hymns*, I.21–23, 26f.

nothing be known."[56] "Moreover, through the discernment which Thou hast bestowed upon me I am come to know that not by the hand of flesh can a mortal order his way."[57]

But the Teacher has not merely perceived man's sinfulness and insignificance before God.

"[I] know that there is hope for that which Thou didst mould out of dust to have consort with things eternal."[58] "I have learned to put hope in Thy mercy."[59] "So I am come to know that in [Thy] loving [kindness] lies hope for them that repent and for them that abandon sin, [and confidence for him] who walks in the way of Thy heart."[60] "None can withstand Thy wrath. Yet, all that are children of Thy truth Thou bringest before Thee with forgiveness, cleansing them of their transgressions through Thine abundant goodness."[61]

The Teacher hints at something of the means by which he has arrived at these perceptions in the Hymns. He not only says of himself what Paul likewise said of himself (Gal. I.15), that God had prepared him from the womb, but also that from his youth up He had enlightened him with "understanding of His judgments"[62]: through His stern direction God had been at work on him. Here the mind of the leading man in the Essene movement is dominated by the God of the Old Testament, the Creator and the All-merciful.

But all these perceptions are now undergirded by a definite theological concept, taken from Iran and fused with the Old Testament heritage into a new unity; this concept, which for the first time allows us to perceive properly the structure of the Essene movement, is that of Predestination. The "Manual of Discipline" contains a fundamental passage which reads:

"All that is and ever was comes from a God of knowledge. Before things came into existence He determined the plan of

[56] *Hymns*, x.2. [57] *Hymns*, xv.12f. [58] *Hymns*, III.20f.
[59] *Hymns*, IX.14. [60] *Hymns*, VI.6f.

[61] The recognition of God's mercy is based upon the Old Testament; cf. the passage from the *Manual of Discipline* quoted on p. 52 below. Cf. also *Zadokite Document* IV.9f.; "According to the covenant which God established with the forefathers to forgive their sins, so God will forgive them (i.e. the men of the New Covenant)" (Trans. Burrows, *The Dead Sea Scrolls*, p. 352); cf. *Zadokite Document*, VIII.14–18; *Hymns*, XVII.12: "In Thine (abundant) mercy Thou has said by the hand of Moses that Thou wouldst forgive (lit. "bear;" cf. Jn. I.29) all iniquity and sin." The one who forgives is always God; there is no sign of a Mediator.

[62] *Hymns*, IX.31, 34; V.15f.—"Prepared from the womb;" XV.15.

them; and when they fill their appointed roles, it is in accordance with His glorious design that they discharge their functions. Nothing can be changed. . . .

"Now this God created man to rule the world, and appointed for him two spirits after whose direction he was to walk until the final Inquisition. They are the spirits of truth and of perversity.

"The origin of truth lies in the Fountain of Light, and that of perversity in the Wellspring of Darkness. All who practise righteousness are under the domination of the Prince of Lights and walk in ways of light; whereas all who practise perversity are under the domination of the Angel of Darkness and walk in ways of darkness. Through the Angel of Darkness, however, even those who practise righteousness are made liable to error. All their sin and their iniquities, all their guilt and their deeds of transgression are the result of his domination; and this, by God's inscrutable design, will continue until the time appointed by Him. Moreover, all men's afflictions and all their moments of tribulation are due to this being's malevolent sway. All of the spirits that attend upon him are bent on causing the sons of light to stumble. Howbeit, the God of Israel and the Angel of His truth are always there to help the sons of light. It is God that created these spirits of light and darkness and made them the basis of every act, the [instigators] of every deed and the directors of every thought. The one He loves to all eternity, and is ever pleased with its deeds; but any association with the other He abhors, and He hates all its ways to the end of time."[63]

Eternal enmity prevails between the two spirits, between their deeds and the men who belong to them:—

"Between the two categories [God] has set an eternal enmity. Deeds of perversity are an abomination to Truth, while all the ways of Truth are an abomination to perversity; and there is a constant jealous rivalry between their two regimes, for they do not march in accord. Howbeit, God in His inscrutable wisdom has appointed a term for the existence of perversity, and when the time of Inquisition comes, He will destroy it for ever. Then truth will emerge triumphant for the world. . . ."[64]

[63] *Manual of Discipline*, III.15–IV.1. For a parallel see *Hymns*, I.7–20.
[64] *Manual of Discipline*, IV.17–19.

Iranian influence is clearly present in this doctrine of the two "spirits."[65] There, not only Ahura Mazda and Ahriman but likewise all men have chosen between truth and falsehood before their birth. Here in Qumran, on the other hand, God stands over the two spirits, having created them both, and has also apportioned to men their lot beforehand. In this way the Iranian outlook is fused with the Old Testament monotheism. The link-up with Iran is clear at two points: first in the terminology, in that the Old Testament title "Satan" does not appear in the cave discoveries, at any rate in recognisable contexts; secondly in respect of content, for in the Qumran texts Belial is not what Satan primarily is in the Old Testament, namely the prosecutor before God, for which there is fundamentally no place in the texts; he is the tempter.

From the long passage from the Manual of Discipline quoted above it is not unequivocally clear in what relationship the individual man stands to the two spirits; whether the first sentences, according to which God has appointed to each his destiny before his birth, are intended in the sense of a predestination of the individual man either to be a son of light or a son of darkness. Other texts give us clear information on this matter. In the Damascus document we read of those who "treat (God's) ordinance as a thing to be shunned":

"Never, from the very beginning of the world, has God approved such men. He has always known what their actions would be, even before the foundations of them were laid. He has anathematised whole generations. . . . Nevertheless, in all of their generations He has ever raised up for Himself duly designated men, so that He might provide survival (i.e. survivors) for the earth and fill the face of the world with their seed."[66]

A passage from the Hymns is equally explicit:

"Thou alone it is that hath created the righteous, preparing him from the womb for the time of Thy good pleasure, to heed Thy covenant. . . . Thou hast [lavished] upon him the abundance of Thy mercies. . . . But the wicked hast Thou created

[65] K. G. Kuhn, "Die Sektenschrift und die iranische Religion," in *Zeitschrift für Theologie und Kirche*, henceforth cited as *Z.Th.K.*, XLIX (1952), pp. 296–316; H. Wildberger, "Der Dualismus in den Qumranschriften," in *Asiatische Studien*, Bern 1954, pp. 163–177; A. Dupont-Sommer, "Le problème des influences étrangères sur la secte juive de Qoumran" in *Revue d'Histoire et de Philosophie Religieuse* XXXV (1955), pp. 75–92.

[66] *Zadokite Document*, II.7–VIII.11.

for the time of Thy wrath, reserving them from the womb for the day of slaughter."[67]

The predestination is therefore a double one, to life and to destruction. All men are sinners alike; even the "Teacher" knows himself as such. But he knows himself as one chosen by God's grace. For this reason all the Hymns begin with "I give thanks unto Thee, O Lord."

"I give thanks unto Thee, O Lord, for Thou hast put my soul in the bundle of life"[68] . . . "I give thanks unto Thee, O Lord, for Thou hast freed my soul from the pit"[69] . . . "I give thanks unto Thee, O Lord, for by Thine own strength hast Thou stayed me, and hast wafted o'er me Thy holy spirit that I cannot be moved"[70] . . . "I give thanks unto Thee, O Lord, for Thou hast cast not my lot in the congregation of the false, nor set my portion in the company of dissemblers."[71]

The individual discerns his election in that God's majesty, man's mortality and God's mercy dawn upon him and lead him to surrender himself resolutely, voluntarily and with his whole heart to the entire Law of God.

This doctrine of Predestination has yet another aspect. One might expect that, even though the "Teacher", knowing himself to be a sinner, has chosen God's ordinance, a wooing love towards all others who, like him, are sinners would result from this. But this is just what we do not find; the "others" are to be hated. The Essenes undertook no universal mission. It was forbidden to acquaint non-members with the principles of the order.[72] The clearest expression of this is again a passage from the Hymns:

"I will admit no comrade into fellowship with me save by the measure of his understanding . . . as Thou keepest him afar, so too will I abhor him."[73]

Only when a man shows himself acceptable to the "divine community," as the Essenes call themselves in the texts, does the writer of the Hymns bestow his love upon him; as long as this acceptability is not apparent, he is worthy of hatred, as it must then be assumed that he is a "son of darkness."

[67] *Hymns*, XV.14–17. See also IV.38; XIII.7ff.; XIV.11–13; XV.13f.; XVI.9f.
[68] *Hymns*, II.20.
[69] *Hymns*, III.19.
[70] *Hymns*, VII.6.
[71] *Hymns*, VII.34.
[72] *Zadokite Document*, XV.10f.
[73] *Hymns*, XIV.18, 21.

These three things then, the radicalised interpretation of the Law, the application of the prophetic predictions to the present time and the conception of predestination work together and find their expression in the fact that the Essenes had drawn together into a community. Those who became members of it were conscious of being God's elect community of the final age, summoned by God to wholesale obedience in order that it might bring repentance to the land and might enable Him to bring about the day of salvation. They know themselves to be the community of the final age which is summoned to the final struggle against the hosts of Belial, and because so summoned, must seclude itself and follow the prescriptions for a monastic way of life.

Initiates into the order have to bring with them three things: their mental, their bodily and their material resources. Their mental resources: for the order constitutes a great community which is corporately enquiring after God's will and in which one member admonishes the other.[74]

"Wherever there be ten men who have been formally enrolled in the community, there is not to be absent from them one who can interpret the (Torah) to them at any time of day or night, for the harmonious adjustment of their human relations. The general members of the community are to keep awake for a third of all the nights of the year reading book(s), studying the Law and worshipping together."[75]

They bring their bodily resources, i.e. their capacity to work, into the community, for it is resolved to stand on its own feet and to be true to itself must do so, in order to be dependent for nothing upon the outsiders, the ungodly, nor to be beholden to them. Their material resources, their money, they bring into the community in order that it may be administered jointly, so that no one has any advantages over another.

Initiation into the community occurs after a two years' novitiate by means of an oath (not through any kind of baptismal rite!), which is apparently renewed every year. In the process "the priests are to rehearse the bounteous acts of God as revealed in all His deeds of power, and they are to recite all His tender mercies towards Israel; while the levites are to

[74] *Manual of Discipline*, v.23–25.

[75] *Manual of Discipline*, vi.6–8. "Torah" = the Pentateuch.

rehearse the iniquities of the children of Israel and all the guilty transgressions and sins that they have committed through the domination of Belial. And all who enter the covenant are to make confession after them, saying, We have acted perversely, we have transgressed, we have sinned, we have done wickedly, ourselves and our fathers before us . . . God has been right to bring His judgment upon us and upon our fathers. Howbeit, always from ancient times He has also bestowed His mercies upon us, and so will He do for all time to come."

Then the priests bless "all that have cast their lot with God," and the levites curse "all that have cast their lot with Belial," saying: ". . . Cursed art thou, beyond hope of mercy. Even as thy works are wrought in darkness, so mayest thou be damned in the gloom of the fire eternal. May God show thee no favour when thou callest, neither pardon to forgive thine iniquities. . . ."

Then those present ratify both blessing and curse with a double "Amen."[76]

In the community each has his definite place at the communal meetings and meals "by the standard of his understanding and performance;"[77] in the process the priests occupy the first rank, in keeping with the origin of the movement in priestly circles. The rule of the communal life, which is preserved in the Manual of Discipline, seeks by means of a detailed code of punishments to safeguard a dignified order, mutual subordination and brotherly love. Here are a few examples:

"One who answers his neighbour with a stiff neck, or speaks with impatience, breaking the foundation of his fellowship by disobeying his neighbour who is registered before him, his own hand has delivered him; therefore he shall be punished for a year."

"A man who without justification knowingly denounces his neighbour shall be punished for a year and set apart."

"One who speaks craftily with his neighbours . . . shall be punished six months."

[76] *Manual of Discipline*, I.21–II.10 *passim*. Cf. I Cor. XIV.16.
[77] *Manual of Discipline*, V.23.

"For one who speaks while his neighbour is speaking the punishment shall be ten days."[78]

The real life of the community pulsed in the meetings of the members, in which no non-member, not even a novice was allowed to participate, because here the elect community of the final age was acting as such. In the meetings, justice was administered, they exhorted one another, studied the Scriptures, prayed, and ate their meal together. To this meal as in ancient times generally, a special significance was attached. Even where there were only ten men present in any place, they met together in table-fellowship, for they also formed the "Community of God." The seating order was laid down in the form that they considered the Messianic banquet of the day of salvation would assume: there the "high priest" and the heads of the priestly families would sit down first, then the "anointed king" with his officers, and then the heads of the families and the sages.[79] The meals, or at least some of them (at festival times?), appear to have been regulated by certain purity rules, judging by the buried animal bones discovered in Khirbet Qumran (see p. 46). This communal eating as an expression of the community-consciousness recalls what Luke in Acts II.46 says of the primitive church in Jerusalem. The Essene meal was as little a sacrament as the meal shared by the primitive church.

The history of this Essene community can no longer be reconstructed in detail from the texts discovered so far. Of the "Teacher" we know well that he underwent manifold persecutions, a fate shared by his community. His chief antagonist was understandably the "wicked priest," i.e. the ruling high priest and prince, possibly Hyrcanus.[80] But whether he died

[78] *Manual of Discipline*, VI.25–27; VII.4f., 9f. (Translation by Burrows, *The Dead Sea Scrolls*, p. 380.)

[79] Barthélemy and Milik, *Cave I*, No. 28a, II.11–22 = IQSa. (Translation by Gaster, The *Scriptures of the Dead Sea Sect*, p. 287.)

[80] The coin discoveries lead us to believe that Khirbet Qumran was built as an Essene settlement during the reign of Hyrcanus I. The Essene community was already in existence at that time. I would suggest the following as a working hypothesis: Josephus recounts a split between the Pharisees and Hyrcanus I; the Talmud ascribes the same event to the reign of Jannaeus. Josephus mentions as the Pharisees' motive the rumour that Hyrcanus' mother had once been a prisoner-of-war, and therefore her son could not be high priest. Josephus cites the same motive later (*Antiquities*, XIII.5 § 372) in respect of a popular uprising against Jannaeus. Could Josephus perhaps have confused two events, namely the Essenes'

a natural death or was executed we do not know: that he was crucified is improbable.[81] After his death the Habakkuk Commentary already makes apparent the suspense into which his adherents were thrown by the delaying of the final age prophesied by the Teacher as imminent. We read there on Habakkuk II. 3b:

"This is addressed to the men of truth, the men who carry out the Torah, who do not relax from serving the Truth, even though the final moment be long drawn out."[82]

The Pharisees

Those of the Hasidim who did not follow the Teacher of Righteousness and did not make the break with the high-priesthood and the temple constituted the sect of the Pharisees. When and in what sense they received this name we do not know. The common origin which links them with the Essenes is still evident in the Habakkuk commentary where, on Habakkuk I. 13b it is said:

"This refers to the 'house of Absalom' and their cronies who kept silent when charges were levelled against the teacher who was expounding the Law aright, and who did not come to his aid against the man of lies when the latter rejected the Torah in the midst of their entire congregation."[83]

---

break with Hyrcanus, the reason for which is no longer apparent, and the Pharisees' break with Jannaeus by reason of the purported captivity of his mother? If so, then no date could be set to the rise of the Essenes and the first appearance of the "Teacher," although it is possible to date the separation from the temple and the founding of Khirbet Qumran, which took place in the reign of Hyrcanus I, as the coins testify. It has so far been scarcely possible to place the emigration to Damascus, and indeed the *Zadokite* Document generally, in its historical setting.

[81] To be deduced from the *Commentary on Nahum* (J.B.L. LXXV (1956), pp. 90f.). The "lion of wrath" in line 5 is Alexander Jannaeus, to whom this title best applies. It is said of him in lines 7f. that he hanged men alive, i.e. crucified them, a thing that had never happened before in Israel (if this completion of an incomplete sentence in the original is correct); this probably refers to the 800 Pharisees whom he crucified. The crucifixion of Jose ben Joezer referred to by E. Stauffer in *Jerusalem und Rom*, Bern 1957, pp. 128ff., and *Zeitschrift für Religions- und Geistesgeschichte* VIII (1956), pp. 250–253, does not therefore enter into the Nahum Commentary's reckoning as being a Syrian act. The view that Jose ben Joezer was the "Teacher" founders upon the fact that with this early assignation there ought to have been more traces of the religious persecution under Antiochus IV.

[82] *Commentary on Habakkuk* VIII.10–12.

[83] *Commentary on Habakkuk*, V.9–12.

The "house of Absalom" and "their cronies" refers presumably to the Pharisees, of whom the writer of the commentary thought that he could have expected them to have gone to the "Teacher's" aid against the high priest (the "man of lies"). Otherwise the Pharisees are characterised in the Qumran documents by the expression "those who seek after smooth things;" herein lies the reproach that whether in relation to the Law or to the Hasmoneans, or to both, they had chosen the easier, smoother and yet more dangerous and slippery path. At any rate the Pharisees did not accept the Teacher's novel heightening of the Law, and also rejected his claim to be in possession of the Holy Spirit. At the same time they rejected the Teacher's belief in an imminent consummation. The time in which they lived was not for them the final age of Belial's dominion, in which the pious must suffer; at that time they did resort to arms, as we shall see in the next chapter. Belial does not appear in the rabbinic writings as the title of the wicked one[84] and the doctrine of predestination gained no currency among them. However, this made it possible for them to leave the door open for their later elaboration of the doctrine of the good and evil "impulse" with which man is created, and for the doctrine of free will and for the mutual balancing of good and evil works. A further point of difference is the fact that Essenism was a priestly movement; Pharisaism on the other hand was of choice a lay movement.

One of the chief motives, however, for the split between Essenism and Pharisaism seems to me to lie in the fact that the latter recognised that the way of the "Teacher" would lead to the monastery and thus to separation from the people. The Pharisees never lost sight of their aim to take in the whole nation and did not desire to lose sight of it; therefore they could not join others on the road to the Essene monastery. That means on the one hand that they shut their eyes to the radicalism of the Teacher and did in actual fact walk along "smooth paths," so that in the long run one can talk not unjustifiably of their "mediocrities;"[85] on the other hand, history has vindicated Pharisaism to the extent that the Essenes did not survive the destruction of Jerusalem, while

[84] *Strack-Billerbeck* VOL. III, p. 521 on II Cor. VI.15a.

[85] H. Braun (see note 34 of this chapter), VOL. I, p. 10.

Pharisaism became immediately afterwards the means of ensuring Judaism's continuity.

We can no longer determine the historical development of Pharisaism in its early days. Two important things are clear, however, in retrospect: for one thing, it strove from its very beginnings to make the "fence around the Law" increasingly impenetrable, but (unlike the Essenes) without committing the details to paper in the early centuries; thus it probably continued in the direct line of the Hasidim. But then again, it carried the transcendentalising process further. Witness to this is the antithesis between "this world" and the "world to come," quite familiar in Jesus' day but missing from the Qumran writings.

CHAPTER 5

THE ZENITH AND END OF THE HASMONEAN DYNASTY

External Events

IT was Hyrcanus' wish that his wife should become queen, but her eldest son, Aristobulus, allowed her to starve to death in prison while he himself assumed sovereignty (104–103 B.C.). He imprisoned three of his brothers and had the fourth, whom he had at first trusted, assassinated, having been made suspicious by his circle of advisers. He bore the nickname of Philhellene. All this clearly shows that the Hasmoneans had by this time become completely transformed into oriental despots.

After his death his widow released the three brothers and appointed the eldest as his successor. He married her, though the Law forbade him, as high priest, to do this. He was called *Alexander Jannaeus* and reigned from 103–76 B.C. He (or perhaps his predecessor) had assumed the royal crown without being of the Davidic line; this confirmed once and for all the purely political outlook of the last of the Hasmoneans. To be king meant at that time to be an absolute monarch. This absoluteness clashed with the Law, which set limits to the power of the king. During his long reign Jannaeus waged war almost uninterruptedly. With varying success he attempted to extend his kingdom to the frontiers of the Promised Land, but he failed to conquer the coast north of Carmel or to gain Ashkelon on the south coast. He conquered the territory east of the Jordan as far north as the Sea of Gennesaret and destroyed those Greek cities whose inhabitants refused to be Judaised. In order to protect the eastern frontier against the Arabs he overstepped the borders of the Promised Land, but did not make the population there Jewish. He fell in an attempt to conquer the territory of the great Greek city of Gerasa.

Not only had he to struggle against enemies without but he had also to struggle for years against opponents within. During his reign there arose dissension with the Pharisees, as the result of an incident which is recounted with divergent detail in our two sources, the Talmud and Josephus, where it is also placed in a different time-setting.[1] But both accounts agree in the fact that the "sages" urged king Jannaeus (or Hyrcanus?) to renounce the high-priestly office, as it was rumoured that his mother had for a time been a prisoner-of-war. It was assumed of a woman prisoner-of-war that she had been abused, and a son of such a woman could not be high priest. The rumour was apparently untrue but for the Pharisees even a possible transgression of the Law, as well as a not completely transparent situation in the life of the high priest's mother, was something to be unconditionally avoided for the sake of conscience. The king for his part felt the demand that he should lay down the high-priestly office, and the grounds for it, to be an insult; he broke with the Pharisees and gave orders that the cult, the administration of justice and other public affairs should no longer be conducted according to the new interpretation of the Law by the Hasidic movement but according to the old usage.

It soon became evident that the mass of the people were already at that time on the side of the Pharisees. At a celebration of the Feast of Tabernacles Jannaeus, the high-priestly king, was pelted by the crowd with citrons from the festive garlands because he had poured out the water from the pool of Siloam not at the foot of the altar but to the side of it. Such were the details at stake when there was serious debate on what might be God's will as laid down in the Law.

The Pharisees, however, rose up against Jannaeus after he had suffered a defeat in battle and fought him with Syrian help (!), thus placing him in extreme jeopardy. But at that

[1] Josephus, *Antiquities*, XIII.10, 5f. (§§ 288–296); B. T. Kidd. 66a; see also Schürer, *Geschichte des jüdischen Volkes*, VOL. I, pp. 271f.; Schlatter, *Geschichte Israels*, pp. 139ff.; J. Jeremias, *Jerusalem zur Zeit Jesu*, henceforth cited as *Jerusalem*, 3 vols., Leipzig/Göttingen 1923–37, VOL. II, B, pp. 12f. For the Hebrew and Aramaic texts relating to this and the following footnotes, together with a German translation, see K. Schlesinger, *Die Gesetzeslehrer*, Berlin 1936. Cf. also footnote (80) of Ch. IV.

moment the nationalistic feelings of many Jews were aroused; they espoused Jannaeus' cause,[2] enabling him to overcome his opponents and took bloody vengeance upon them: he had eight hundred of them crucified and their wives and children slaughtered before their dying eyes. Eight thousand of his opponents fled.[3] Even then he felt that the Pharisaic movement had not been stifled as a result, and on his death-bed advised his wife, who was to follow him, to come to terms with the Pharisees.

Thus he was succeeded by his wife, *Alexandra* (76–67 B.C.). She allowed her eldest son, Hyrcanus II, to exercise the high-priestly office. Following the advice of her husband she made peace with the Pharisees and dealt sharply with the originators of the blood-bath, to the disapproval of her youngest son. When Alexandra died the latter seized the crown and the high-priesthood by force and reigned as Aristobulus II from 67–63. His brother Hyrcanus lived as a private citizen. In the year 64 Pompey, the Roman, swept through the near east, in order to subject the remainder of the Syrian realm to Rome. The two brothers then placed their dispute before him, while at the same time the Pharisees sent a deputation requesting him to put Judea under Roman jurisdiction. The irresolute attitude of Aristobulus and his adherents obliged Pompey to capture Jerusalem (it was then that he actually entered the Holy of Holies in the Temple). Aristobulus was sent to Rome as a captive and Hyrcanus installed as high priest.

Aristobulus' sons, like their father, who succeeded in fleeing from Rome, tried long and often to defend the freedom of their country against Rome, as their forbears did against the Syrians. But they failed time and again. The winner in all this was a third party, namely *Antipater* the Idumean. Like all Idumeans his forefathers had been compulsorily Judaised in the Maccabean wars. He was thus regarded by pious Jews as only a half-Jew; and he for his part did not share the Jewish nationalistic feelings of those who fought with Aristobulus and his sons for the freedom of Judea. It was therefore an easy matter for him who, to begin with, had only been governor

[2] The reason for this reaction is probably indicated by a find from Qumran: the Syrian king Demetrius sought to enter Jerusalem, according to the *Commentary on Nahum* ch. II (*J.B.L.* [LXXV], 1956, p. 90).

[3] Josephus, *Antiquities*, XIII.14, 2 (§§ 379–383).

of Idumea under Aristobulus, to submit to the Romans and always to defer to them. So he finally became governor of the entire Jewish territory along with his sons Phasael and Herod.

Aristobulus' son Antigonus (his father Aristobulus and his brother Alexander had meanwhile been killed by the Romans) now attempted in 40 B.C. to win back the throne and kingdom of his fathers with the help of the Parthians, the hereditary enemies of Rome. Phasael died and Herod managed to flee. He betook himself to Rome and had Judea transferred to him as a kingdom by the Senate. After a struggle lasting three years he conquered it and then reigned unmolested as *Herod the Great* until his death.

The Expansion of Jewry

The intervention of the Romans under Pompey resulted initially in a substantial diminution of the Jewish state. The towns with Greek culture were again set free. With these the whole coastal area, Samaria, the Greek cities on the eastern bank of the Jordan and Scythopolis on its western bank were lost; only Joppa was eventually restored to Hyrcanus II.

The early Maccabees had been among the first to seek an understanding with Rome. Even in their day we see a great expansion of Jewry. 1 Maccabees xv.15–23 records a letter from the Roman consul, Lucius, to the Egyptian king and also to Syria, Pergamum, Cappadocia, Parthia and a large number of other countries and cities. In it the addressees are requested to do nothing against the Jews; thus we see how widespread they already were at that time. We are informed of the existence of Jews in Rome in 139 B.C. Before Pompey's march through Asia Minor Cicero mentions that "temple-monies" flowed from every province and from Italy.[4]

A series of factors contributed to this vigorous expansion:

1. The desire for children had widely diminished in Greco-Roman circles, but not in the Jewish community; there was also the fact that Judaism keenly rejected the ancient practice of child-exposure.

[4] Cicero, *Pro Flacco*, xxviii; cf. Schürer, *Geschichte des jüdischen Volkes*, vol. iii, pp. 58f. On the expansion of Jewry see G. Rosen, *Juden und Phönizier. Das antike Judentum als Missionsreligion und die Entstehung der jüdischen Diaspora*, Tübingen 1929; G. Kittel, *Die historischen Voraussetzungen der jüdischen Rassenmischung*, Hamburg 1939.

2. In the changing fortunes of war many Jews were sold as slaves and, since they were unpopular as slaves on account of their sabbath observance, were frequently set free.

3. There was also the wanderlust which lured Jews from the small and not very fertile land of Palestine into the wider world, and the attractiveness of the Jewish religion.

In the Psalms of Solomon[5] 1.3 "Sion" looks back on the Maccabean age with the words:

"I thought in my heart that I was full of righteousness, Because I was well off and had become rich in children. Their wealth spread to the whole earth, And their glory unto the end of the earth."

The Jewish Law was at the same time a civil code. It was a matter of life and death to the Jews of the Diaspora whether they had the possibility of living according to their law. The Romans had denied the Greeks the right of association as being the source of political intrigues. It was thus an extraordinarily successful consequence of Antipater's and Herod's policy of friendship to the Romans that Caesar explicitly exempted the Jews from these restrictions and permitted them to observe their sabbaths, to live according to their laws and to assemble in their synagogues. They were also exempt from military service, and could judge their own causes before their own courts.

Testimonies from the 1st Century B.C.

The rabbinic writings give us a series of anecdotes relating to leading scribes of this initial period. Two may be quoted here. They concern Simeon ben Shetach at the time of Jannaeus and his contemporary Juda ben Tabbai. The latter had fled to Alexandria; when he embarked on the ship for his voyage home, he asked one of his pupils accompanying him (like Jesus' disciples) what faults his landlady Deborah had. He answered that she squinted in one eye. "Double is your sin," was the reply. For one thing the pupil had placed his master under suspicion of staring at a strange woman, and, for another, he had eyed her himself.[6] The rabbi's question had

[5] On the *Psalms of Solomon*, see p. 141. (All quotations from the *Psalms of Solomon* and other Pseudepigrapha are taken from R. H. Charles, *Apocrypha and Pseudepigrapha of the Old Testament*, 2 vols. Oxford 1913, VOL. II. Tr.)

[6] *J.T. Hag.*, II.2 = 77d.

concerned merely her actions, her attitude to the Law. The struggle against the lewd glance was waged resolutely.

It is related of R. Simeon ben Shetach that he once bought an ass from an Ishmaelite. His disciples came and found a precious stone suspended from its neck. They said to him: "Master, *the blessing of the Lord, it maketh rich*" (Prov. x.22). R. Simeon ben Shetach replied: "I have purchased an ass, but I have not purchased a precious stone." He then went and returned it to the Ishmaelite, and the latter exclaimed of him, "Blessed be the Lord God of Simeon ben Shetach."[7] The rabbis regarded it as important to ask themselves: How do strangers speak of my God because of my actions? ". . . that they may see your good works and give glory to your Father who is in heaven."

Under the impact of the destruction of the Hasmonean dynasty the *Psalms of Solomon* were written, a collection, preserved in Greek, of eighteen hymns which give us a profound insight into the piety of a devout Jew of the first century B.C. In Psalm I the unknown author allows Zion itself to speak:

> "I thought in my heart that I was full of righteousness,
> Because I was well off and had become rich in children . . .
> But they (the children, especially the Hasmoneans) became insolent in their prosperity,
> "And . . .
> Their sins were in secret,
> And even I had no knowledge (of them)."[8]

Psalm II begins with the judgment that the intervention of Pompey and, with it, of the Romans, had brought upon Jerusalem:

> "When the sinner waxed proud, with a battering ram he cast down fortified walls,
> And Thou didst not restrain (him).
> Alien nations ascended Thine altar,
> They trampled it proudly with their sandals;

[7] *Deut. R.*, III.3.

[8] *Ps. Sol.*, I.3, 6f. The last two lines make clear that this is not an Essene speaking: the Essene movement perceived the sins of the Hasmoneans early on. But for the same reason these words cannot be those of a Pharisaic writer.

Because the sons of Jerusalem had defiled the holy things of the Lord,
Had profaned with iniquities the offerings of God.
Therefore He said: Cast them from Me."

The godly man submits himself to this judgment upon Jerusalem:

"(And yet) I will justify Thee, O God, in uprightness of heart,
For in Thy judgments is Thy righteousness (displayed), O God.
For Thou has rendered to the sinners according to their deeds,
Yea according to their sins, which were very wicked,
Thou hast uncovered their sins, that Thy judgment might be manifest;
Thou hast wiped out their memorial from the earth.
God is a righteous judge,
And He is no respecter of persons."[9]

The Essene Movement and Apocalyptic

In the previous chapter we paid heed only to those finds at Qumran that gave us information about the first period of the Essene movement which stood under the dominating influence of the "Teacher of Righteousness." But in the caves there were discovered—unfortunately in some cases only in fragments—another series of different writings, some of which have been more completely preserved than others by various Christian Churches. A number of common features justify us in considering these writings together as a unity and differentiating them from the earlier Qumran writings. We can start with the fact that the writings discovered in the caves are all linked with the Essene movement in one or other of its stages.

The first characteristic, then, of the writings we are now to consider is that the "Teacher" is no longer mentioned. We are therefore transported to a later stage in the Essene movement, to the middle or second half, say, of the first century B.C. The second feature common to these writings is their pseudepigraphic character, i.e. they are writings with a false (Greek

[9] *Ps. Sol.*, II.1–4, 15–18.

pseud-) signature (*epigraphē*). They purport to be revelations to men of long past ages, Enoch or Moses, or *dicta* perhaps of the patriarchs. The fact of this pseudonymity is surprising; for the "Teacher" was conscious of possessing the Holy Spirit, and therefore did not consider it necessary to invoke alleged revelations to men of past ages; even the writers of commentaries on Biblical writings did not so camouflage themselves. But men in the Essene movement now regard it as necessary to invest themselves with alien authority. This signifies a difference not only in time but also in essential content as compared with the early days of the Essene movement. The writers are linked by means of their pseudonymity with the Hasidim, for the book of Daniel and the Vision of the Seventy Shepherds are also pseudepigrapha. The third common feature of the writings under review is that they all contain apocalyptic material. Apocalyptic ideas are those which concern revelation[10] of things hidden from ordinary men. One thinks mainly in this respect of revelations concerning the future, particularly of individual acts in the final drama. But in this connexion we must define the concept of apocalyptic more precisely. It concerns revelations about things in the divine world of beyond; for the Jewish cosmology this comprises everything that lies above the "firmament" of Genesis I.7: rain, snow, hail, lightning and their angels, the course of the sun and the moon, the paths of the stars, as well as angels and demons, and the various heavens, paradise and hell, and the abodes of the righteous and the unrighteous before the final judgment. The transcendental background of world-history, the coming of evil into this world and the form that its ending will take, finally, of course, the events of the end, the resurrection of the dead, the annihilation of the wicked, the great world-judgment and the situation at the day of salvation: all these lie within the scope of apocalyptic. In their preoccupation with apocalyptic ideas the later Qumran writings also link up with the Hasidic movement, for the Vision of the Seventy Shepherds saw in Genesis VI.1ff. the invasion of evil powers into this world, but the doctrine of the two spirits created by God as taught by the "Teacher" left no room for the further development of these ideas. It was only some time after his

[10] Apokaluptein (Gr.) = to unveil; apokalupsis = unveiling.

death that the apocalyptic tendencies and, with them, the transcendentalising process were developed further.

Of these writings we shall only discuss the three which were already known to us earlier in their entirety.

The so-called *Book of Jubilees* derives its name from its division of world-history from the Creation into periods of jubilee.[11] An "angel of the presence" narrates to Moses the contents of Genesis I to Exodus XII interposed with apocalyptic material. The emphasis lies upon the fact that the commandments of God are eternal laws observed even by the angels and valid for all times, even in heaven, as for example the law of the Sabbath.

The so-called "*Testaments of the Twelve Patriarchs*" are preserved for us in various languages and purport to contain the last testaments of the patriarchs, Reuben, Simeon, Levi, Judah, etc. In each "Testament" a patriarch, with reference to what is said of him in Genesis, holds up a virtue before his sons, or warns against a vice; a vista of the end-period forms the conclusion in each case. The textual tradition often diverges widely, and the few finds in the caves which contain parts of this document make it clear that they had a lengthy history prior to the detailed form in which they are known to us, and have undergone much Christian interpolation which it is difficult to separate with accuracy.

The third work is the so-called *Ethiopic Book of Enoch*, of which lengthy portions are also preserved for us in Greek. It contains a collection of various apocalyptic themes; one part, the so-called "Parables," was not found at Qumran and may therefore stand at a further remove from the Essene movement; we shall consider it separately at the close of this section.

The book offers revelations made to Enoch. Large portions are focussed upon the fall of the "sons of God" in Genesis VI.1ff. and their provisional and final judgment; in other parts Enoch tells of a heavenly journey in which he has surveyed the various heavens and the laws, paths and "portals" of the sun and moon; in admonitory sections the righteous are warned to be faithful to the Law and to cleave firmly to the will of God; the unrighteous are confronted with their future

[11] A year of jubilee delimits a period of seven times seven years; cf. Lev. XXV.8ff.

judgment, and the righteous with the coming glorious resurrection.

In these writings we find, first of all, crucial ideas recurring from the earlier Qumran writings, for example—the solar calendar and the strict consecration of the sabbath. The praise of the simple life of the countryman recalls the simplicity of the Essene mode of life, and when it is then said in this context that physical tiredness caused by work forbids the arousing of desire for a woman[12] we are reminded of the celibacy of the order, which is made more comprehensible in another context by an unfavourable judgment upon women in general.[13] The setting of Levi over Judah, the priesthood over the kingship, finds particular expression in the "Testaments," but recurs also in the Book of Jubilees.[14]

The governing watchwords for man's total behaviour occur here too, as in the earlier Essene writings: walk perfectly, repent with one's heart and soul, do not turn to the right or to the left from any of God's ways, circumcise the heart;[15] likewise love for the neighbour has a special place in these texts. But then something new soon appears: hatred for the ungodly does not recur in our texts, and the duty to love extends beyond the limits of the order. Noah himself is supposed to have instilled in his children, the ancestors also of pagan peoples, the love of their neighbour, and in Abraham's blessing upon his children Ishmael and Isaac we read:

"And he commanded them that they should observe the way of the Lord; that they should work righteousness, and love each his neighbour . . . . Let them not commit fornication with (any woman) after their eyes and their heart. . . . I implore you, my sons, love the God of heaven, and cleave to all His commandments. . . . Serve ye the most high God, and worship Him continually; And hope for His countenance

[12] *Test. Issachar.*, III.5. On the simple mode of life see *Test. Judah*, XXVI.3.

[13] *Test. Reuben.*, V.1–4. There is a similar Essene verdict upon women in Josephus, *War*, II.8, 2 § 121.

[14] *Jub.*, XXXI.13–20; XXXII.1, 3; XLV.16.

[15] *Jub.*, XIX.13; XXIII.10; XXVII.17; XXXV.21. *Test. Levi*, XIII.1; *Test. Issachar*, VII.6; *Jub.*, I.15, 23; XX.3; *Jub.* I.23. Even the stereotyped expression "plant of uprightness," which appears in the earlier Qumran texts, is to be found here—*Jub.*, I.16; XVI.26; XXI.24; XXXVI.6; *Enoch*, X.16; LXXXIV.6; XCIII.5, 10. The cliché "good mind" appears in the Testaments, e.g. *Test. Benjamin*, V.1; VI.5.

always, And work uprightness and righteousness before Him, that He may . . . grant you His mercy."[16]

In the "Testaments" appears not only the juxtaposition, familiar to us from Jesus' lips, of love for God and for one's neighbour,[17] but any limitation on love for the neighbour is removed and men are warned to love even the sinner and the enemy:

"For the good man hath not a dark eye (cf. Mt. VI.22f. and Lk. XI.34–36); for he showeth mercy to all men, even though they be sinners. And though they devise with evil intent concerning him, by doing good he overcometh evil, being shielded by God; and he loveth the righteous as his own soul."

"If therefore ye also have a good mind, then will both wicked men be at peace with you, and the profligate will reverence you and turn into good."[18]

The doctrine of the two spirits created by God and of absolute double predestination must have receded into the background by this time. The texts also make this clear: the fall of the sons of God in Genesis VI.1ff. plays a part in all the three writings mentioned and signifies the decisive invasion of evil into this world:[19] the guilt lies in their fall, for they were created good.[20] Dualistic overtones are to be detected, of course, but without the predestination connected with them in the Manual of Discipline: man stands between the two spirits,[21] or there are two ways, two modes of action given to him;[22] at the same time man is given freedom of decision; this theme runs through the admonitory sections of the writings: "For if a man flee to the Lord, the evil spirit runneth away from him."[23] Election, which in the earlier writings applied only to the sect, now applies again to the whole of Israel: no evil spirit is given

[16] *Jub.*, XX.2, 4, 7, 9. In the subsequent verses special commandments relating to the sacrificial cult are given to Isaac himself.

[17] *Test. Dan.*, V.3; *Test. Issachar*, V.2; VII.6.

[18] *Test. Benjamin*, IV.2, 3; V.1.

[19] The Fall (of Adam and Eve) is not regarded as the decisive event; see *Jub.* III.

[20] *Enoch*, XV.4–7.

[21] *Test. Judah*, XX.1.

[22] *Test. Asher*, I.3.

[23] *Test. Simeon*, III.5. *Zadokite Document*, XVI.4f. offers a parallel; this document in general contains many reminiscences of the apocalyptic writings.

power over Israel, and yet the children of Israel will forsake God;[24] sin is created by man himself.[25]

Apart from the name Belial (Beliar) there also appears the name of Satan, or the abstract conception, "Mastemah";[26] it is noteworthy how, alongside the Old Testament names, Satan also appears in his Old Testament guise of accuser.[27]

It is in line with the apocalyptic character of the writings under discussion that we also hear a great deal about the events of the end, first of an intermediate state between death and resurrection,[28] then of the great cosmic judgment upon the fallen angels, of the resurrection and the judgment upon the ungodly and of the salvation prepared for the righteous. The detailed picture of the resurrection is still twofold. The Book of Jubilees envisages that the bones of the righteous will rest in the earth, but their spirits will possess great joy.[29] Heaven and earth and all creatures upon earth will be renewed like the luminaries of heaven. Jerusalem will then have a new temple: here again the era of salvation appears to mean a return of paradise to this earth,[30] and no clear distinction is drawn between long life in the era of salvation and eternal life.[31]

Texts about the Messiah are astonishingly sparse. Only the Testaments of the Twelve Patriarchs make any pronouncements upon the subject; they anticipate a future high priest and a future king; the former will teach the Law and offer sacrifice on behalf of Israel. The texts are, however, of the unanimous conviction that evil will one day be abolished, and that that will be God's work alone; no Messiah-figure intervenes here; this probably accounts for its complete omission from the Book of Jubilees.

The same considerations do not apply to the part of the

[24] *Jub.*, xv.32.

[25] *Enoch*, xcviii.4—"I have sworn unto you, ye sinners, as a mountain has not become a slave . . . even sin has not been sent upon the earth, but man of himself has created it."

[26] Mastemah is also mentioned in *Zadokite Document*, xvi.5.

[27] *Jub.*, i.20; xlviii.15, 18. Satan = enemy, opponent; Mastemah = obstruction.

[28] *Enoch* xxii.

[29] *Jub.*, xxiii.31.

[30] *Jub.*, i.29; *Enoch*, xxv.4–6; cf. *Enoch*, x.17–19.

[31] *Enoch*, v.9; x.17; xxv.6.

Ethiopic Book of Enoch which has not so far been discovered in the caves, and therefore probably does not stem from the Essene movement, namely the so-called *Parables of Enoch.*[32] Apart from the apocalyptic material with which we are already acquainted, we are confronted for the first time with the figure of a heavenly Messiah. He is called the Elect, the Chosen One, particularly however, with reference to Daniel VII, the Son of Man. Of him we read:

"And there (i.e. in heaven) I saw One who had a head of days.
And His head was white like wool (cf. Dan. VII.9),
And with Him was another being whose countenance had the appearance of a man,
And his face was full of graciousness, like one of the holy angels."

Enoch is then told:

"This is the Son of Man who hath righteousness,
With whom dwelleth righteousness. . . .
Because the Lord of Spirits (i.e. God) hath chosen him,
And whose lot hath the pre-eminence before the Lord of Spirits in uprightness for ever. . . ."[33]
"Yea, before the sun and the signs (i.e. of the Zodiac) were created,
Before the stars of the heaven were made,
His name was named before the Lord of Spirits.
He shall be a staff to the righteous whereon to stay themselves and not fall,
And he shall be the light of the Gentiles,
And the hope of those who are troubled of heart. . . .
For he hath preserved the lot of the righteous. . . .
For in his name they are saved. . . .
In those days downcast in countenance shall the kings of the earth have become,
And the strong who possess the land because of the works of their hands,
For on the day of their anguish and affliction they shall not (be able to) save themselves,

[32] *Enoch* XXXVII–LXXI.

[33] *Enoch*, XLVI.1–3.

And I will give them over into the hands of Mine elect:
As straw in the fire so shall they burn before the face of the holy. . . ."[34]

"And in those days a change shall take place for the holy and the elect. . . ."[35]

"And the faces of [all] the angels in heaven shall be lighted up with joy. . . ."[36]

"Blessed are ye, ye righteous and elect,
For glorious shall be your lot.
And the righteous shall be in the light of the sun,
And the elect in the light of eternal life:
The days of their life shall be unending,
And the days of the holy without number."[37]

This passage re-echoes ideas from Deutero-Isaiah; here the subject-matter is a Messiah who is more than a king over his people; here the transcendentalising process is carried to its logical conclusion.

[34] *Enoch*, XLVIII.3–9 *passim*.
[35] *Enoch*, L.1.
[36] *Enoch*, LI.4.
[37] *Enoch* LVIII.2f. E. Sjöberg, *Der Menschensohn im äthiopischen Henochbuch*, Lund 1946.

Chapter 6

THE RULE OF HEROD. THE ZEALOTS

Herod's Kingdom

In 40 B.C. Herod acquired in fief from the Romans the Hasmonean kingdom as pruned by Pompey. It therefore embraced, in the first instance, Judea, Idumea, Perea and Galilee. Rome was at that time standing on the brink of a new civil war, that between Octavian and Antony, which ended in victory for Octavian, the later Caesar Augustus, and put an end to the long period of civil wars. Herod stood on the side of Antony, and, as his vassal, had to put up with a diminution of his kingdom. A series of favourable circumstances resulted in his being able to introduce himself to Octavian, after the decisive battle at Actium in 31 B.C., as one who, even though under orders to Antony, had rendered good service in the struggle against Arabian tribes, and had proved helpful even to Octavian after the latter's victory. So he won the confidence of the first Roman emperor and was clever enough to maintain this confidence (except for a short period of estrangement) and consolidate it. Not only did he regain his kingdom in its old proportions but, in addition, the whole coastal plain (with the exception of Ashkelon), and Samaria including the "Great Plain;" moreover he later received a personal present from Caesar in the form of purely Gentile territories in north-east Palestine, namely the provinces of Trachonitis, Auranitis and Batanea, where he was to put a stop to banditry and thus protect the trade route to Damascus. In Trachonitis he settled a permanent colony of Babylonian Jews. Furthermore he acquired another area around Paneas, later to be known as Caesarea Philippi. On the other hand the region of "Decapolis" ("Ten Cities") did not come under his jurisdiction, except for Hippos and Gadara.

Herod's Reign and its Objects

The first object of his reign was the safety of his throne, which he achieved, in the fashion of the age, by unscrupulous means. First, he had forty-five of the leading partisans of the Hasmoneans executed and confiscated their property. Antigonus was beheaded by Antony. Herod made the grandson of Hyrcanus II and Aristobulus, also named Aristobulus, high priest in defiance of the Law. When he learned, however, of the popularity of this youth, the last male member of the Hasmonean family, he cunningly had him drowned in Jericho. From a marriage with a granddaughter of Hyrcanus, Mariamne, he might, at first, have hoped for a strengthening of his position amongst the Jewish people. But eventually he had her and her sons executed, along with all who still had a drop of Maccabean blood in their veins. Even the aged Hyrcanus, recently returned from the Parthians, died on Herod's orders, and only five days before his own death he had his eldest son, Antipater, killed. Contributory factors in these measures against the members of his own house were the pride of the Hasmonean descendants in their royal blood, the game of intrigue on the part of Herod's sister, Salome, and a natural mistrust on the part of the king, nourished by the consciousness of his "bourgeois" origins. In the last resort it was always a matter of the security of his throne. Every revolt against his régime was broken by force and by heavy punishments; many were liquidated in prison, either publicly or secretly. Informers kept their ears open amongst the populace, and Herod himself is supposed to have mingled frequently amongst the people incognito, in order to sound out their opinions. A system of fortresses up and down the land, together with a citadel on the north-west corner of the temple area, the Antonia, a fortified palace in the north-west of Jerusalem, and a mercenary army consisting of Thracians, Gauls and Teutons, were intended to protect his throne. One of the most important garrisons was Samaria. Herod even had Gentile troops stationed in the great plain between Samaria and Galilee. Jewish troops were not reliable enough for him.

The second object of his reign was the welfare of his people. However cruelly Herod combated every threat to his power and position, he strove just as strongly, on the other hand, to care for his country. He colonised infertile districts, he beautified the cities and during a famine he threw himself into its amelioration with great energy and resource, and to this end gave away his valuable plate. The city of Jerusalem particularly gained in brilliance and dignity under him. He had the temple there reconstructed, a work lasting many years from about 22 B.C. onwards, and the temple area enlarged. Even today one views the gigantic task with amazement: in parts the foundations go to a depth of 45 metres and its surface area measures a good 480 by 300 metres! For Caesarea, Jericho and a few other cities, but especially for Jerusalem, he laid on a water supply and also had a theatre and amphitheatre built there. He had the graves of the patriarchs in Hebron and, north of it, the wood of Mamre, generously enlarged.

But his provision for his people's welfare went far beyond these purely external matters. He felt and acted like a Jew. When he was forced to besiege Jerusalem in order to conquer his kingdom, he sent sacrificial animals into the city for the besieged population, so that the temple cult could be carried on undisturbed. He had his sons educated with Jewish families in Rome. In connexion with the reconstruction of the temple he had a thousand priests trained as stonemasons, in order that they could build where only priests had access. When the Arab Syllaeus asked for the hand of his sister Salome in marriage, the match foundered on Herod's demand that Syllaeus should adopt the Jewish Law. But of special importance is the fact that he did not deny his Judaism even in the face of the Romans.[1] He allowed nothing that contradicted the Jewish belief in the *one* God to enter specifically Jewish territory. No portrait of Caesar was imported into Jerusalem, nor did he permit the minting of any coin with Caesar's image. He even used his influence successfully on behalf of the Jews in the Roman Empire and succeeded in enabling the Jews in the Diaspora to live henceforth according to the Law. After his death the Romans maintained this same attitude towards the land of Palestine as well as to the Jews in the Diaspora. That was one of the most important consequences of his reign. A

[1] A. Schlatter, *Die Theologie des Judentums nach dem Bericht des Josephus*, henceforth cited as *Die Theologie des Judentums*, Gütersloh 1932, p. 187: "The impression that he (Herod) made upon the ruling Romans was also based upon the manner in which he proved himself free of scrupulosity although unashamedly a Jew."

sign of the status that the Jewish king procured for Judaism in the eyes of the Romans is the fact that Augustus' son-in-law, Agrippa, came to Jerusalem in 15 B.C. and made a great sacrifice to the God of the Jews in the temple. The Jewish people welcomed him on that occasion with jubilation.

The third object was the opening up of his country and people to Greek culture. Herod steeped himself in it deliberately. He surrounded himself with a circle of cultured Greeks and had them introduce him to Greek, i.e. Gentile, culture in philosophy, rhetoric and history. He had no scruples about erecting a temple in Samaria in honour of and for the veneration of Augustus, and a similar one in Rhodes for the Pythian god Apollo. In one of the great cities of the Roman Empire, Antioch, a majestic double colonnade on both sides of the main street derived from him, and he generously supported the famous Olympic Games. Whole cities rose up in fresh glory at his command; thus, the city of Sebaste, i.e. "City of Augustus," was created out of the old Samaria, and Caesarea, i.e. "City of Caesar," was created out of Strato's Tower on the coast, a twelve-year task. This he provided with an artificial harbour and adorned with a temple to Augustus and Roma, i.e. Rome the Divine. There, as in Jerusalem, he founded games to be held every four years; in this connexion he probably kept the gladiatorial combats, so hated by the Jews, at a distance from the holy city, but not animal-baiting and charioteering, which were equally taboo.

Just as Herod wished to be both Jew and Greek in his own person, so it was his aim generally to lead Jews and Greeks into harmonious co-existence. In the newly built city of Caesarea he gave Jews and Greeks identical civil rights. The Jew was intended to remain a Jew and yet be open to the influence of the superior Hellenistic culture and education. Consequently he introduced the circus games into Jerusalem and fitted out his palace in Jericho with all the refinements of the art of living. The antithesis between Jews and Samaritans seems to have lost its edge in Herod's time.

The Verdict upon Herod

The portrait of Herod's character fluctuates throughout history, and that both in ancient and in recent times. For

Klausner,[2] his reign was an uninterrupted rule of blood, and his political terrorism could only compete with, say, the horrors of the French Revolution.[3] Willrich, on the other hand, refers to the recognition that Herod received from Augustus and Agrippa, whose judgment carried more weight than that of the Pharisees.[4] In the struggle that had smouldered openly and under the ashes between the Jews themselves and against Rome in the period between Pompey and the Jewish War of A.D. 66–70, there had been only *one* real time of peace, the time of Herod. Every disaster had come upon the Jews only on account of their animosity towards the foreigners, and because they did not know how to use the freedom intended for them.[5] Josephus begins his characterisation of Herod with a reference to the dichotomy of his nature. He places his generosity and his kindheartedness in antithesis to his cruelty and harshness and traces both back to his ambition and vainglory. And because the Jews regarded justice more highly than fame the Jewish people had no respect for him, nor he for the Jews.[6] This verdict is certainly not unfounded, but we must distinguish between two things: the personal character of Herod and the essential problem of his reign.

His life-portrait appears very dark because of his death sentences upon members of his own family and the massacre of the children in Bethlehem (upon the historicity of which no verdict can be reached). The suspicions of the *parvenu* stained his rule with much blood and made it in many respects akin to a reign of terror. But one cannot say that Herod took a delight in sentences of death and acts of cruelty. The sums that he spent on beautifying cities within and without Palestine were, to be sure, astoundingly large, but Herod did not suck his

[2] J. Klausner, *Jesus of Nazareth: his life, times and teaching*, henceforth cited as *Jesus of Nazareth*, trans. H. Danby, London 1925, pp. 135ff. Klausner's opening sentence in Book II, Ch. I reads "The Maccabeans built up a Jewish Palestine: the Herodian kings destroyed it," p. 179.

[3] Klausner, *Jesus of Nazareth*, p. 151.

[4] H. Willrich, *Das Haus des Herodes zwischen Jerusalem und Rom*, henceforth cited as *Das Haus des Herodes*, Heidelberg 1928, p. 134. For the latest findings on Herod see S. Perowne, *The Life and Times of Herod the Great*, London 1956. Further literature in *Die Religion in Geschichte und Gegenwart*, henceforth cited as *R.G.G.*, 3rd edn., Tübingen 1957 *et seq.* and *Evangelisches Kirchenlexikon*, Göttingen 1956 *et seq.* under "Herodes."

[5] Willrich, *Das Haus des Herodes*, pp. 163, 165.

[6] *Antiquities*, XVI.5, 4 (§§ 150-159).

country dry; he had other sources of income. The tax revenue in Palestine does not appear to have been greater under him than before him, and he also did much for the economic prosperity of the land. He did indeed have ten wives, most of them simultaneously, but we hear nothing of erotic excesses.[7] The real shadow that lay upon his reign was cast by the fact that he wanted to win over the Jewish people, and he did not win them over, nor was it in his power to do so. This brings us to the essential problem of his reign.

There were circles in Judaism who adopted a cool or rejecting attitude to the Law of their fathers, and strove for an emancipation of the Jewish community, a complete assimilation to Greek culture. Apart from these Jews in name only to whom Herod, who was at best still very much a Jew, was a "barbarian," there were other circles in Judaism who welcomed Herod's reign. They could point to the fact that his sovereignty gave the Jewish people a share in the glory of Hellenistic-Roman culture, without restricting it in its freedom to live out its faith. They could quote the fact that the Jews throughout the Roman Empire were unhindered in their freedom to practise their religion and to assemble in their synagogue communities; that in Palestine the Temple worship was daily able to take its prescribed course undisturbed and that even Herod did not interfere unnecessarily with the administration of justice as laid down in the Law. Anyone could observe the sabbath as he wished, could give tithes as he thought fit, could take a ritual bath whenever he considered himself defiled, could recite the Shema and make the sacrifices which the Law prescribed. Such would have been the thoughts of the Sadducees.

But the mass of the people stood under the influence of the Pharisees. When, towards the end of his reign (possibly in connexion with the census of Quirinius?), Herod imposed on his subjects an oath of allegiance to Caesar and to his own policy, the Essenes and the Pharisees refused to take it; Herod exempted the Essenes from the oath and punished the Pharisees merely with a fine.[8] The relative triviality of the

[7] In *Antiquities*, XVII.11, 2 (§ 309) Josephus cites the posthumous charge against Herod laid by the Jews before Augustus to the effect that he had defiled virgins and had outraged married women, but he does not adduce any concrete example in support of this.

[8] Josephus, *Antiquities*, XV.10, 4 (§ 371); *Antiquities*, XVII.2, 4 (§ 42).

punishment shows that Herod did not fear any armed revolt on the part of the Pharisees, but understood the religious motive for their attitude.

Herod saw in the Jewish Law not the will of God but the Law and the customs of the Jewish people, which the Jews had as much right to hold as the other nations their laws and customs. So he was able to see to it that the Jews in the Diaspora were given the possibility of living according to their Law. But this national Law of the Jews had its limits in the exigencies of politics. The Jewish Law forbade, for instance, the sale of thieves abroad; Herod, however, decreed that order could not be secured in Palestine unless he allowed thieves to be sold abroad. The Law provided that the office of high priest should be for life; certainly Herod did abide by the legal requirements in connexion with the election of the high priest, but he fixed their term of office according to his own predilection. He feared of course that a high priest exercising life-long office would be able to create a dangerous position of power for himself. By far the majority of the Jewish people, however, saw God's will expressed in the Law, which could never be transgressed for political ends, and therefore saw in Herod's attitude nothing but a "dissolution of their religion."[9] A compromise was impossible on this score, and Herod was unable to win over his people despite great concern for their welfare.

The Zealots

Even though Pharisaism was of the opinion that Herod was causing the death of piety by his rule, it did not take it to the logical conclusion of active revolt. Just as it had arisen as a movement of repentance, so it interpreted the domination of Herod and subsequently that of the Romans as a punishment of God and as a summons to repentance. It awaited the end of all foreign domination through God's intervention, when guilt would be expiated and the nation would be totally restored to the way of the Law; for this reason it threw itself with all the greater zeal into ascertaining exactly what God's will according to the Law was in the many varied situations of daily life. Two of the best known Pharisaic scribes lived in Herod's day, Hillel and Shammai, whom we shall meet later.

[9] Josephus, *Antiquities*, xv.10, 4 (§ 365).

The question of what was God's will was also asked by a new movement, which appears on the scene at the beginning and the end of Herod's reign. When Herod was forced to conquer his country, he had to overcome bitter resistance in Galilee. His opponents despised him on account of his humble origins, and a number of them preferred voluntary death to subjection, although Herod offered them an amnesty. Josephus calls these men robbers. What kind of "robbers" these were is indicated by an event that fell at a time when Herod was as yet only procurator of Galilee. He had a "robber chief," Ezekias, arrested and executed with his comrades. Hyrcanus II indicted him before the Sanhedrin[10] on account of this high-handed procedure. Herod appeared with an armed escort, and the Sanhedrin did not dare to condemn him.[11] He would hardly have attempted to exert his influence thus in connexion with ordinary robbers; it had much more to do with a religiously based liberation movement.

When Herod was already lying at the point of death two distinguished scribes by the name of Judas and Matthias taught their disciples that they had to abrogate every measure that the king had introduced against the Law even if they encountered death in the process. And when the rumour spread abroad that Herod had died, a host marched to the temple and tore down the golden eagle that Herod had put up there and chopped it into pieces. Judas and Matthias were taken prisoner and declared before Herod:

> "It ought not to be wondered at, if we esteem those laws which Moses had suggested to him, and were taught him by God, and which he wrote and left behind him, more worthy of observation than thy commands. Accordingly, we will undergo death, and all sorts of punishments which thou canst inflict upon us, with pleasure. . . ."[12]

Herod had Judas and Matthias burnt alive.

At this point the opposition to Herod began to flare into active resistance. These men therewith abandoned the Pharisaic line. Here are the beginnings of the movement which came

[10] Sanhedrin, properly "synedrion," is the Greek name for the "supreme council."

[11] Josephus, *Antiquities*, XVI.15, 5 (§§ 427–430) and IX.2–5 (§§ 159–177).

[12] Josephus, *Antiquities*, XVII.6, 3 (§ 159).

together under the banner of the *Zealots*. They were at one with Pharisaism in the proposition that God's will was to be performed unconditionally. But the question *what* was to be done now when God's will was not being performed amongst the people on account of the ruler—later on account of the Romans—was answered differently, and therefore a compromise between Pharisaism and the Zealots was impossible.

The determination to reject at all costs every ruler over Israel but God alone seemed to the Zealots to be just that element that was lacking in the piety of Pharisaism, if that total obedience was to be offered that would bring about God's intervention and the messianic age.[13] This movement produced prophet after prophet who spoke of the imminent fulfilment of the Old Testament prophecies, and gave rise time and again to men who believed themselves called to lead the Jews against the pagan world power of Rome.

When, after Herod's death, Augustus was faced with the problem of the succession he was confronted not only by Herod's sons, who had been bequeathed the succession in his will, but also with a large deputation of Jews, who asked for Judea to be placed directly under Roman dominion. They complained of the king's mode of life and his rule of violence, while Herod's closest friend and collaborator, Nicholas of Damascus, accused the Jews of being by nature difficult to govern, of obeying their rulers reluctantly and wanting always to have the upper hand.[14] Here again Herod's principles of government and the outlook of the Jewish people recoiled against each other. To the Jews a direct subordination to Rome appeared to be the lesser evil; they expected from her more freedom to live according to the Law than from the rule of a half-Jew. They might also have promised themselves a juster rule from Rome; and the fact that whatever a Roman governor might do contrary to the Law he did as a Gentile and not as a Jew, was always easier to bear. On the other hand, the advantages that Herod's rule had created for them carried little

[13] Josephus says of the "fourth sect" of the Jews, the Zealots: "These men agree in all other things with the Pharisaic notions; but they have an inviolable attachment to liberty; and they say that God is to be their only Ruler and Lord." *Antiquities*, XVIII. 1, 6 (§ 23).

[14] Josephus, *War*, II.6, 2 (§ 92); *Antiquities*, XVII.11, 3 (§ 316).

weight in their eyes, and they had no time for the grandeur of Greek culture.

Not long after Herod's death the so-called *Assumption of Moses* was written. In it Moses prophesies to Joshua the fate of his people up to the time of the sons of Herod. After them it anticipates a period of godlessness and persecution. Then a man of the tribe of Levi named Taxo will, with his seven sons, surrender willingly to death in fidelity to the Law. Thereupon the time of salvation will appear, and the devil will be no more. This document gives its verdict upon Herod the Great:

"An insolent king . . . a man bold and shameless: he shall judge them (i.e. the Jews) as they shall deserve. And he shall cut off their chief men with the sword. . . . He shall slay the old and the young, and he shall not spare. Then the fear of him shall be bitter in their land."[15]

[15] *Ass. Mos.*, VI.2ff. Parts of the document suggest Essene authorship, but no traces have so far been found of it in the Qumran caves; the standpoint of the author must therefore remain a matter of doubt.

CHAPTER 7

THE SONS AND GRANDSONS OF HEROD

HEROD died in 4 B.C. Augustus had foreseen that unrest would set in after his death and ordered the governor of Syria, Varus, to march into Palestine. The son of the above-mentioned Ezekias, Judas, did in fact raise the standard of revolt and occupied Sepphoris in Galilee, which Varus then conquered and destroyed. The fate of Judas is uncertain; according to Acts v.37 he perished. Varus marched on to Jerusalem where Herod's son Archelaus had to deal with insurrections. The governor's withdrawal was the signal for a great rebellion, by means of which several Jews hoped to assume the royal crown. During the fighting the halls in the temple square were burnt down and the temple treasury plundered. Varus eventually restored order and had 2,000 Jews crucified.

Herod's will required Caesar's ratification. It provided that his kingdom should be divided between three of his sons: Judea, Idumea, Samaria and the title of king should go to Archelaus, his son by one of his ten wives named Malthake; Galilee and Perea should go to his blood-brother, mentioned in the New Testament as Herod Antipas, the governor of Jesus' native province; the area in the north-east of Galilee was to fall to a half-brother of both, whom Cleopatra had borne to Herod, named Philip. After he had listened both to Herod's heirs and to the representatives of the Jewish people Caesar gave judgment essentially in terms of the will as drawn up by Herod although the Greek cities of Gaza on the coast and Hippos, together with Gadara to the east or south-east of Lake Gennesaret were annexed to the province of Syria.

The reign of *Archelaus* only lasted about ten years. Augustus had held out to him the prospect of the royal dignity only on condition that he would give evidence of having the necessary aptitude. But his conduct of office rendered him so vulnerable to attack—according to Josephus he was accused of cruelty and lust for power[1]—that a Jewish and Samaritan deputation to Augustus was able to demand and secure his deposition. In A.D. 6, his territory was placed under a Roman governor. The only mention of Archelaus in the New Testament is in Matthew II.22, where Joseph, for fear of him, does not return to Bethlehem but goes to Nazareth. From what is said of him, Joseph's fears were well-founded.

Least in alignment with the New Testament world was the reign of *Philip*. It was kindly, just and peaceful. Like all Herodians Philip had made a name for himself as a builder of cities; the Caesarea Philippi mentioned in Mark VIII.27 was a new foundation that he took in hand on the site of the ancient Paneas. At the point where the Jordan flows into the Lake of Gennesaret, he had the new city of Julias constructed in the neighbourhood of the fishing village of Bethsaida. As the Jordan formed the boundary of his territory, there was on the other side of the river, almost opposite Bethsaida, a customs post (Capernaum). Philip's gentle and just reign had significance for the life of Jesus in that Jesus was safe from ambushes within his territory, which could be reached from Capernaum in about an hour. As this kingdom was predominantly Gentile the crossing over into it meant at the same time a withdrawal from Jewish publicity. Philip died in A.D. 34; his kingdom belonged from A.D. 37–44 to Agrippa I and from *circa* 53–100 to Agrippa II.

The one who is best known from the New Testament is *Herod Antipas* who was awarded Galilee and Perea. He was a true son of his father; Jesus calls him a "fox" (Lk. XIII.32). He associated himself with a complaint on the part of the Jews against Pilate on account of an insult to Jewish religious sensibilities; his coins avoided the human image so offensive to the Jews. As a new capital in place of Sepphoris, destroyed on the death of Herod the Great, he founded Tiberias on the

[1] *Antiquities*, XVII.13, 2 (§ 342). On the Herodians see, most recently, S. Perowne, *The Later Herods*, London 1958.

Lake of Gennesaret. He provided it with a race-course, and a palace adorned with animal images, which was an offence to the Law-abiding Jews, but also had a synagogue built there. When the excavations were going on for the building of the city an ancient burial ground came to light at the projected spot. This meant that the planned city was from the very start defiled and defiling in the eyes of the pious (cf. Numbers XIX.16). Herod Antipas lost no sleep over this, but simply bent his energies to finding a motley cosmopolitan population for his new capital city.

Even in his marriages he showed himself to be a true son of his father. He was married to a daughter of the Arabian king Aretas. When he visited his half-brother Herod[2] in Rome on one occasion he fell in love with his wife Herodias, who was a granddaughter of Herod the Great and had a daughter Salome. Antipas divorced his first wife and married Herodias. This later caused war between him and his first father-in-law, and brought down the reproach of John the Baptist upon him: "It is not lawful for you to have your brother's wife." (Mk. VI.18, after Lev. XVIII.16.) This woman was the immediate cause of the loss of his kingdom.

This is connected with the destiny of a grandson of Herod the Great, *Agrippa*. This man, who was born in about 10 B.C., had idled away his time in Rome, Palestine and elsewhere, had become steeped in debt and was unable to settle down anywhere. He was associated in Rome with a distinguished man, Gaius, and once expressed the hope that Gaius might become emperor. When that fact became known, he was thrown into prison, but when Gaius really did become Caesar, he took up his friend's cause, and conferred on him the kingdom made available a few years previously through the death of Philip, together with the title of king (A.D. 37). This elevation of rank left Herodias no peace; she prevailed upon her husband to travel to Rome and to plead for the kingly title. But Agrippa had already taken precautions and indicted him before the emperor. Gaius deposed him from office and exiled him to Lyons, as it is known today. This exile, during which he died, Herodias voluntarily shared with him. His kingdom, however, was taken over by Agrippa.

[2] Not Philip as Mk. VI.17 erroneously states.

The latter also contributed after Gaius' assassination (A.D. 41) to the fact that Claudius ascended the throne, and for this he received in gratitude Judea, Idumea and Samaria, so that from 41 till his subsequent death in A.D. 44 the kingdom of Herod was once more in the hands of a single member of the Herod family. He knew how to win favour with the pious. He offered large and correct sacrifices and had the penal requirements carried out exactly in accordance with the Mosaic Law. "He loved to live continually at Jerusalem, and was exactly careful in the observance of the laws of his country. He therefore kept himself entirely pure: nor did any day pass over his head without its appointed sacrifice."[3] He himself brought the first fruits to the temple. He even protected the Jews in the Diaspora. Whereas the day of Herod the Great's death was a day of rejoicing for the Pharisees, the Gentile cities of Palestine, such as Caesarea and Sebaste, in their turn greeted the news of the death of Agrippa I with jubilation. It fits in with the picture we receive of him that Luke connects the persecution of the Christian Church with the fact that he wished to show himself in a pleasing light to the Jews (Acts XII.3). To be sure, his Jewish correctness stopped at the borders of Palestine. He had a theatre built in Berytus and instituted gladiatorial contests there, he had statues of his daughters set up in Caesarea and Sebaste, and the coins minted by him outside Jerusalem carried a likeness—all in antithesis to the conception of the Law held in pious Jewish cities. His attitude is indicated by his title: "Great King, Friend of Caesar, staunch Friend of the Romans."

His reign came to an abrupt end, recorded in substantially the same terms both in Acts XII.21–23 and Josephus.[4] He died in A.D. 44 after a brief and agonising illness.

His son *Agrippa II* was at that time only 17 years old, and the Roman emperor was dissuaded from making over his father's kingdom to him; he did however use his influence with Caesar as a private citizen on behalf of the Jewish people. In about A.D. 50 he received the kingdom of his uncle, a blood-brother of his father, around Chalcis, together with the

[3] Josephus, *Antiquities*, XIX.7, 3 (§ 331). A revealing light is thrown on Acts XXI.23ff. by Josephus' mention in *Antiquities*, XIX.6, 1 (§ 294) of Agrippa's payment of the expenses of fulfilling the Nazarite vow as a sign of his piety.

[4] *Antiquities*, XIX.8, 2 (§§ 343–350).

oversight of the Jerusalem temple and the right of appointing the high priest. In about A.D. 53 the kingdom of Philip and some other territories with, after the death of Claudius (A.D. 54), some more Palestinian cities were transferred to him. He is the Agrippa before whom Paul, according to Acts XXVI, gave an account of himself. He also conducted himself to a certain extent like a Jew. He died about A.D. 100.

Chapter 8

PALESTINE UNDER ROMAN PROCURATORS

The Principles of Roman Administration in Palestine

After the deposition of Archelaus Judea, Idumea and Samaria and, after the death of Agrippa I, the whole of Palestine, were placed under Roman procurators of the equestrian order, who were directly responsible to Caesar. The procurator of Syria, however, could intervene in special cases. This form of administration was applied to provinces with peculiar characteristics. It was the general policy of the Romans that the population of the subject provinces should be allowed the right to self-government and their own customs, and that they should only reserve to themselves military defence, the superintendence of taxes and the administration of justice, a system that also tended to develop in one form or another in the colonies. Thus the Jews in Palestine had, under Roman administration, their own constitution with a high priest and the Sanhedrin at the head, but the Romans could intervene at any time when they felt it necessary. Following the example of Herod, they nominated and dismissed the high priest, but adhered to the legal provisions in connexion with the election of persons to the office. They later transferred the right of nominating the high priest to Herod of Chalcis and subsequently to Agrippa II. They allowed the Sanhedrin to hold and to terminate its own meetings and to dispense justice, but reserved to themselves the confirmation of death sentences and also the right to suspend the Sanhedrin. They did not interfere with the temple cult, but used the Tower of Antonia lying at the north-west corner of the temple area as a barracks, from which they could intervene in cases of emergency, as the story of the arrest of Paul shows (Acts xxi.31ff.). They left the synagogue worship and the whole organisation of the learning and study of the Law completely untouched. Thus, as under Herod, the Law could be taught and observed in both private and ceremonial life. Pharisaic scriptural learning also flourished at that time; Acts mentions the distinguished Rabbi Gamaliel (Acts v.34; xxii.3). Even the status of Jerusalem as the centre of the total Jewish community remained undisputed; a poll-tax of a double drachma, as mentioned in Matthew xvii.24ff., came annually into the temple treasury in Jerusalem from every Jew in Palestine and the Diaspora. But the Romans did lay claim to a certain oversight of the administration of the monies, which oversight they likewise transferred later to Agrippa II. This, however, remained a bone of contention; an act of interference with the temple treasury was the immediate occasion of the Jewish War. Only on *one* matter did Rome take a consistent stand: the recognition of its supreme sovereignty. The *manner* in which the Jews were obliged to make this recognition was not oppressive: they were not required to participate in the Caesar-worship customary elsewhere. Rome was content that they should take the oath of allegiance and that a daily sacrifice should be offered for the emperor in the temple. The suspension of this sacrifice in the year 66 was tantamount to a declaration of war. In the actual Jewish territory Rome only maintained a weak army of occupation; a cohort was garrisoned in Jerusalem and in fortresses up and down the land there were smaller garrisons; the nucleus of the troops was based on Caesarea, in order to spare Jewish feelings.

The Attitude of the Jews to the Roman Occupation

With what has been mentioned so far the basis for tolerable relations might have been laid. But the reality was different, and that from both sides. The Romans fundamentally despised the Jews with their manifold legal susceptibilities and, like a master-race, exercised jurisdiction with superior pride, without striving to achieve a real understanding of the peculiarities of this people. The Jews for their part regarded themselves as the people whom God had chosen before other nations on account of their righteousness, and therefore considered that freedom was due to them. That God, as they now saw it, was punishing them with foreign domination because of their sins did not in their eyes alter Israel's superiority to the Gentiles and particularly to the Romans. Indeed, if the latter abused their sovereignty over the Jews, then their sin was greater than Israel's, and the Jews believed themselves entitled to hope for God's intervention in their favour.

Typical of this attitude is IV Ezra III.25ff., written in A.D. 70, under the impact of the destruction of Jerusalem:

"The inhabitants of the City (i.e. Jerusalem) committed sin . . . and so thou gavest thy city over into the hands of thine enemies. Then I said in my heart: Are their deeds any better that inhabit Babylon? Has he for this rejected Sion?. . . . Have the deeds of Babylon been better than those of Sion? Has any other nation known thee beside Israel? Or what tribes have so believed thy covenants as those of Jacob? . . . Now, therefore, weigh thou our iniquities, and those of the inhabitants of the world, in the balance and so shall be found which way the turn of the scale inclines."

The manners and customs of the subject races, to which the Romans paid regard as far as was possible and politically expedient, were, to the Jews, not merely manners and customs but God's commandments. Every infringement of these could awaken the determination of the whole people to fight to the death. What, of course, the matters were for which they would have to hold out to the very last, was disputed; but the question became urgent whether the recognition of Roman sovereignty by the act of paying taxes was not already in any circumstances a sin to avoid, being against the first commandment, according to which there was for Israel only one Lord—God.

The History of Palestine under Roman Administration

After the deposition of Archelaus, Coponius was sent to Judea as its first procurator; with him came Quirinius, in order to carry out a census of property. The high priest Joazar persuaded the Jews with difficulty not to offer them any resistance, while the Judas already mentioned (see p. 92) together with Zadok, a Pharisee, sought to stir up the people with the argument that the census denoted slavery; he pointed out that God would acknowledge them if they chose the way of freedom without regard to trials and difficulties, i.e. if they refused to have themselves assessed. Josephus places the actual beginning of the Zealot party at this point.[1]

It is important to notice that the opposition to Roman rule set in even before the Jews could have had untoward experiences with the Roman procurators, and that for centuries they paid taxes without a murmur first to the Persians and subsequently to the Ptolemies and Seleucids; but the new doctrine arose that even the act of paying tax was an infringement of the first commandment. Whoever refused the taxes had to flee and stay in hiding. Thus Zealotism developed as an underground movement. To the Zealots their attitude appeared to be one of obedience to God; accordingly, those who did not share it were ungodly and had no right to live. The Maccabean forces of liberation served as an example to the Zealots. Just as the numerically weak forces of the Maccabeans had nonetheless brought freedom in face of Syrian overlordship, so the Zealots counted on God's help in the struggle against the superior weight of Rome; just as Jonathan and his kin were forced to withdraw for a time into the solitude of the hills, so likewise the Zealots; just as the Maccabees "destroyed the ungodly out of Israel" (I Macc. IX.73), so the Zealots did not shy from using violence and murder against their opponents among their own people. The Maccabean revolt arose in face of a prohibition of the Jewish religion; with the Zealots, however, it was a question of an axiomatic non-recognition of Roman sovereignty, even if the Romans had exercised every possible consideration for the Jewish religion. But in fact the procurators played in increasing measure their part in offending the Jews' religious susceptibilities and making them feel the pressure of alien domination.

Valerius Gratus (15–26) and Pontius Pilate (26–36) stayed in office for particularly long periods. This accorded with the

[1] *Antiquities*, XVIII.I, I (§§ 6–9). The chronological setting of the census in Josephus is irreconcilable with Lk. II.I. For an older bibliography on the census see Schürer, *Geschichte des jüdischen Volkes*, VOL. I, pp. 508–543; most recently H. Braunert, "Der römische Provinzial-zensus und der Schätzungsbericht des Lukas-Ev." in *Historia* VI (1957), pp. 192–214; E. Stauffer, *Jesus, Gestalt und Geschichte*, Bern 1957, pp. 26–34; also, by the same author, *Jerusalem und Rom*, Bern 1957, p. 133, note 3.

policy of the Emperor Tiberius, who changed procurators as little as possible in order to spare the provinces. He compared the procurators with flies which have settled on the wounds of the victim of a sudden attack, in order to suck his blood. If they are left alone, they gradually become sated and plague the poor man less; if, however, they are scared away well-meaningly, then fresh and still hungrier flies arrive, and the torture begins again. This makes clear how the procurators behaved towards their provinces.

Of the procurators of the first period, i.e. until the reign of Agrippa I, we have precise information only about *Pontius Pilate*. Agrippa called him "by nature unbending and severe with the stubborn, and reproached him and his conduct of office for "the taking of bribes, wanton insolence, rapacity, outrages, countless and continuous murders, endless and most painful cruelty."[2] He symbolised in a special way the contempt with which the Romans regarded the legal scrupulosity of the Jews. Prior to him the Romans, in deference to Jewish feelings, avoided bringing the standards of the legion bearing images of Caesar into the holy city, Jerusalem. Pilate was pleased to regard this as a weakness. He therefore introduced the standards by night, in order to confront the Jews with a *fait accompli*. But the consequences were unexpected: for five days and five nights the people besieged him in Caesarea with requests to revoke the measure. On the sixth day Pilate ordered the masses on to the race-course, and, when they did not desist from their pleadings, had soldiers encircle them with drawn swords. Then they prostrated themselves and bared their necks, prepared to die rather than suffer the profaning of Jerusalem's sanctity. Pilate thereupon relented, because Caesar would not have accepted a blood-bath graciously. When Pilate some time later raided the temple treasury for money to build an aqueduct to Jerusalem he was again surrounded in Jerusalem by a screaming mob. On that occasion he had soldiers wade into the crowds with cudgels, and abided by his measure. He later had gilt votive shields set up in the former palace of Herod in Jerusalem, and nothing would persuade him to remove them. But the Jews turned to Tiberius who, as a witness to his displeasure, ordered the shields to be brought

[2] Philo, *Embassy to Gaius*, XXXVIII (§§ 301 f.).

back to Caesarea.[3] The respect that the procurator had to pay Caesar throws light upon the trial of Jesus, during which the Jews, according to John XIX.12, charged Pilate menacingly with no longer being a friend of Caesar's if he let Jesus go. We have no evidence from other sources for the uproar in connexion with Barabbas' arrest (Mk. XV.7) and for the blood-bath mentioned in Luke XIII.1.

Pilate's procuratorship ended in a manner typical of him. A Samaritan prophet volunteered to show his compatriots the sacred vessels of the first temple, buried, so they believed, on Mount Gerizim; thereupon they assembled armed, in order to march up the mountain. Pilate intervened, killed many and had the leading men of the prisoners whom he had taken executed. The Samaritans, however, complained about him to the procurator of Syria, Vitellius, who deposed Pilate and sent him to Rome for reckoning. Despite the commitment of Roman official opinion to this course, it is clear that messianic ideas had a part to play in this matter: even in Revelation XI.19 the appearance of the ark of the covenant in the temple is a symbol of the dawning of the time of fulfilment.

The reign of the Emperor Gaius Caligula (37–41) brought heavy trials upon the Jews in Alexandria and Palestine. He was morbidly intent on being venerated as a god. The Jews were exempted for the sake of their faith from participation in the emperor-cult. In Alexandria anti-semitism was vented in Jewish pogroms. Jewish houses and shops were destroyed, and their synagogues profaned, wherever they were not immediately torn down, by the setting up of images of Caesar. In Palestine Gentiles had erected an altar to Caesar in the predominantly Jewish coastal town of Jamnia, and the Jews had destroyed it. When Caligula learnt of this, he ordered the procurator of Syria, Petronius, to erect an image of Caesar in the temple at Jerusalem. This may have been the "abomination that makes desolate" of which Daniel had prophesied, and at which Paul himself hints in II Thessalonians II.4. The whole populace fell into uproar and besieged Petronius with fervent requests that he should desist from his plan. Only through cunning and, in the end, bold delaying tactics,

[3] On Pilate see Josephus, *Antiquities*, XVIII.3f. (§ 55ff.); *War* II.9, 2 (§§ 169–171); Philo, *Embassy to Gaius*, XXXVIII (§§ 299–305).

together with the intervention of Agrippa I in Rome and the murder of Caligula, did the imperial decree remain unexecuted, and it was only by chance that Petronius got away with his life.[4] For the Jews it was a sign of God's ability to assail their enemies and protect their friends. Flaccus, the procurator, who was implicated in the pogrom in Alexandria, had to die shortly afterwards on Caligula's orders, while Caligula himself came to a violent end, whereas the prudent and, to the Jewish mind, accessible Petronius was almost miraculously rescued.

The official garments of the high priest (cf. Exod. XXVIII) were actually for the Jews a "symbol of their religion."[5] Herod, Archelaus and the Romans had custody of them, thus to maintain the upper hand over the Jews. They, for their part, felt this to be an almost intolerable interference with their religious freedom. After the deposition of Pilate they therefore requested from Vitellius the handing over of these garments, and he acceded to their request. Also at the request of the Jews, he avoided contact between Jerusalem and his troops on the march against the Arabian king. The first procurator after the death of Agrippa I, Cuspius Fadus, took back the vestments, although he had to return them to the Jews when they appealed successfully to Caesar.

It was under the same *Cuspius Fadus* that the Theudas, mentioned anachronistically in the book of Acts (v.36), appeared, and marched to the Jordan with a host of adherents, promising that the river would part at his word, as it did once under Joshua. Behind this lay the belief that the events which preceded the entry of the children of Israel into the promised land would repeat themselves at the coming of the messianic time of salvation. To that extent Theudas was himself a prophet, who believed himself capable of proclaiming the coming of the time of salvation. Cuspius Fadus, however, had him and his followers set upon by his cavalry, and Theudas lost his life in the process.

The next procurator, *Tiberius Alexander*, was a member of a leading Jewish family who had placed himself completely at the service of the Romans. He succeeded in arresting the sons of Judas the Galilean and had them crucified. He was followed

[4] Josephus, *Antiquities*, XVIII.8 (§§ 257–309); Philo, *Embassy to Gaius*, XXX–XLIII (§§ 197–348).

[5] Jeremias, *Jerusalem*, VOL. II B, pp. 3f.

by *Cumanus* (until A.D. 52), during whose term of office we are told of some clashes occurring between the occupation troops and the Jewish populace. At a Passover festival a Roman soldier ridiculed the festival crowds with an indecent gesture. Cumanus attempted to appease the mob, aroused by this act, but was himself reviled, whereupon he took violent action; many Jews lost their lives in the resulting stampede. When, conversely, an imperial official was attacked and robbed near Jerusalem, during his term of office, the procurator had the villages near the seat of the crime plundered. In the course of this plundering a roll of the Law was torn up with contemptuous words by a soldier. He had to be executed at the request of the Jews.[6]

A third incident cost Cumanus his office. Samaritans had ambushed Jewish festival pilgrims. Cumanus, bribed by the Samaritans, had not intervened, whereupon the Jews took the law into their own hands, attacked Samaritan villages and massacred the inhabitants. Both parties then appealed to the procurator of Syria, who took sharp measures and despatched the leading Jews and Samaritans to the emperor in Rome, where the advocacy of Agrippa II procured for the Jews their rights and brought about the dismissal of Cumanus from office.

His successor was the *Felix* mentioned in the book of Acts, an imperial freedman, i.e. a former slave. The Roman historian Tacitus says of him that "in every way of cruelty and lust he used a king's power (i.e. his procurator's office) in a slave's spirit."[7] He was married three times, one of his wives being Drusilla, a daughter of Agrippa I whom he seduced from her first husband, king Azizus of Emesa, shortly after her marriage (cf. Acts XXV.24–26).

Felix took violent measures against the increasingly strong party of the Zealots, caught their leader Eleazar by trickery, sent him to Rome, and had many others crucified. During his period the Egyptian mentioned in Acts XXI.38 appeared on the scene. This was an Egyptian Jew who had promised his followers that, even from the Mount of Olives, the walls of Jerusalem would fall down at his bidding. Felix dispersed his followers with his soldiery and the Egyptian himself escaped. At about this period the Zealots transformed

[6] Josephus, *Antiquities*, XX.5, 4 (§§ 113–117).

[7] *Historiae*, V.9.

themselves into the "Sicarii," i.e. dagger-men. Armed with tiny daggers they mingled amongst the crowds and struck down their opponents, amongst them the high priest Jonathan.[8] Josephus tells us, without mentioning names, of "charlatans and impostors" who incited the people to accompany them into the desert, where they would see God's wonders. The words of Matthew xxiv.26 "So, if they say to you, 'Lo, he (i.e. the Messiah) is in the wilderness,' do not go out," and Mark xiii.22, "False Christs and false prophets will arise and show signs and wonders," fit in with this situation, in which one messianic movement gave way to another.

Also under Felix's successor, *Festus*, a man of just disposition, a prophet appeared who desired to lead people into the desert where he promised them salvation; this movement was likewise suppressed by force.

Festus died suddenly during his term of office. Ananus, the high priest, utilised the interval until the arrival of Festus' successor Albinus, in order to have James, the Lord's brother, and some others condemned and stoned. This procedure, however, did not have the approval of the Pharisees, who denounced Ananus to Albinus. Agrippa II then had Ananus deposed.[9]

The last two procurators before the Jewish War were *Albinus* and *Gessius Florus*. They are accused particularly of bribery and greed for money. Albinus is supposed to have received money from both parties, the Zealots and their opponents, and Florus to have plundered whole cities and communities. It was during Florus' term of office that the war broke out which led to the destruction of Jerusalem and the ruin of the temple.

[8] Josephus, *Antiquities*, xx.8, 5 (§§ 163f.). The situation in those years, when an assassination of opponents of the Law could be publicly discussed, throws clear light upon the attack against Paul mentioned in Acts xxiii.12ff.

[9] Josephus, *Antiquities*, xx.9, 1 (§§ 200–203). Apart from *Antiquities*, xviii.3, 3 (§§ 63f.), the famous and controversial *Testimonium Flavianum*, this passage contains the only reference in Josephus to Christians and Christ. It must be genuine, whereas the Testimonium, at least in its present form, can hardly be attributed to Josephus. Older bibliography in Schürer, *Geschichte des jüdischen Volkes*, vol. i, pp. 544–549; more recently, H. Windisch in *Th.R.*, *N.F.I.* (1929) pp. 276ff., ii (1930), pp. 207ff.; W. Bienert, *Der älteste nichtchristliche Jesusbericht*, Halle 1936, pp. 8ff.; H. W. Kars, "Der älteste nichtchristliche Jesusbericht" in *Theologische Studien und Kritiken*, cviii (1937–38), pp. 40–64; F. Scheidweiler in *Z.N.W.*, xliii (1950–51), pp. 176–178; xlv (1954), pp. 230–243.

Chapter 9

THE FALL OF JERUSALEM

The War A.D. 66–70.

The superficial causes of the Jewish War were relatively slight. Like Pilate, Florus drew seventeen talents out of the temple treasury. The Jews resisted him and contemptuously collected alms for him. Florus reacted sharply, but the unrest grew even greater. Agrippa II hastened to the scene and attempted to pour oil on the troubled waters. His efforts eventually foundered on the fact that the people were indeed willing to submit to Rome but not to its procurator Florus. With the decision to suspend the daily sacrifice on behalf of the emperor, and the mowing down of a Roman cohort which had been promised an unmolested departure, the war became a reality. The struggle remained essentially confined to Palestine; the Diaspora in the Roman Empire and the Jewish community in Babylon rendered no help. The news of the beginning of the revolt led to pogroms against the Jews in some Greek cities in and around Palestine; in Damascus 18,000 Jews are said to have been killed in the process. In return the Jews in Palestine took vengeance as far as possible on the Greek cities.

Implicated in the revolt were the provinces of Judea, Idumea, Perea and Galilee—in the main, therefore, the areas inhabited exclusively by Jews. The war began with a defeat of the Syrian procurator, Cestius. This appeared to the Jews to set the divine seal upon the righteousness of the war. Vespasian led the campaign on the Roman side. First Galilee, where Josephus had organised the revolt, then Perea and the greater environs of Jerusalem were mopped up. The death of Nero and the resulting confusion delayed the attack on

Jerusalem itself, and for three years it remained unmolested. When Vespasian became emperor in 69 he transferred the conduct of the war to his son Titus, who made to besiege Jerusalem early in the year 70. After four months of extremely bitter fighting, the temple area was taken by storm. The temple went up in flames. A month later the whole city was in Roman hands. In Rome, Titus celebrated a triumph in which the pillaged temple vessels were carried along. In Palestine a few fortresses still remained to be overcome; this was the task of the procurator. The fortress of Masada by the Dead Sea held out longest. Eventually, after a three year siege, the Romans built an embankment, in order to storm the fort, which was built on steep cliffs, and breached the walls, whereupon the whole garrison, man, woman and child, did themselves to death, in order not to fall into the enemies' hands alive.

The Underlying Causes of the Jewish War

Instead of the details of the war, which Josephus has described for us with precision, only the most important aspects of it will be portrayed as a key to an understanding of the events. The underlying cause of the war lay, in the first place, in the equivocal justice which the Roman occupation brought with it. This derived not merely from some procurators who were particularly greedy for power or money, but from Rome itself. No clear line had been consistently laid down and pursued from there. The Jews had come to learn that they could achieve their ends through the intercession of influential persons at the imperial court even in defiance of the procurator's wishes, although at the same time they had to learn that their opponents could likewise get their own way there, even apart from the question of what was justice.[1] Both factors inevitably undermined the authority of Rome and its procurators.

In the second place, however, the Jews brought the elements of a catastrophe upon themselves. The Zealots were gaining influence with the people in increasing measure. They believed

[1] The erratic nature of this justice is illustrated by Acts xxv.9–11. When Festus suggests to Paul that he should let himself be tried in Jerusalem, i.e. before the Sanhedrin, under his presidency, Paul sees himself compelled to appeal to the imperial court.

that, by consistent rejection of Rome and by waging war against their opponents within Judaism, they could render the obedience to God that would guarantee them God's help. To that end men appeared in their midst who believed themselves commissioned to prophesy the imminent coming of the Messiah and with it the end of Rome's power, and to show the people the "signs from heaven" that would precede and herald this turn of events. The Pharisees had nothing to offer as a counterweight to this movement which would put the Zealots in the wrong spiritually as they also were striving for mundane power on the part of the people of Israel and hoped to achieve it by means of perfect fulfilment of the Law. Zealotism was only a radical form of Pharisaism.

The misrule of the procurators certainly raised the confidence of the Zealots. For the time of salvation was to be preceded by a great period of trial. The more the procurators oppressed the Jewish people in Palestine and the more the resistance to them could be viewed as a struggle for the Law so much more confident was one of seeing the approach of the time of salvation.

Along with these general causes there was another particular cause. "When will the kingdom of God come?" Jesus was asked. He denied that it would come with "signs to be observed" (Lk. XVII.20f.). It was widely held at that time that the coming of the time of salvation was susceptible to observation and calculation. Such calculation played a part in the Jewish War:

"But what more than all else incited them to the war was an ambiguous oracle, likewise found in their sacred Scriptures, to the effect that at that time one from their country would become ruler of the world," writes Josephus.[2] He does not say what part of the Old Testament this refers to; it may even have nothing to do with any passage mentioning a particular number (such as Dan. IX.24), but with some other prophecy. At any rate, the calculation of the time of salvation, combined with the hope of mundane political power for Israel, gained epoch-making authority.

Thus the Jewish War probably arose by chance; it could

[2] *War*, VI.5, 4 (§ 312); similarly Tacitus, *Historiae*, V.3 and Suetonius, *Vespasian*, IV.

have come just as easily earlier on, or, when it did arise, it could still have been avoided. There is also no sign of any figure who might have considered himself to be the Messiah. Only Menahem of the tribe of Judas the Galilean (a member of the Davidic line?) made himself out to be king of Israel in Jerusalem, but he was soon murdered. But the war was certainly a struggle for the Law, and was waged to the very last in the confidence that God, although He might well allow his people to fall into desperate straits in this struggle, would subsequently send the great turning-point of history as an act of deliverance. When in the year 70 the final assault on the Temple itself was imminent and the situation, humanly speaking, was hopeless, a "prophet" appeared with the message that God's salvation would now manifest itself. And when the Temple was taken and went up in flames, the survivors demanded of Titus that they be allowed to withdraw unhindered into the desert—even there they still hoped for God's intervention.[3]

The endeavour to order everything according to the Law was apparent in many ways during the war. The fact that the Herodians and the Romans appointed the high priest was at variance with the Law. At the beginning of the war, therefore, a high priest was chosen by lot. Josephus set up an orderly judicial system in Galilee, forbade looting and the killing of compatriots. In Tiberias the animal-images in Herod's palace, so offensive to the Law, were removed.[4] In the middle of the war there was murderous internecine strife in Jerusalem. As the war was naturally in the judgment of those waging it a struggle for the Law, those who rejected it appeared in their eyes to be enemies of the Law; they were persecuted and assassinated, particularly the leading priestly circles and the owners of large estates. But even those who were bent on waging the war decisively split into two, at times even three parties, which fought bloodily among themselves and were united only in their opposition to the Romans. Social and personal factors certainly played a part in these internal struggles, but they appeared under the banner of a struggle for the proper fulfilment of the Law. And as God's help was to be expected only

[3] Josephus, *War*, VI.5, 2; 6, 3 (§§ 285, 351).

[4] Cf. the typical scene in Josephus, *Life*, XXVII (§§ 134 f.).

from total obedience to the Law, there was an inexorable struggle when one group considered that the other was not fulfilling the Law wholeheartedly or correctly.

Jesus and the Primitive Church

In the decades which preceded the destruction of the Jewish temple John the Baptist appeared, Jesus exercised his ministry and the primitive Church was alive. "The kingly rule of God is at hand": with this message the Baptist appeared on the scene. That was intelligible to the Jews. What was new, however, was the fact that this divine rule would not be brought about by repentance but that the summons to repentance flowed from the imminence of the divine rule. It was exactly the reverse of what the Jews thought right up to the great War and after. New also was the fact that this message contained no political overtones: the tax-collectors in the Roman service were not required to surrender their occupation. Also new was the fact that the Baptist summoned everyone, the pious and the sinners, to repentance, and proclaimed the forgiveness of sins to them in the baptism of repentance. Sadducees and Zealots, Pharisees and Essenes were linked together in the common repentance and the gaze of all of them was directed towards the divine rule instituted by God alone. If the nation really had obeyed the call of John the Baptist an end would have been put to the struggle of each against all, and the temerarious struggle against Rome, and they might have waited jointly for Him who baptised with fire.

When the Pharisees asked Jesus: "Is it lawful to pay taxes to Caesar or not" (Mk. xii.14), they were asking in effect whether the Zealot underground movement had God on its side when it rejected every acknowledgement of Roman rule. In His reply Jesus drew His enquirers' attention to the fact that Caesar was only demanding back something of what he and Roman rule had given to the nations and they, in their turn, had accepted: a uniform currency; and this itself was part and parcel of the world-trade assured by Rome and indeed almost a symbol of it—a trade in which the Jewish people had a rich share. But furthermore the Zealot refusal to pay taxes was, on account of the sacrifices connected with it, only an isolated part of Jewish legalism along with many others.

In adding "render to God the things that are God's," Jesus was saying that God in no way desires parts of Jewish legalism, neither money, nor sacrificial animals, nor even stricter sabbath observance, but the whole man. The Zealots' question was based on a false presupposition. God's will would not come on the basis of redoubled human efforts, nor on the basis of a tax-refusal that would render men homeless and destitute; it came, rather, when Jesus called sinners to himself with authority, it came when He let Himself be nailed defencelessly to a Cross, it came when He gathered around Him a body of unknown men, it came when He summoned His people to repent, repent even of its political hopes. Hence we understand also why Jesus forbade Himself to be acknowledged as Messiah in the atmosphere at that time so pregnant with politico-messianic expectations.

The primitive Church in Palestine saw its task as the proclamation to its compatriots of atonement and faith in Jesus Christ, in whom alone "salvation" subsisted, even for the nation as a whole. It likewise held aloof from the politico-messianic hopes of its nation, and subsequently also from the war against Rome; if the Letter of James stems from the Lord's brother, then in ch. IV.1–12 he regarded the struggles and disputes which rent Palestinian Jewry before the outbreak of the Jewish War as the consequence of human passions (Jas. IV.1), and viewed the request for the coming of the kingdom of God upon earth as an evil request that was animated by selfish motives (Jas. IV.3).

The Result of the War

Those who could escape from Palestine fled to Alexandria and sought to stir up the Jewish community there. In this they were certainly unsuccessful, but as a precaution the Romans closed the Jewish temple in Leontopolis at that time.

Weightier still were the consequences of the war for Palestine. The regard that the Romans had paid to the Holy Land and the Holy City now ceased. Judea became a Roman province under a senatorial procurator, and a legion was posted to Jerusalem. Pagan worship penetrated into Jerusalem with it. The temple lay in ruins, and any reconstruction of it was unthinkable. The temple tax that all Jews had sent annually to Jerusalem had now to be paid to the pagan god Jupiter in Rome. The Sanhedrin and with it the handling of justice according to peculiarly Jewish norms was no longer protected. The Sadducean, Essene and Zealot parties disappeared and only Pharisaism remained.

Josephus and Johanan

Pharisaism became the saviour of Judaism. Certainly the Pharisees took part in the War once it became inevitable, but the conduct of two figures who stand in greater or less proximity to it and with whom we are more closely acquainted is significant, namely Josephus and Johanan ben Zakkai. *Josephus,*[5] born in 37–38 A.D., was descended from a distinguished priestly family. In his youth he made himself familiar with the ideas of the Pharisees, Sadducees and Essenes, and spent three years in the desert with a hermit called Bannus; he returned to Jerusalem and joined the Pharisees. At the beginning of the War he was sent to Galilee, there to organise the struggle with Rome. He defended himself doughtily against the Romans in the town of Jotapata. When they finally penetrated into the city, he saved himself with forty comrades in a cistern; there they all resolved to die voluntarily and not to surrender to the Romans. At the instigation of Josephus, lots were drawn to decide in what order they should die; he was left together with another man, and surrendered to the Romans, whereupon he saluted the enemy field-marshal Vespasian with the cry of "Imperator." Thus he predicted his subsequent emperorship as ordained by God, which, when Vespasian became emperor, brought him freedom, Roman citizenship and various honours from the Romans. Thereupon he gave up the politico-messianic hope; how much he had to sacrifice of his personal convictions at the same time we cannot tell.

In any event, a like decision on the part of the rabbi *Johanan ben Zakkai*[6] arose out of a different sense of responsibility. He

[5] On Josephus see, apart from the historical works, especially *Realencyclopädie*, ed. A. F. von Pauly and G. Wissowa, IX.2 (1916), pp. 1934–2000 (Hölscher); H. St. J. Thackeray, *Josephus, the Man and the Historian*, New York 1929; Schlatter, *Die Theologie des Judentums*.

[6] On Johanan ben Zakkai, see the highly informative monograph by A. Schlatter, *Jochanan ben Zakkai, der Zeitgenosse der Apostel*, henceforth cited as *Jochanan ben Zakkai*, Gütersloh 1899.

had himself carried out of Jerusalem as one dead, and came by this subterfuge to the Romans, who gave him shelter. Here also the manner in which he saved his life causes raised eyebrows, but the way in which he acted was in the interest of the whole nation. He could no longer share the Zealot hope that God would intervene miraculously on behalf of His people; perhaps the bloody self-laceration of the besieged had shown him that it was wrong to expect God's help in this situation. He then recognised it as his task to cater for the maintenance of the study of the Law as the basis for the future existence of his people. So he abandoned the lost city—another task awaited him.

The figure of Josephus has been clarified for us through the fact that he wrote the history of the war in Greek and, in another comprehensive work, portrayed and made available to the Greeks and the Romans the history of his people from the dawn of humanity. In the process he adhered more closely to the Biblical narrative than the Hellenistic-Jewish writers mentioned earlier; but even his work flattens out the Biblical account and is often apologetic in the undesirable sense. His gaze is directed at the Roman world, and he goes to great lengths to accommodate himself to their level of understanding. Rabbi Johanan's gaze, on the other hand, is directed only to Israel and its God-given Law. He saw more correctly than Josephus that in it lay the only guarantee of his people's future survival.

Palestinian Judaism after the Fall of Jerusalem

In Jamnia, west of Jerusalem, those who rejected this struggle, the leaders of Pharisaism, gathered together with the consent of the Romans while the war was actually being fought. They managed to ensure that, even after the destruction of the Temple and the disappearance of the high priest and the Sanhedrin, leadership of the Jewish community remained in Palestine. The place of the Sanhedrin was taken by the assembly of the leading scribes. To enable them to act unitedly and also, probably, to single out one man to act as a spokesman to the authorities, they created the office of "prince." Under his guidance various points of controversy amongst the scribes were now resolved, particularly the struggle between the schools of Hillel and Shammai. The scope of the canon was laid down, and scruples regarding, in particular, the Song of Songs, Ecclesiastes and Esther were at the same time overcome. Sadduceeism was declared heretical and the Jewish Christians were excluded from the synagogue fellowship since a petition for their destruction was incorporated in the "Eighteen Benedictions" (see p. 157) that were to be recited daily and also had their place in the synagogue worship.

Through the fall of the Temple lengthy portions of the Old Testament Law and the precepts that the Pharisaic tradition had added became inoperable; no more sacrifices could be offered, no more passover lambs could be slain and no more Nazarite vows fulfilled. Pilgrimages to the great festivals ceased. Pharisaism viewed this consciously as a state of transition and strove to keep alive the remembrance of the temple arrangements and the course of the cult; above all, it preserved the memory of how justice was to be handled according to the Law, even though there existed no possibility, or only a slight one, of putting it into practice. Consequently, the scribal teaching became to a high degree a matter of theoretical debate irrelevant to life, the cultivation of mere tradition, and discussion of unrealisable possibilities. Part of the temple cult and the festival observances was taken up into the synagogue worship.

A few writings from the period after 70 give us insight into the shock that the lost war and the destruction of the temple had caused. Unknown men, writing pseudonymously as Biblical figures who had experienced the fall of Jerusalem in Nebuchadnezzar's day, expressed their own and their nation's anguish and sought to console themselves and their people. Of those writings that have come down to us IV *Ezra* is, next to the so-called *Syriac Apocalypse of Baruch*, the most devastating witness to their inward struggle with the fate that had overtaken them. National disaster awakens the acute sense of the sinfulness of the individual as well as of the people, and of the greatness of the Fall that Adam brought upon humanity. But even this work gives no other answer than that every man is answerable for his deeds and freely chooses life or death for himself. It still remains for the Jewish people to separate themselves from the Gentile peoples, and for the devout individual to separate himself from the ungodly, and the main task of the

Messiah is still to exercise judgment upon the Gentiles and the ungodly. Even after Rome's victory the expectation of its imminent fall and the hope of Israel's elevation remained as strong as ever.

Even in Pharisaism we see a profound shattering of confidence in personal achievement but we also see how the efforts to fulfil the Law in every detail were at the same time intensified. The principle that every man works out his own destiny was often upheld with something approaching inflexibility. From one of the leading Pharisaic scribes between A.D. 70 and 135, Akiba, there has come down a monumental metaphor that expresses the freedom to sin or not to sin and likewise shows that Akiba (and all Jewry with him) expected salvation or damnation only from man himself, and ascribed no significance to the Messiah for one's own spiritual life: "The shop stands open and the shopkeeper gives credit and the account-book lies open and the hand writes and every one that wishes to borrow let him come and borrow; but the collectors go their round continually every day and exact payment of men with their consent or without their consent, for they have that on which they can rely; and the judgment is a judgment of truth; and all is made ready for the (messianic) banquet."[7]

It was this Akiba who taught that human righteousness was to be measured by the preponderance of good works over bad, and who thereby helped to overcome the shock that the fall of Jerusalem caused (see pp. 218ff.).[8]

The Final Struggles and their Effects

Though rejecting Zealot activism, Pharisaism nevertheless wrestled for the perfect fulfilment of the Law that was to bring about the intervention of God and the redemption of Israel. The signs of the times seemed to indicate that the age of salvation and the judgment of the Gentiles were still to come, yet there were to be violent struggles after the year 70. When the emperor Trajan began a large-scale attack against the Parthians in 114, all Jewry watched the course of the campaign with tense anticipation. For upon the Parthians, the

[7] *M. Ab.* III.17.

[8] On Akiba see P. Billerbeck in *Nathanael* 1916 and 1917; on the earlier scribes as a whole see W. Bacher, *Die Agada der Tannaiten*, VOLS. I and II, Strassburg 1884, 1890.

only oriental power that the Romans could not subdue, rested many a quiet hope of the beginning of Rome's downfall (cf. Rev. IX.13ff.). Consequently, it only required the rumour that the campaign was not going well with Trajan, for the Jewish community (particularly in Egypt, Cyrenaica and Cyprus) to be moved to a large-scale uprising in which both sides behaved with unheard-of cruelty and which was stifled in rivers of blood. The favourable status that the Jews had in Alexandria was lost at this time.

Only half a generation later, in A.D. 132, the most terrible struggle the Jews ever waged broke out. It was probably occasioned by the permission the emperor Hadrian gave for the rebuilding of the temple in Jerusalem.[9] Leader in the struggle was a certain Simon, in whom Akiba saw the Messiah and to whom he applied the passage in Numbers XXIV.17f.:—

> "A star shall come forth out of Jacob,
> and a sceptre shall rise out of Israel;
> it shall crush the forehead of Moab,
> and break down all the sons of Sheth.
> Edom shall be dispossessed
> Seir also, his enemies shall be dispossessed,
> while Israel does valiantly."[10]

Naturally objections were raised to viewing this Simon, the "son of a star" (Aramaic: "Bar-Cocheba"), as the Messiah. But Jews from every part of the world flocked to enlist under his banner. The whole of Palestine fell into his hands; worship at the altar in Jerusalem was resumed, conducted by a priest Eleazar.[11] Coins were minted with the name of Simon, Prince of Israel, bearing a star, some also bearing the name of Eleazar and dated according to the years of the "freedom of Israel," or "Jerusalem."[12] The war lasted three years, and Hadrian

[9] See my essay "Der Jupitertempel auf dem Tempelplatz in Jerusalem" in *Theologische Blätter*, X (1931), pp. 241–250 and H. Bietenhard in *Judaica*, IV (1948) pp. 57ff., 81ff., 161ff.

[10] We must notice in this connexion that "Edom" was the current pseudonym amongst the Pharisees for Rome, so that they found the conquest of Rome prophesied in this passage.

[11] Eleazar is the same name as Lazarus.

[12] Along with the finds at Khirbet Qumran there were found south of Qumran, at Wadi Murabba' at, letters of Simon Bar Cocheba dating from the period of the war, *Revue Biblique*, LX (1953), pp. 245–267; 276-294; LXIII (1956), pp. 45–48.

was obliged to summon his most capable general. Fifty castles and 985 fortified villages had to be taken separately. So bitter was the fighting that the emperor, in his letters to the Senate, did not use the customary formula of introduction: "It fares well with myself and the army." Eight hundred and fifty thousand men are said to have died in Palestine at that time. The last battle took place around the mountain stronghold of Bittir, with whose capture in A.D. 135 hope in the "son of a star," to whom the nations would render subjection, subsided.

Now, in A.D. 135, the Jews were forbidden to enter Jerusalem and its surroundings and to practise their religion; it was forbidden to circumcise children, to possess the Law and to celebrate the festivals. Martyrdoms now became numerous.

On Exodus xx.6 we read: "These are the Israelites who live in the land of Israel and give their lives for the commandments. 'Why are you led out to be killed?' 'Because I have circumcised sons of Israel.' 'Why are you led out to be burnt to death?' 'Because I have been reading the Torah.' 'Why are you led out to be crucified?' 'Because I have eaten unleavened bread.' 'Why are you beaten with the scourge.' 'Because I have carried the festive branch at the Feast of Tabernacles.'"[13]

Akiba also died a martyr's death at that time in his old age. The account of his death is moving.

"When R. Akiba was taken out for execution, it was the hour for the recital of the *Shema*, and while they combed his flesh with iron combs, he was accepting upon himself the kingship of heaven (i.e. reciting the *Shema*). His disciples said to him: Our teacher, even to this point? He said to them: All my days I have been troubled by this verse, '*with all thy soul*,' (which I interpret) 'even if He takes thy soul.' I said: When shall I have the opportunity of fulfilling this? Now that I have the opportunity shall I not fulfil it? He prolonged (as was customary) the word *echad* ('One' in 'Hear, O Israel, the Lord thy God is One. . . .') until he expired while saying it."[14]

Antoninus Pius (A.D. 138–161) rescinded the prohibition of the circumcision of Jewish children; on the other hand, the prohibition of Jewish access to Jerusalem remained in force still longer. This city was now completely rebuilt out of

[13] *Mekilta Ex.*, xx.6 quoted Strack-Billerbeck, VOL. I, p. 395.

[14] *B.T.Ber.*, 61 b quoted Strack-Billerbeck, VOL. I, p. 224.

the ruins as a Gentile city under the name of Aelia Capitolina.

The effect of these events on Judaism was that it consciously abandoned the messianic hope and concentrated even more upon the Law. Its three pillars were now the Canon together with the Law, the synagogue and rabbinic learning which preserved Judaism as an entity. The story is told of a rabbi who, at the cost of his life, ordained some disciples and so kept the chain of tradition unbroken.[15] Even apocalypticism was now completely suppressed as it distracted one's gaze from concentration upon the Law. Thus the writings which gave expression to it were preserved only through the intermediacy of non-Jewish circles. Of the new ideas Pharisaism only retained those that had some connexion with the fulfilment of the Law: the belief in the resurrection of the dead and in the universal world-judgment; the whole unsettling quest after the superterrestrial backgrounds to world history and the history of the individual subsided. Judaism limited itself with great consistency to one matter: the Law. The things that the earlier teachers had expressed as their interpretation of the Law were now collected and discussed. Thus the foundations of the Talmud were laid. With it Judaism found expression for its own peculiar character; with it Judaism reached the goal towards which it had been striving ever since the Babylonian captivity.

[15] *T.B.Sanh.*, 13 b quoted Strack-Billerbeck, VOL. II, pp. 649f.

Part II

PALESTINE IN JESUS' DAY

INTRODUCTION

Let us survey first the total extent of Jewry in New Testament times. In the former Babylon, by now part of the Parthian kingdom, lived a numerous Jewish community which was not molested by its government and was exempt from the various changes of fortune to which its compatriots in the Roman Empire were exposed. The link between Babylonian Jewry and Palestine was never broken; e.g. the well-known scribe, Hillel, went from Babylon to Jerusalem, while Josephus, on the other hand, wrote his account of the Jewish War in the first instance for the Jews in the east. In the Roman Empire, Palestine was the centre of the Jewish community which was to be found scattered beyond Palestine's borders throughout the Empire, from the Nile to the Tiber, particularly in Egypt, Syria and Asia Minor. Cities like Rome, Alexandria, Antioch and Ephesus had an especially large Jewish population. The proportion at that time of Jews to the total population of the Roman Empire has been estimated at 7 per cent., and their numbers about 4 to 4½ millions, but these estimates are naturally vague.

When the Old Testament wishes to describe the extent of the "Promised Land" it uses the phrase: "from Dan to Beer-sheeba" (e.g. I Sam. III.20). That was a distance of about 145 miles as the crow flies, just a little further than from Glasgow to Newcastle. In breadth Palestine stretched from the coast to beyond the Jordan although it was never Israelite to that extent at any one time. Thus, if the ideal area of the Promised Land was slight, the region inhabited exclusively by Jews in New Testament times was even slighter. It comprised Judea, larger in area as compared with the time of the return from the Babylonian captivity, together with Idumea, Galilee and Perea. This did not include any of the coastal plain, whose numerous cities had a varying proportion of Jewish inhabitants, nor Samaria and the so-called "Great Plain" between Galilee and Samaria, the most fertile part of Palestine. Capernaum, where Jesus began His public ministry, was the most outlying part of the purely Jewish territory, and the most distant from Jerusalem. It lay near the border of Philip's kingdom with its cosmopolitan population. Matthew IV.15f. recalls, therefore, the ancient prophecy of Isaiah: "The land of Zebulun and the land of Naphtali, toward the sea, across the Jordan, Galilee of the Gentiles—the people who sat in darkness have seen a great light. . . ."

The cramped conditions of Palestine are variously reflected in the New Testament. From Jerusalem to Nazareth it was a good three days' march, whereas a car can cover the distance today in a few hours. It took the soldiers only a single night to bring Paul from Jerusalem to Antipatris (Acts XXIII.31), the border of the exclusively Jewish territory, which was half-way to Caesarea by the Sea. The few hours that lay by Palestinian custom between death and burial sufficed to fetch Peter from Joppa to Lydda (Acts IX.38f.). Even more cramped were the conditions in Galilee. According to John IV.46f., the official at Capernaum, the border city, could hasten in one day from there to Cana in the centre of Galilee and arrive shortly after midday ("at the seventh hour"), even though it did not allow him time to get back home on the same day. The three cities "where most of his mighty works had been done" (Matt. XI.20ff.), Chorazin, Bethsaida and Capernaum, were scarcely more than an hour's distance from each other.

Chapter 10

THE POLITICAL SITUATION

The Roman Administration

It was, as we saw, important for the situation of Palestinian Jewry that the political administration in the proper sense, and it alone, lay outside the jurisdiction of the Jews: either in the hands of the Romans or in those of the Herodians who were only to a qualified extent recognised as Jews. Both the Romans and the Herodians had an *army* in Palestine. Of the former, only the so-called "auxiliary troops" were stationed there, recruited not from Roman citizens but from the country itself. These were picked especially from the regions of Samaria and Caesarea, as the Romans did not recruit Jews as soldiers, on account of their sabbath-observance.

It was the proud boast of the Romans that they brought "peace" to their subject peoples, and they therefore maintained only a skeleton army of occupation in the provinces. So it was in Palestine. The majority of the troops were stationed in Caesarea, where the procurator also had his official residence; to them belonged the centurion Cornelius (Acts x and xi); Paul was handed over to a centurion of this cohort (Acts xxvii.1) after the commandant of the Jerusalem garrison had sent him to the procurator (Acts xxiii.23–35). The Roman garrison of Jerusalem had a strength of about 700–1,000 men; it was stationed mainly in the fortress of Antonia at the north-west corner of the temple area, which, then as now the source of many a disturbance, could be easily surveyed and supervised from that point; thus the "tribune" Lysias was able to intervene immediately, when Paul was about to be lynched in the riot (Acts xxi.27–40). The soldiers who crucified Christ were members of this garrison unit.

The Herodians also had troops at their disposal; thus we find a centurion stationed at Capernaum; he was, like Cornelius, a Gentile. Luke's account of him (Luke VII.4f.) indicates that he too was deeply impressed by the Old Testament faith.

Alongside the concern for peace and security in the land, the Roman and Herodian authorities had two other special tasks. One was the collecting of *taxes and custom duties*. About the collection of taxes we need only say that there were two main types of direct tax: a tax on land profits and a poll-tax.[1] The customs were levied at the provincial borders, as, for example, in Capernaum on the border between the kingdoms of Herod Antipas and Philip, and in the area of Jericho on the border between the Roman procuracy of Judea and Perea, which belonged to Antipas. The "chief tax collector," Zacchaeus, would have leased the right to levy taxes in this whole border region, and further farmed out the right to collect taxes individually to tax-collectors at the separate customs posts. The amount for which the taxes were farmed out was fixed by levy; the tax-collectors were responsible for any deficit, while any surplus stood to their credit. There was presumably a customs tariff, but many a door was opened to arbitrariness and deceit. In the Talmud tax collectors were equated with robbers; the New Testament classes tax collectors and sinners together. In Judea a factor which contributed to the contempt shown to tax collectors was that they worked for the occupying power.

In the matter of the *administration of justice*—and here we come to the second task of the authorities—rulers in the ancient world were completely autonomous. That applied to the Herodians within certain limits, as they held their authority in fief from Rome, and on this account invoked the emperor's decision in particularly important cases. The procurators had complete jurisdiction over the indigenous population and could pronounce the death sentence or pardon at will. Roman citizens could demand that their cause should come before the imperial court in Rome. Such an appeal to the emperor's court meant that the case was withdrawn completely from the

[1] F. C. Grant in *The Economic Background of the Gospels*, Oxford 1926, p. 105, estimates the percentage of income-tax levied upon the Jewish people in Jesus' day for the Romans and the Temple at roughly 30–40 per cent, if not higher.

procurator's sphere of authority, in fact, he no longer had the power to set the prisoner free (Acts xxvi.32).

Jewish Self-government

As it was Roman policy to preserve as far as possible the characteristic life and self-government of the subject peoples, the judicial system in Palestine, so far as it concerned non-political affairs, was left in the hands of the Jewish authorities; only death sentences required to be confirmed by the procurator; that is clear from Jesus' trial.[2] The criterion by which the Jews ordered their public affairs was the Old Testament Law with its juridical stipulations, cultic statutes and ritual decrees.

This Law was implemented so far as this could be achieved by the methods open to the judicial administration, i.e. by the Sanhedrins (EVV "council"). These were the local authorities in those towns and villages which were inhabited exclusively by Jews. The prime method of punishment was flogging inflicted, according to II Corinthians xi.24, upon Paul five times, followed by expulsion, mentioned in John ix.22, xii.42, xvi.2 and Luke vi.22. The book of Acts says that Peter and the other apostles also suffered the penalty of flogging (Acts v.40). The Old Testament further provided for various kinds of death penalty, e.g., for blasphemy, the penalty of stoning, as was inflicted upon Stephen, perhaps without Roman sanction. Where the circumstances did not warrant an execution, they contented themselves with expulsion, and left it to God Himself to preserve the honour of His name through the sudden death of the sinner.[3]

In smaller places the Sanhedrin consisted of seven members; more serious cases came before a college of twenty-three persons. For the protection and maintenance of order in the temple there was a temple police force armed with clubs, who participated in the arrest of Jesus (Mk. xiv.43, 48). They were responsible to the "captain of the temple" (Acts iv.1; v.24).

Of special significance was the Sanhedrin of the city of Jerusalem, the "Supreme Council." We have seen how after the return from the Babylonian captivity the governor was

[2] On the trial of Jesus see J. Blinzler, *Der Prozess Jesu,* 3rd edn., Stuttgart 1960 and the bibliography listed there; Paul Winter, *On the Trial of Jesus,* Berlin 1961.

[3] See Strack-Billerbeck, vol. iv, pp. 233–333 on expulsion from the synagogue.

aided by the "elders," i.e. the heads of families (see p. 20) and how after the disappearance of the governorship the high priest assumed ever greater prominence and even secured entry for the heads of the priestly families into the council of elders. The "scribes" then entered as the third element in the leadership, being versed in the Law.

Whenever these three, "the elders and chief priests and scribes" are mentioned in the New Testament together, the "supreme council" is meant: thus Matthew XVI.21, XXVII.41; Mark VIII.31, XV.1; Luke IX.22; Acts IV.5. Frequently, however, mention is made only of "the chief priests and scribes," with the same meaning. At first sight the plural "the chief priests" is surprising, as there was only one in office at any one time; the expression signifies the current holder of the office, together with the past high priests and the holders of some of the higher temple offices.[4]

As long as the temple remained standing and the supreme council was in office the high priests and the high priestly families exercised great influence, although the reputation that the Pharisees enjoyed amongst the people often compelled them to give way, as Acts v.34–40 shows.

Legally the supreme council had jurisdiction only over Judea, but in practice its authority extended beyond the borders of Palestine. It was able to send Paul with warrants to Damascus and expected the Jewish community there to act on his instructions; when Paul arrived in Rome the Jews there told him that neither had they received letters regarding his case from Judea, nor had any brother who had been there reported about him (Acts XXVIII.21). The letters from Judea would have come from the supreme council, and the brother would have to have been sent by them; the Jewish synagogue in Rome would then have acted on these instructions (cf. p. 133).

[4] Jeremias, *Jerusalem*, VOL. II B, pp. 17ff.

CHAPTER II

THE SOCIAL SYSTEM

The Patriarchal Order

AMONGST all the peoples of the ancient world we find in historical times a *patriarchal order of society*, which gave the husband and father power over wife and children. In the Roman Empire we encounter at that time a widespread emancipation of women and children. In Judaism, however, the position of the husband and father was protected by such passages as Genesis III.16 ("he shall rule over you"), Exodus XX.12 ("honour your father and your mother"), while reverence for age was protected by such passages as Leviticus XIX.32 ("You shall rise up before the hoary head"); in New Testament times the patriarchal order continued virtually undiminished. The division of the Palestinian Christian congregations into "old" and "young" (Acts v.6 and 1 Pet. v.1, 5) testifies to the regard for age.[1] The commandment to honour one's father and mother was regarded throughout Jewry as one of the most important commandments; both Josephus and the Talmud testify to this. Even Herod is supposed on one occasion to have invoked the Old Testament commandment that a disobedient son should be stoned. Josephus characterises the proper bearing towards one's parents with the same word as that used in relation to God: piety.[2]

As the Law provided definite penalties for insubordinate sons (Ex. XXI.15, 17), the question arose for the scribes as to

[1] A. Schlatter, *The Church in the New Testament Period*, trans. P. P. Levertoff, London 1955, p. 35. The episode in which the whole Jewish people draws up before Petronius in order to petition him is significant (see p. 102); they arrange themselves into six groups: "old men," "young men," children,—"old women," "women in the prime of life," virgins; Philo, *Embassy to Gaius*, XXXII (§ 227).

[2] Greek *eusebeia*; Schlatter, *Theologie des Judentums*, pp. 169f.; for rabbinic passages on the veneration of parents see Strack-Billerbeck, VOL. I, pp. 705ff.; Josephus, *Against Apion*, II.27 (§ 206).

when the cursing or smiting of parents punishable by death had taken place, whether with the "cursing" God's name had to be uttered, whether with the "smiting" an injury had to be inflicted on the parents, or whether the cursing of the mother alone (and not the father also) rendered a man culpable.[3] Such considerations, necessary for any human court of justice, were a result of the fact that the Old Testament Law contained both ethical and juridical stipulations.

This factor plays a part in the Corban pericope in Mark VII.1ff. By uttering the votive formula *Corban* a son who was in duty bound to maintain his parents could declare his contribution to their maintenance to be a sacrifice devoted to the temple from which the parents could not then derive the slightest benefit. In the process it was not even necessary for the means withdrawn from the parents actually to be given to the temple. The rabbis decided that such declarations of intent were binding in law.[4] Jesus says that this juridical stipulation, the "tradition of the elders," i.e. accretion of tradition, abrogated the commandment to honour one's parents and therefore conflicted with God's commandment. The rabbis were not enabled by their juridical casuistry to regard such a vow as completely and utterly immoral, in conflict with God's will and therefore null and void.

The Status of Women

The Old Testament itself indicates in some passages that a lower status was accorded to the woman as compared with the man; thus the mother, for example, is "unclean" longer after the birth of a daughter than after the birth of a boy. In Judaism we find, and not only in the Talmud, some unfavourable judgments upon woman who, according to Josephus, is "in all things inferior to the man."[5] The rabbis[6] say that the woman is in many ways frivolous and unteachable.[7]

[3] Strack-Billerbeck, VOL. I, pp. 709–711; see also G. F. Moore, *Judaism in the First Centuries of the Christian Era, the Age of the Tannaim*, 3 vols., Cambridge (Mass.), 1927–30, VOL. II, pp. 134f.

[4] Strack-Billerbeck, VOL. I, pp. 711ff.

[5] *Against Apion*, II.24 (§ 201). Josephus characterises the attitude of the Essenes towards women with the statement that the former were "persuaded that [they] could not keep their plighted troth to *one* man;" see ch. V, footnote (13).

[6] Rabbis are the pharisaic scribes.

[7] *B.T. Shab.*, 33 b quoted Strack-Billerbeck, VOL. III, p. 611.

The differing status of man and woman is also clear both in the cult and in their relationship to the Law. Women were allowed admittance to the courtyard of the temple only up to a certain limit (the "Court of Women"); they could offer no sacrifice; they did not count when it was being determined whether the quorum of worshippers necessary for a synagogue service was present, and in the synagogues they were kept separate from the men. Yet they participated in the sabbath meal and in times of emergency the whole community prayed jointly with the women and children.[8] In connexion with the Law the women, together with minors and slaves, were pledged to observe all the negative prohibitions, but not to keep all the positive commandments, and that because they were subordinate to the authority of another, namely, their husband. Women were not even obliged to study the Law; we therefore hear of only one instance, in the second century A.D., of a woman learned in the scriptures. Women could not lay testimony before a court of law. The fact that women followed Jesus is without precedent in contemporary Judaism. One of the earliest rabbinic sayings from pre-New Testament times reads: "Talk not much with a woman" (cf. Jn. IV.27), and the later gloss refers it explicitly to the wife.[9] An anecdote about Akiba, however, should keep us from making a one-sided judgment: on one occasion, he was returning home after a long absence, his wife ran towards him, fell on her face and kissed him. His disciples wished to repulse her, but Akiba said: "My [learning] and yours are hers;" she had borne a long separation from him while he devoted himself to study of the Torah.[10]

Marriage

The marriage age was low, 18–24 years for the man, 13–14 years for the girl. The patriarchal social order was manifest here in the fact that the father gave his daughter to a man for wife. Paul speaks in I Corinthians VII.36–38 of the responsibility of the father or guardian in relation to the marriage of a girl.[11]

[8] Cf. also the common petition of the whole population laid before Petronius.

[9] *M.Ab.* I.5.

[10] *B.T. Ned.*, 50 a quoted Strack-Billerbeck, VOL. III, p. 610.

[11] The exegesis of the passage is greatly disputed; see G. Kümmel in *Festschrift für R. Bultmann*, Berlin 1954, pp. 275–295.

The man marries the woman; she *is* married. The man can divorce his wife; the wife *is* divorced. Thus, according to Jesus the man who divorces his wife is guilty when the marriage with her is broken off (Mt. v.32 literally) and she is free to marry again; the woman herself has no say in the matter.

The woman is transferred from the father's authority to that of the husband. Josephus and the Talmud agree in saying that the wife is controlled by the husband's will. The betrothal is preceded by the conclusion of the marriage contract. This involves the settlement of three matters; first, the marriage portion, which remains the property of the wife;[12] then the dowry, which becomes the property of the husband, and finally the marriage settlement (Heb. *ketubha*), i.e. the determining of the sum of money which must be paid back to the wife in the event of divorce or the death of the husband. This consisted of a basic assessment, the value of the dowry and, in certain circumstances, supplements to the basic assessment. This marriage settlement could on occasions add up to a considerable amount. After the conclusion of the marriage contract the betrothal took place by means of an appropriate declaration on the bridegroom's part, which conferred upon the woman the legal status of wife. Betrothal could therefore only be dissolved by divorce; if the bridegroom died, the bride ranked as a widow. The marriage was concluded by the fetching home of the bride to the bridegroom's house. These things are important for the appraisal of the birth-story of Jesus.

Regarding *divorce* Deuteronomy xxiv.1 lays down that the husband, if he finds "any indecency" in the wife and wishes to divorce her, must give her a bill of divorce. This stipulation was originally conceived as a protection for the wife, in that the divorce in this way received a legal form. The rabbis laid down the formalities of the bill of divorce in minute detail; the delays connected with it doubtless prevented many a premature divorce. Another obstacle to an all too hasty divorce was the fact that in this case the husband had to pay the wife the marriage settlement.

In New Testament times a difference of opinion arose between the schools of Hillel and Shammai regarding the

[12] Perhaps the ten "coins," of which the woman in the parable in Lk. xv.8 lost one, represents part of her marriage portion.

meaning of the expression "any indecency" in Deuteronomy XXIV.1. The latter regarded only marital infidelity on the part of the wife as legitimate grounds for divorce while the former applied the Old Testament phrase to anything in his wife that displeased the husband. The laxer conception was represented not only by such a man as Akiba, but also by Josephus and Philo. Accordingly there was at that time no Jewish marriage that could not be dissolved by the husband in a completely legal manner by the handing over of a bill of divorce.[13]

The wife could give the husband no bill of divorce, but merely compel him in certain cases to hand over one to her. It is a mark of Greek influence that amongst the Herodians even wives dissolved marriages. It should not go unmentioned that many rabbinic sayings have been preserved which warn against hasty divorce.[14]

For the man it was regarded as a duty to marry; even the widower had to marry again. It was rare for a scribe to remain unmarried. Thus it is surprising that Jesus had not married even by the age of thirty, and we are at least permitted to ask whether Paul was not a widower.[15] Whilst the husband had to feed, clothe and maintain his wife, the wife's duty was to carry out the household tasks, and also to wash her husband's feet, a task which the slaves could not be compelled to do.

The woman's place was in the home; girls were confined to the women's boudoirs. In the Jewish literature of the pre- and post-New Testament period frequent expression is given to the endeavour to limit social intercourse with women as much as possible.[16] Along with Jesus' word concerning the lustful glance we can quote many a parallel from this body of writings; they reveal that the attempt was made to avoid the lustful glance by the greatest possible limitation of opportunities to

[13] Strack-Billerbeck, VOL. I, pp. 312ff.; Josephus, *Antiquities*, IV.8, 23 (§ 253); cf. *Life*, LXXVI (§ 426); Philo, *On the Special Laws*, III.5 (§ 30); Schlatter, *Theologie des Judentums*, p. 166; Jeremias, *Jerusalem*, VOL. II B, pp. 243f. The question which the Pharisees, according to Mt. XIX.3, posed to Jesus was precisely the question which divided the schools of Hillel and Shammai. Mark's Gospel, written for the Roman reader, omits the decisive words "for any cause."

[14] Strack-Billerbeck, VOL. I, p. 320.

[15] Cf. J. Jeremias in *Z.N.W.*, XXV (1926), pp. 310–312 and E. Fascher, *ibid.* XXVIII (1929), pp. 62–69.

[16] Schlatter, *Theologie des Judentums*, p. 169; by the same author, *Der Evangelist Matthäus*, Stuttgart 1929, pp. 175–177.

meet with the opposite sex.[17] There existed no legal prohibition of polygamy; in the case of the Levirate marriage the Law explicitly sanctioned it, and it was taken for granted for the majority (see p. 49). The Old Testament ensured that the then widespread custom of exposing new-born children found no place in Judaism.

The Social Divisions of the Nation

Jesus Sirach concludes his "praise of the fathers" with the praise of the high priest Simon, who was "the pride of his people" (Sir. L.1). The Hasmoneans had at that time combined the royal and high priestly offices in themselves. As the Herodians, being half-Jews and non-Aaronites, could not possess the highest office of the cult, the high priests gained greater influence as the spiritual representatives of the people. The best proof of this is the fact that Herod, like the Romans, allowed no life-office of high priest. Nevertheless his official position and the presidency of the Sanhedrin always gave the high priest great distinction, as Acts XXIII.2–5 testifies. Next to him the chief priests succeeded in winning political power and wealth.[18] In contrast to them stood the mass of ordinary priests, who only had to do service in Jerusalem at festivals and for two weeks in the year, and were thus obliged to practise a trade, usually a handicraft, in their home district. The priest Phanni, whom the Zealots elected high priest by lot at the beginning of the Jewish War, was a stone mason and completely uneducated. The total number of priests amounted to over 7,000 men, the Levites about 11,000.[19]

Next in importance to the priests stood a series of distinguished land-owning families, who formed the "elders" of the Jerusalem Sanhedrin.

To the high priests and the elders there was added in the course of time another group, who based their influence upon their knowledge of the Law: the scribes. These not only existed amongst the Pharisees; the reference in Mark II.16, puzzling at first glance, to the "scribes of the Pharisees" is

[17] Cf. the anecdote about Juda ben Tabbai quoted on p. 61 and Jub. XX.4 quoted on p. 66.

[18] Jeremias, *Jerusalem*, VOL. II B, pp. 40ff.

[19] Jeremias, *Jerusalem*, VOL. II B, pp. 61–68.

informative. Even the Sadducees and the "sects" had "scribes," although the pharisaic scribes, like the Pharisees generally, had the broadest influence amongst the people and in the New Testament stand dominatingly in the foreground. Their influence rested upon the fact that knowledge of the Law was essential for legal, ceremonial and daily affairs. "Rabbi" was the title given in their honour, a title that the people frequently applied to Jesus, and which Jesus in Matthew XXIII.7f. forbids His disciples to assume.

The Divisions of the People from the Standpoint of Purity[20]

Purity formed an important mark of distinction, particularly blood-purity. Prior esteem was given to the Israelites of pure descent, who were divided into priests, Levites and (full-) Israelites. The importance which is attached to the genealogies in the books of Ezra, Nehemiah and Chronicles shows the stress that Jewry laid upon the knowledge of the blood-connexion of its members to the people of Israel. Paul knows that he belongs to the tribe of Benjamin; the Zadokite Document orders the members of the community to be registered in divisions: priests, levites, Israelites and proselytes.[21] Knowledge of one's genealogy was particularly important for the priests, as they could marry only a girl who was a full Israelite. Even though it is impossible to account for the difference between the genealogies of Jesus in Matthew and Luke, that Jesus was of the Davidic line is certain; indeed, towards the end of the first century, the emperor Domitian had the "kinsfolk of the Lord" hauled before him as being of the Davidic line and therefore politically suspect.[22]

Only pure-bred Israelites could occupy posts of honour, and belong to the Sanhedrins, or be of those who were heads of the community or custodians of alms. Participation in the "merits of the fathers" was based upon blood-membership of the people of Abraham. Elijah would prepare for the coming of the Messiah, so it was thought at that time, by restoring the blood-purity of the people, i.e. clarify cases where membership of the Israelite race was erroneously denied or acknowledged.[23]

Then there was a number of despised trades. Whoever

[20] Jeremias, *Jerusalem*, VOL. II B, pp. 141ff. [21] *Zadokite Document*, XIV.3–12.
[22] Eusebius, *Ecclesiastical History*, III.20. [23] Strack-Billerbeck, VOL. IV, pp. 792ff.

practised them was not permitted, even though he was a full Israelite, to give testimony in court. To these belonged the shepherds, tax-collectors and customs men; they were trades which gave rise particularly to the temptation to deceive. The New Testament shows us the contempt which was borne towards the customs men. Some other trades were condemned as particularly loathsome, of which that of the tanner was one. Acts therefore does not stress for nothing the fact that Peter lodged with a tanner (Acts x.6).

Of the Israelites who could not boast of pure descent, the most important group was that of the *Proselytes*, i.e. those who had come over to Judaism with every formality, circumcision, baptism and the offering of a sacrifice (see p. 142f.). They could not marry into priestly families nor could they occupy most of the public offices. For the attainment of "righteousness" they were thrown upon their own merits, as they were not credited with the righteousness of the fathers. In other respects, however, they stood on a level with the full Israelites; amongst the scribes we find sons of proselyte women.

Jesus' parables presuppose that there were *Jewish slaves*. A Jew could not be sold to a Gentile master as a slave, an arrangement that the Romans in the various wars did not disturb, though Herod did so in his administration of justice (see p. 88). According to the Old Testament a Jewish slave was only like a wage-earner who had sold his labour for a definite period, for in the "sabbatical year" his master had to release him. In other respects, too, his legal position was better than that of Gentile slaves.[24]

The position of Gentiles bought as slaves was different, even when, as probably happened in most cases, they, as slaves, had been made Jews by baptism and circumcision. They were and remained the unprivileged possession of their masters; the commandment applies to them only insofar as this did not detract from their master's rights. They could not appear as witnesses nor could they enter upon a valid marriage with Jewish women. They were not set free in the sabbatical year, and could receive corporal punishment (Mt. xxiv.51 mg.).

[24] Jeremias, *Jerusalem*, vol. ii B, pp. 184ff.; 217ff.; Strack-Billerbeck, vol. iv, pp. 698ff.

Chapter 12

THE CULTURAL AND ECONOMIC SITUATION

The Cultural Situation

Galilee, Judea, Idumea and Perea were equally islands of Judaism in a sea of non-Jewish culture. The bearers of this culture were the Hellenistic cities. Between Judea and Galilee lay the province of Samaria with Sebaste, built by Herod, a city to which Herod had imparted all the brilliance of a Greek cultural city. On the coast of the Mediterranean Sea Gaza and Ashkelon must receive particular mention as Hellenistic cities. Joppa was predominantly, Caesarea by the Sea partly, Jewish. North of Carmel, alongside the western boundary of Galilee, lay the Gentile towns of Ptolemais (= Akko), and Tyre and Sidon with their extensive territory, trodden by Jesus Himself. Between Samaria and Galilee, on the western bank of the Jordan, lay the important town of Scythopolis, whose Jewish inhabitants refused to take part in the revolt against Rome but were nonetheless massacred by their suspicious Gentile fellow-citizens. On the eastern shore of Lake Gennesaret lay Hippos and, to the south-east, Gadara while, beyond Perea, Gerasa deserves special mention. These cities belonged to the league of the so-called Decapolis ("Ten Cities"), which maintained the Roman Empire's border watch upon the desert. North-east of Galilee Philip had created centres of Hellenistic culture in Julias and Caesarea Philippi, the place of Peter's confession.

Even in the territory settled exclusively by Jews the Herodians introduced Greek culture: in Jerusalem there was an amphitheatre, a theatre and a hippodrome; the same three amenities, hallmarks of foreign culture, existed in Jericho.

In Galilee Tiberias was, as we saw, built by Herod Antipas in the same spirit, and promoted to the status of a capital city. Finally, the great trade route linking Damascus with Egypt ran through Galilee. Thus, Helleno-Roman, i.e. Gentile, culture surged round the tiny areas occupied exclusively by Jews.

One must picture these circumstances as being hardly any different from what, by analogy, they were by the first decades of this century in Palestine. European culture had made its way into the towns and given rise to hotels, cinemas, business houses and administrative buildings; European languages were understood there, while in the country, away from the great towns and highways, there was hardly any discernible contact with European culture; there traditions, customs and conceptions going back thousands of years, and primitive methods of farming and craftsmanship had remained unaltered, and even in the indigenous parts of the cities (Jerusalem for instance) the new age had penetrated only fragmentarily and superficially. Conditions in Jesus' day must be conceived in similar terms: the villages in Judea and Galilee were little affected by the tide of the "new age" of those days.[1]

This was true of Sadducean circles most of all. In varying measure the Jews were ready to welcome this exotic culture that radiated from the cities. Ananias the high priest had the indictment againt Paul presented by a (Greek) "spokesman" (Acts XXIV.1). A certain Justus of Tiberias, who played a part in the war against Rome, possessed a Greek education. The festivals drew vast hordes of festal pilgrims from every country in the Empire to Jerusalem; the Pentecost story gives a detailed list of the regions from which Jews came into the "Holy City" (Mt. IV.5). This and the numerous great edifices with which Herod had adorned it made it an international city which, at the same time, steadily retained its peculiarly religious significance as the city of the temple. Here one could hear the Greek language in the streets; here there were synagogues for Diaspora Jews (Acts VI.9; IX.29). Here the Jews expected Paul to speak to them in Greek, but were even more quiet when he

[1] A. Alt, "Die Stätten des Wirkens Jesu territorialgeschichtlich betrachtet," in *Beiträge zur biblischen Landes- und Altertumskunde*, (= *Z.D.P.V.*), LXVIII (1949–51), pp. 51–72.

had recourse to Aramaic (Acts XXII.2); Josephus similarly spoke Aramaic, in order that everyone could understand him when, on Titus' orders, he called upon the city to end its revolt against the Romans.[2] Here "Greeks" came to Jesus (Jn. XII.20ff.); here there were even Jews who possessed the Roman knighthood. Here arose the complaint of the "Hellenists," i.e. the Greek-speaking Jewish Christians, that their widows were being neglected (Acts VI.1ff.). Even amongst Jesus' Galilean disciples there were two who bore Greek names: Andrew and Philip. In the Talmud the number of imported Greek and Latin words is very high, particularly those which describe the things of material culture. But Greek conceptions also infiltrated into the mental climate of the rabbis and the apocalyptic literature.[3]

In the main, however, the Jews in Palestine, and especially the Pharisees, set their faces wherever possible against Greek culture. After Herod's death the Jews demanded the removal of the Greeks;[4] when Josephus, acting on orders, was about to destroy the palace of Antipas with its animal images the populace stole a march on him. At the beginning of the war it was resolved at the instigation of the Zealots to do away with the Greek language in Palestine.[5]

It is no longer possible to ascertain how far Jesus' contacts with Greek culture went. We do not know when and to what extent He understood Greek. The Joanna mentioned in Luke VIII.3 as being in Jesus' circle of disciples cannot, on account of her husband who held a major office under Herod Antipas, have remained entirely unaffected by the alien culture, and if the apostle John was known to the high priest (Jn. XVIII.16) he would thus have been influenced to a certain extent by the wealth and culture of the household. The outlook of Levi the tax-collector, and even more Zacchaeus, would have been broadened by their profession. In general, however, the group that followed Jesus about Palestine belonged

[2] *War*, VI.2, 1 (§ 96).

[3] R. Meyer, *Hellenistisches in der rabbinischen Anthropologie*, henceforth cited as *Hellenistisches*, Stuttgart 1937.

[4] Nicolaos of Damascus, Fragment 5 in C. Müller, *Fragmenta historicorum graecorum*, VOL. III, Paris 1883, p. 353 = Fragment 136 in Jacoby, *Die Fragmente der griechischen Historiker*, VOL. IIA, Berlin 1926, p. 424.

[5] Meyer, *Hellenistisches*, p. 137.

to the simple classes of the people, unexposed to Greek culture.

The Economic Situation

Jesus' parables give us frequent glimpses into the habits of life of the simple people. The lamp on the stand gives light to all in the house (Mt. v.15); the "house" is therefore only a room, as is the case there with Arabs today. The woman in the parable sweeps her whole "house," i.e. precisely this one room, in order to find the lost "coin" (Lk. xv.8); the whole family sleeps together on the one bed (Lk. xi.7). Of course, Jesus' parables reflect other conditions also; the wicked servant owes his master ten thousand "talents," about three million pounds sterling (Mt. xviii.24). The mode of life of Agrippa I before he became king casts a certain light upon this. In the parable of the dishonest steward (Lk. xvi.1ff.) we hear of a bailiff who cheats his absentee master and merely by altering bills of contract puts the farmers so much into his debt that they guarantee him a carefree retirement.[6]

The rich landowners, who liked to spend an enjoyable life in the cities, would probably have heard about Jesus only by hearsay.[7] But the Lord has them in mind in the parable of the rich fool (Lk. xii.16ff.); this "woe to you that are rich" applies to them (Lk. vi.24). And, to the Jewish men of affairs who roam the world on business, James says that their life is a mist that soon vanishes (Jas. iv.13–17). Thus the manifold variety of Palestinian life is reflected in the New Testament.

Throughout Palestine cultivation of the soil, and of the vine and olive formed the principal agricultural occupations, to which, of course, handicrafts formed an indispensable adjunct. Galilee's fertility was famed, but one must not apply European standards in this respect; everywhere the ground was stony, and the crust of soil above the rocky base was in most places very thin, as the parable of the sower presupposes. The largest

[6] When in 1928 I was standing upon the so-called Little Hermon looking down into the fertile "Great Plain," our party of tourists was joined by some Arabs who told us that the whole village lying at our feet used to belong to some rich fellow-tribesmen in Beirut who had sold it to the Jews. This clarified for me the situation in many of Jesus' parables where the master goes abroad and the loyalty of the servants must stand the test in his absence.

[7] J. Herz, "Grossgrundbesitz in Palästina im Zeitalter Jesu," in *Palästina Jahrbuch*, xxiv (1928), pp. 98–113.

areas of cultivation were the Great Plain between Galilee and Samaria and the region north-east of Lake Gennesaret, along with larger and smaller plains situated here and there in the highlands of Palestine. Important moreover was the fishing industry which is still maintained today on the western and northern shores of Lake Gennesaret, and is mentioned also in the Gospels. Vine and olive cultivation in the Jordan valley near Jericho contributed to the prosperity of this district in New Testament times.[8] A great part of Judea is mountainous desert offering only a temporary and meagre living to nomads with their herds and a place for bandits to practise their mischief. The road from Jerusalem down to Jericho was then as now devoid of humanity. By the "wilderness" in which Jesus was tempted is probably meant the mountainous desert of Judea.

Of importance for Judea was the fact that, since the Maccabean period it had an access to the Mediterranean Sea of which it was only temporarily deprived by Pompey's intervention. Herod, moreover, had installed a large harbour in Caesarea, protected by artificial constructions. By this means favourable conditions were created for commerce.[9] Furthermore, if one takes into account the circle of Greek cities, centres of Greek culture, which surrounded Palestine and even penetrated it, and if one goes on to ponder the number of Jews in the Decapolis and in the Palestinian coastal towns, it appears as if the Jewish terrain at that time, together with its economic development, was totally unable to escape the influence of Greek culture.

Caution, however, is advised by the antagonism so keenly felt between Jews and non-Jews in the Greek cities in and around Palestine, which evolved at the beginning of the great war into savage massacres on both sides.[10] As far as Jesus' life was concerned it is no coincidence that we have no mention in the Gospels of Jesus entering any large town apart from

[8] L. Mowry, "Settlements in the Jericho Valley during the Roman Period," in *The Biblical Archaeologist*, XV (1952), pp. 26-42. On the whole subject cf. G. Dalman, *Sacred Sites and Ways: Studies in the topography of the Gospels*, trans. P. P. Levertoff, London 1935.

[9] Klausner, *Jesus of Nazareth*, p. 188.

[10] The conduct of the inhabitants of Scythopolis is especially revealing, Josephus, *War*, II.18, 3 (§§ 466–468).

Jerusalem and that Jesus' words of commission to His disciples presuppose that they would only enter such places as, being totally Jewish, could act in common either in accepting or rejecting them (Mk. VI.11). Jesus' activity was directed for preference to the highlands of Palestine whose numerous villages had a purely Jewish population.

Part III

THE RELIGIOUS SITUATION

CHAPTER 13

FACTORS COMMON TO ALL JEWS

The Jews as a People: the Proselytes

THE religious situation of the Jewish people in the New Testament period does not appear as a rounded whole; tendencies and "parties" of many kinds make it impossible to give a unified picture of it. Before we therefore portray the individual groups, we must first isolate that which was common to all Jews, that which made the Jews essentially "Jews." In the process we shall have to direct our attention to the Diaspora also, as the factors common to all can be more clearly seen there.

The Jews were a people, and a people, in fact, that had been welded together by a common history. This does not require us to portray the historical events in which the tribes of Israel grew together and which historical research feels able to reconstruct from many clues, for the decisive thing is the Jewish people's own understanding of their history as it has been moulded by the scriptures. The Jewish people were conscious of being chosen out of every nation on earth by a personal and historically potent act of God (Deut. VII.6); they were conscious that this election had a goal, salvation for all nations: "In you all the families of the earth will be blessed" (Gen. XII.3 mg.). The highlights of this historically potent divine action are, firstly, the basic event of Abraham's call, God's covenant with him and the circumcision given as a token of the covenant; secondly, the deliverance from the "furnace of Egypt," and the making of the covenant at Sinai, in which the will of God was made known to the people in laws and they swore obedience (Exod. XXIV.3); and finally, later, the construction of a temple in Jerusalem, which then became the only shrine of worship and sacrifice. Thus the scriptures, which contained the history of this people and the Law to which it was subject, were the chief reason for its existence.

The external token of incorporation into this race was the token of the covenant with Abraham, *circumcision*. The Jews who abolished it under Antiochus IV wanted thereby to be absorbed into the other nations (1 Maccabees I.11ff.). This might have meant the end of the Jewish people as a race with a particular history and a particular mission. For the Jewish Christians who had left the synagogue the question later arose, therefore, whether they ought not to do away with circumcision, but Paul advised them against it (1 Cor. VII.18). Through circumcision (which also involved ritual immersion and sacrifice) a Gentile could be incorporated into the Jewish people, and become a son of the Abraham-covenant, a "proselyte,"[1] and was thus made subject to the Law (Gal. V.3). The question therefore arose for the Galatian Christians whether it was not necessary for them to be incorporated into the people of Abraham through their adoption of circumcision, in order to have a legitimate share in the blessings promised to it; this view was represented among members of the primitive Church, but rejected by the first apostles at the so-called "Apostolic Council" (Acts XV). The tractate in the Talmud regarding proselytes clearly shows in its introduction that the man who came over to Judaism thereby belonged to this people and had a share in its history. The beginning of this tractate reads:

"The man who wishes to be converted we do not accept immediately. We say to him: 'Why should you become converted? Do you not see that this people (are) more meek, subdued and lowly than all the peoples, and that sicknesses and afflictions befall them? They bury sons and sons' sons; they are slain because of circumcision and (ritual) immersion and because of the other commandments.'"[2]

[1] On "Proselytes" see Schürer, *Geschichte des jüdischen Volkes*, VOL. III, pp. 150–188; Jeremias, *Jerusalem*, VOL. II B, pp. 191–207; Strack-Billerbeck, index under "Proselyten," VOL. IV, part II, p. 1254; article by K. G. Kuhn in *Th.W.*, VOL. VI, pp. 727–745.

[2] *B.T. Gerim*, I.1.

Of course the proselyte could not talk of the patriarchs as "our fathers;" that was only possible to his descendants. Proselytes are mentioned in the New Testament in Matthew XXIII.15, Acts II.10, VI.5 and XIII.43. More numerous than proselytes were those who took part in the synagogue worship and observed many Old Testament commandments, but were not received into the Jewish people by circumcision, the so-called "God-fearers" (Acts X.2; XVII.4, 17; XVIII.7 etc.); these were not in consequence regarded as Jews.[3]

Instruction in the Scriptures

The scriptures bore record of the particular history of the Jewish people and the Law imposed upon it. Accordingly the fact that instruction in the scriptures was given from earliest youth, was a token of how very conscious the Jews were of having the foundation of their racial existence in this history. Three stages must be distinguished in this instruction: the parental home, the school and the synagogue.

The foundation was laid by the instruction and training given in the *parental home*. "From childhood you have been acquainted with the sacred writings" writes Paul to Timothy (II Tim. III.15), and Josephus says:

"The result, then, of our thorough grounding in the laws from the first dawn of intelligence is that we have them, as it were, engraved on our souls."[4] The rabbis held that children should obey the laws as soon as it could be individually expected of them. At about the age of 13 the Jewish boy was pledged to keep all the commandments.[5]

In order to provide everyone with access to the sacred writings there were *schools*. Reading practice began with Leviticus.[6] One cannot ascertain for sure how far all boys were equally and as a matter of principle obliged to attend school in Jesus' day. According to Luke IV.17 Jesus could read the scriptures. For girls at any rate the obligation to attend school did not exist. The parental home and attendance at the synagogue services generally sufficed to provide them with knowledge of the Law.

[3] Strack-Billerbeck, VOL. II, pp. 715–723.
[4] *Against Apion*, II.18 (§ 178). [5] Strack-Billerbeck, VOL. II, pp. 144–147.
[6] Strack-Billerbeck, VOL. III, pp. 664–666; Moore, *Judaism*, VOL. I, pp. 308–322.

In every town and village in Palestine and the Diaspora, in fact wherever Jews lived together in groups or in sizable numbers, there were *synagogues.*[7] "For from early generations Moses has had in every city those who preach him, for he is read every sabbath in the synagogues" (Acts xv.21). Larger cities like Jerusalem had several synagogues; in ancient Rome we know of at least thirteen.[8] Acts vi.9 mentions the synagogue of the Freedmen (Libertines) and of the Cyrenians and Alexandrians in which Diaspora Jews banded together with their compatriots.

The arrangement of the synagogue was simple. Wherever possible water was near at hand on account of the ritual washings. In Philippi Paul went out of the city on the sabbath day to a river bank because he assumed that if there were no synagogue there, the Jewish colony being too small to justify the building of one, there would nevertheless be a place of prayer; this assumption proved correct (Acts xvi.13). A school room was frequently attached to the synagogue. In the synagogue itself the most important thing was the "ark" in which the rolls of the sacred writings were kept.[9]

Synagogue worship took place on the sabbath forenoon; further services were held in the afternoon and on the second and fifth days of the week. The service comprised: confession of faith, prayer, scripture reading, address and blessing. Something more detailed will be said later about the confession of faith and prayer. The scripture reading consisted of two parts, one from the Torah (= the Pentateuch), which developed early into a three-year cycle, and one from the "prophets," which in Jesus' day was probably selected at random. Along with the reading went a verse translation made by another from the original Hebrew text into the Aramaic dialect. In the Diaspora only the Greek translation was read out.

[7] Strack-Billerbeck, vol. iv, pp. 115–188; S. Krauss, *Synagogale Altertümer*, Berlin-Wien 1922; Moore, *Judaism*, vol. i, pp. 281-307.

[8] J.-B. Frey, *Corpus inscriptionium iudaicarum*, vol. i, Rome 1936, lxxff.

[9] The synagogues discovered in Palestine date from the post-New Testament period; see E. L. Sukenik, *Ancient Synagogues in Palestine and Greece*, London 1934. The Theodotos inscription from Jerusalem, which relates to the building of a synagogue there, derives, on the other hand, from the New Testament period itself, see *ibid.* pp. 69f. and Table xvia. On synagogues see further, E. L. Sukenik, *The Present State of Ancient Synagogue Studies*, Jerusalem 1949; E. R. Goodenough, *Jewish Symbols in the Graeco-Roman Period*, New York, vol. i, 1953, pp. 178–267; vol. ii, 1953, pp. 70–100.

In Jesus' day the sermon was probably, in the main, rather brief. It explained individual points in the passage read, it expounded an idea drawn from the whole passage and exemplified and illustrated it by a plethora of citations from the Old Testament (Jdth. VIII.19ff.; I Macc. II.50ff.; Heb. XI). It was full of an earnest desire to expound the scriptures and to activate the will. But the one thing which no exposition could read out of the Old Testament, namely the assertion, "Today this scripture has been fulfilled in your hearing," could only be said by One who, as the Son, had the authority to say it and those to whom He gave that authority.

There were no professional readers and preachers. Anyone could read and address a word to the congregation. The ruler of the synagogue was responsible both for appointing the reader and for outward order (Acts XIII.15). The synagogue attendant was there to take out and to put away the great scripture rolls (Lk. IV.20).

Jewish Exclusiveness

The history recorded in scripture, while it bound the Jewish people together, also cut it off from the outside world. "There is a certain people scattered abroad and dispersed among the peoples in all the provinces of your kingdom; their laws are different from those of every other people," says Haman to king Ahasuerus in the Book of Esther (III.8). The cause of the Maccabean Wars lay in the attempt of some Jews to abolish this separation from the Gentiles. It was this separation which time and again aroused the enmity of other nations against the Jews. We shall only mention here a few of the things common to all Jews which marked them off from the other races of antiquity. There was, first of all, the *belief in God*, not so much, perhaps, the abstract worship of God so unintelligible to many men of those days—this could still appear to be a certain type of philosophical wisdom—as rather the categorical rejection of the worship of any other god including the deified emperor. As the whole of civil life was closely bound up at that time with (Gentile) religion, this attitude meant that a Jew in the Diaspora could hardly or only to a limited extent participate in the civil life of his city. But it meant even more that all commercial traffic between Jews and Gentiles was grievously hindered. This is clear from what Paul writes in I Corinthians VIII–X regarding "food offered to idols." Meat sacrificed to idols was not merely forbidden to the Jews as not being ritually slaughtered, but because, over and above this, it was the flesh of animals which had been sacrificed to pagan gods. The question whether they ought to eat such meat disquieted Jewish Christians. And what went for food offered to idols went also for much else; e.g. with regard to wine it had to be asked if any of it had been poured out as a libation to gods, etc. The events in Alexandria (see p. 102) showed how much the rejection of the emperor-cult—from which the Jews were exempt—antagonised the Gentiles.

In several passages of the Old Testament it was commanded that certain texts should be carried as a token of remembrance and fixed to the doors of houses. Three of these passages, Deuteronomy VI.4–9; XI.13–21 and Numbers XV.37–41, were combined into a *confession* that every Jew had to recite twice a day; it was called the "Shema," after the initial Hebrew word of Deuteronomy VI.4.[10] This confession, of which Jesus reminds the enquiring scribe in Mark XII.29f., was a confession of faith in the one God of Israel. Akiba the martyr died with this confession upon his lips (see p. 117); it was recited at every synagogue service, and with it every Jew daily confessed his faith anew in the God of his fathers and thus drew a line between himself and the Gentile world.

The *sabbath*[11] was another common factor which particularly impressed the Gentiles. It was of paramount concern to the Jews in the Diaspora that they should not be required to appear in court on the sabbath or to take receipt of dues of money or grain on this day. The Jews in the Diaspora were exempt from military service, even if they possessed Roman citizenship; this was also connected with their sabbath-observance, which forbade them to undertake lengthy marches on the sabbath.[12]

[10] On the Shema see Schürer, *Geschichte des jüdischen Volkes,* VOL. II, pp. 528f., 537f.; Strack-Billerbeck, VOL. IV, pp. 189–207.

[11] Schürer, *Geschichte des jüdischen Volkes,* VOL. II, pp. 551–560; Moore, *Judaism,* VOL. II, pp. 21–39; Strack-Billerbeck, Index under "Sabbat," VOL. IV, part II, p. 1257.

[12] Cf. the collection of Roman decrees in favour of the Jews, Josephus, *Antiquities,* XIV.10, 8ff. (§§ 213ff.); cf. XVI.2, 3, 4 (§§ 28, 45–47).

A further feature uniting all Jews were the precepts which they had to observe with regard to *the pure and the impure.* This had to do, first, with forbidden food such as pork, and with foods which were connected with the worship of idols, and, secondly, with animals which were pure in themselves but not ritually slaughtered, i.e. with things "strangled" and the taking of blood (Acts xv.20, 29; xxi.25). Underlying this were certain definite Old Testament prohibitions. Thus, for example, in the periods of persecution under Antiochus IV Epiphanes Jews laid down their lives because they refused to eat "impure" foods (I Macc. I.62f.; II Macc. VI.18f., VII); in the first chapter of Daniel, Daniel and his friends are praised because they abstained from the eating of any kind of meat at the Persian court.[13] In Mark VII.15–23 Jesus abrogates this whole conception of impure and pure foods, which judgment Paul solemnly invokes in Romans XIV.14.

In view of this unequivocal word of Jesus it was in the interests of love and solidarity with their people and not of the Law that the early Jewish Christian Churches still adhered to the food-regulations and laid down the rule for the very mixed Jewish and Gentile Christian Church at Antioch and the Syrian churches that converted Gentile Christians should, *inter alia*, refrain from "what is strangled."

Besides what was "impure," i.e. forbidden to be eaten, there were also many kinds of "uncleanness" which could befall human beings and also inanimate objects, even without any intention on the part of the affected person.[14] Thus leprosy, for example, or leprous-like marks on human beings, clothing and houses rendered them unclean; the men had to quit society, the houses were torn down and the articles of clothing destroyed. The decision as to whether anything was leprous in this sense or not, as also the declaration of purity, which was combined with sacrifices, had to de made by a priest (Mk. I.44).[15] Furthermore, anyone who touched the carcase of an impure animal or even the sheets in which it

[13] Cf. Josephus, *War*, II.8, 10 (§ 152); *Life*, III (§ 14).

[14] Schürer, *Geschichte des jüdischen Volkes*, VOL. II, pp. 560-565.

[15] Even if the priest was not a member of the Qumran movement, he had to pronounce the verdict regarding purity, although the "overseer" instructed him beforehand upon the detailed interpretation of the Law according to the mind of the Essene movement, *Zadokite Document*, XIII.4–7.

had been carried, was unclean. This impurity was removed from human beings by means of a bath in the evening; clothes had to be washed and vessels purified or broken to pieces. A human corpse, however, conveyed the most serious impurity. A person who found himself in a room containing a dead body, and likewise every uncovered vessel in it were unclean, and this impurity was transferred by contact to others. The same thing obtained with women's menstruation. Even a birth rendered the mother contagiously unclean for one or two weeks; the termination of this period, during which she was not allowed to come to the temple, was marked by a sacrifice (Lk. II.22–24). In certain cases the ashes of a red heifer were required for purification (cf. Num. XIX and Heb. IX.13; on the whole matter see, especially, Lev. XI–XV; Num. V.1–4, XIX).

Even though most impurities could be removed by a ritual bath which the affected person took himself (he was not baptised but took the purifying bath himself), and even though a Jew in the Diaspora could not excape a levitical defilement, nevertheless Mark VII.3f. indicates, in a note intended for the Gentile Christian Church in Rome, what an abundance of regulations "all the Jews" observed with regard to the pure and impure. But that again rendered their relations with the Gentiles more difficult (cf. Jn. XVIII.28; Acts x.28), binding them together and cutting them off from the Gentiles at the same time.

The Jews differed from the Gentiles of their day in respect of other matters also, and these they stressed with pride: suicide was anathema to them, abortion and child exposure unknown, and the duty to work recognised.[16] Paul impressed the last matter upon his churches from the very beginning and emphasised it by his own example. Even the rabbis, at any rate in New Testament times, worked with their hands.

The Jews as a Civil Group

Among the privileges which the Jews in the Diaspora had, not the least was *the right to exercise their own jurisdiction* according to their Law, i.e. the Old Testament. For them, this did not have merely to do with the fact that the Gentile courts judged according to a different law from that of the Old Testament,

[16] Josephus, *Against Apion*, II, 24 (§ 202); XXXII (§ 234); *Sybill.*, II.272f.

but also with the ability to maintain without hindrance the validity of their Law within their own ranks by means of legal measures. Even in Palestine under the Herodians and the procurators they possessed this right, although they found it hard to bear when Herod, when he interfered with the administration of justice, failed to judge in accordance with the Old Testament. A limit was set in *one* respect to their jurisdiction both in Palestine and the Diaspora: death sentences had to be confirmed by the procurator, and it is doubtful whether in the Diaspora death sentences could be laid before the procurator at all. But whatever the limitations in respect of individual matters may have been, the Jews everywhere possessed a jurisdiction over their own affairs which extended beyond matters of cult and ritual, and this gave to Jewish communities up and down the Roman Empire the character of a civil group.

The Roman state accorded the Jews merely the possibility of dispensing justice amongst themselves according to their own laws; it did not, however, place its sanctions at their disposal. The administration of synagogue justice rested therefore, at any rate in the Diaspora, upon the authority which it had amongst the Jews both as a body and as individuals. The sending of Paul to Damascus and Acts xxviii.21 (see p. 123f.) show how strong it was. Even Roman citizens like Paul submitted to sentence by Jewish communities, in fact, according to II Corinthians xi.24, the apostle suffered the synagogue punishment of flogging five times. The verdict of the synagogue communities served, firstly, to settle the disputes of their members amongst themselves. As a result, when members of the Corinthian synagogue became Christians and boasted of their freedom from the Law they also considered it a proof of their freedom and spiritual "competence" to lay disputes with other members of the congregation before a Gentile court (I Cor. vi.1ff.). The synagogue court served, secondly, to punish transgressions of the Law and actions contrary to the Jewish religion. The methods of punishment were flogging and expulsion;[17] the latter meant that association with the

[17] Strack-Billerbeck, vol. iv, pp. 293–333; C. H. Hunzinger, *Die jüdische Bannpraxis im neutestamentlichen Zeitalter* (Dissertation, Göttingen 1954; see *Th.L.Z.* lxxx [1955] pp. 114f.).

expelled person was extensively prevented for a definite period. After A.D. 70 all intercourse with heretics and Christians was avoided. This went so far that Rabbi Ishmael (before A.D. 135) forbade his nephew Eleazar ben Dama, when the latter was bitten by a snake, to have himself healed in the name of Jesus; when he died he congratulated him on going home "in peace."[18] Thus after 70 the cursing of heretics and Christians was also taken up into the daily prayers; as these were prayed in the synagogue no heretic or Christian could any longer attend the synagogue. Thus the synagogue, by its exercise of discipline, both held its members together and kept them faithful to the Law.

The Scriptures and their Exposition

Through the scriptures the Jews were incorporated as a people into a particular history; through the scriptures they were bound together and marked off from Gentile ways. Some observations, therefore, about the *Canon of the Jews*[19] ought to follow at this point.

The title by which the Old Testament is referred to in the New, "the scriptures" or "holy scriptures" or possibly even "the law" goes back to corresponding Jewish expressions. The phrase "the Law and the prophets," on the other hand, is rarely found amongst the rabbis. It arose through the fact that for a long time no comprehensive title existed for the third part of the Canon (see p. 26). By the "prophets" in the expression "the Law and the prophets" Luke XXIV.44 means to describe the books of Joshua, Judges, Samuel, Kings and Isaiah, and thus "the psalms" refers to all writings apart from the Law and the prophets. Jesus Sirach calls them in the prologue to his book "the other books of our fathers;" II Maccabees II.13 calls them "the writings of David." Later the expression "the Writings" became customary, so that the Canon was described as the "Law, Prophets and Writings." The "Law," Hebrew "Torah," here comprises the Pentateuch, the "Prophets" the books of Joshua, Judges, Samuel, Kings, Isaiah, Jeremiah, Ezekiel and the twelve Minor Prophets (thus without the book of Daniel); the "Writings" consist of the

[18] Tos. Hull., II.22f quoted Strack-Billerbeck, VOL. I, p. 36.
[19] Strack-Billerbeck, VOL. IV, pp. 415–451.

books of Ruth, Psalms, Job, Proverbs, Ecclesiastes, Song of Songs, Lamentations, Daniel, Esther, Ezra and Nehemiah, together with the books of Chronicles. When Jesus speaks in Matthew XXIII.35 of all the righteous blood shed on earth, from the blood of innocent Abel to the blood of Zechariah, who was murdered between the sanctuary and the altar, the reference is to the first and last murder recounted in Jesus' Bible; the murder of Zechariah comes in II Chronicles XXIV.20f., and thus in the last book of the Hebrew Bible.

The Pentateuch stood in the eyes of the Jews on a far higher plane than the other writings, since it was directly of divine origin. The other parts of the scriptures had arisen by divine inspiration. The Apocrypha were certainly known in Palestine, but no canonical authority was attributed to them there; information as to what was God's will, how God had acted in the past and how He would act in the future could not be validly derived from them. Compared with the Pentateuch the other canonical writings had, however, only a complementary significance.

As the text of the Law had remained fixed from time immemorial and nothing more could be added once the Canon was complete, the need arose to adapt it to ever new life-situations. As it also contained judicial law, the administration of justice had to be modelled upon it. All this demanded a thoroughgoing preoccupation with, and study of it. This obligation lay upon the scribes who, as we have seen, were not necessarily Pharisees at the same time. The scribes had to be able to apply the Law of the Pentateuch to judicial, cult, ritual and other situations as they arose in order to rank as legal experts in court and to be at the disposal of priests and laymen as counsellors and pastors. In general they had no fixed professional status and we know of many pharisaic scribes who followed a trade; this was also true of Paul (Acts XVIII.3).

There was no special academy for the training of scribes, only, instead, a kind of easy pupil-teacher relationship similar to that in the Middle Ages at the beginnings of the universities. To outsiders the relationship between Jesus and His disciples must have seemed similar to that between a scribe and his pupils.

The Temple and its Cult

"So populous are the Jews that no one country can hold them, and therefore they settle in very many of the most prosperous countries in Europe and Asia both in the islands and on the mainland, and while they hold the Holy City where stands the sacred temple of the most high God to be their mother city, yet those which are theirs by inheritance from their fathers, grandfathers, and ancestors even farther back, are in each case accounted by them to be their fatherland."[20]

With these words Philo is saying in effect that the spiritual centre for all Jews was Jerusalem, the city of the temple. Thither, to the great festivals, came innumerable hordes of Jewish pilgrims from every country where Jews lived. Compared with it the temple in Leontopolis in Egypt had no particular importance; Philo and the Egyptian Jews and even the Ethiopian eunuch went to Jerusalem. At the centre of the festivals stood the temple. But this bond, however obvious it may have been and however great the joy, pride and veneration that were attached to the sight and the very thought of the temple, was not as indissoluble as the bond of the scriptures. Well may the Jews have defended the temple in the wars of 66–70 and 132–135 with the utmost tenacity and grim resolution, in the belief that it would not be destroyed; but when it fell in ruins, Judaism itself did not collapse—that would have happened, however, if the scriptures had been lost. We need, therefore, at this point to say just a little about the temple, the priesthood and the cult, in order to clarify the situation at the time of Jesus and the apostles.

History testifies abundantly to the fact that with its rise in outward brilliance and prestige the spiritual weight and significance of an institution decline. The collapse of the temple occurred in a period of special prosperity for everything that was connected with it. It had probably never, as long as it had been built, received more in the way of taxes and revenues, gifts and sacrifices, recognition and fame even amongst the Gentiles, than in the period in which it was to fall. A numerous priesthood, divided into twenty-four divisions, and an even greater multitude of Levites saw to it that day

[20] *Flaccus*, VII (§§ 45f.). The Jew, Philo of Alexandria, wrote in the first half of the 1st century A.D.

by day and year by year an extensive and highly differentiated worship took place smoothly. Let us try to survey it.

The temple was the shrine at which *sacrifices* were offered. Those who returned from the Babylonian captivity at first erected merely an altar "to offer some burnt offerings upon it" (Ezra III.2–6). That was the most important thing. Even in New Testament times the temple was primarily the shrine of sacrifice.

Amongst the many types of sacrifice,[21] the burnt-offering took first place, while amongst the many objects of sacrifice that of atonement was paramount. Twice a day, morning and evening, a burnt-offering was made called "the continual offering" (Heb. "tamid"). At this principal offering, surrounded on sabbath and festival days by a variety of other offerings, the congregation was present. The whole of Palestine was divided into twenty-four divisions whose inhabitants, together with a class of priests, were "on duty" in turn, in the sense that they appointed deputies who were obliged to be in attendance at the temple as representatives of all the Jews in their region and thus of all Jews generally. These deputies were called "men of attendance."

This service is described in Sirach L, where the high priest himself does duty, which was not the rule; it is also referred to in Luke I.8–22. The making of the incense-offering was a special honour which fell to a priest only once in his lifetime; he was then alone in the sanctuary while he made the incense-offering, as did Zechariah. The priestly course of Abijah mentioned in Luke I.5 was the eighth.[22]

The act of sacrifice itself was set in a framework of praise, reading of the Ten Commandments and prayers, and concluded with the priestly blessing (Lk. I.22). The hours of the "Tamid-offering" were also the chief hours of prayer.

In Acts III.1 Peter and John go accordingly to the temple at the time of the afternoon "Tamid-offering" in order to pray. Devout people prayed in the street if they happened to find themselves there at the time of prayer (Mt. VI.5).

[21] O. Schmitz, *Die Opferanschauung des späteren Judentums und die Opferaussagen des Neuen Testaments*, Tübingen 1910; Strack-Billerbeck, VOL. I, pp. 396f.; II, pp. 71–76; III, pp. 696–700; Moore, *Judaism*, VOL. I, pp. 497–506; further information in E. Sjöberg, *Gott und die Sünder*, Stuttgart, 1939, p. 176, note 1.

[22] Strack-Billerbeck on Lk. I.5ff., VOL. II, pp. 55ff.

The atoning power of the cult was especially prominent on the great *Day of Atonement*,[23] which was observed shortly after the Jewish New Year festival. On this day only the high priest, and he alone, was permitted to enter the Holy of Holies; on this day the guilt of the community and every defilement that clung to the temple was thought to be taken away. On this day the people "humiliated" themselves through fasting. The letter to the Hebrews refers to this festival in great detail, and it is also mentioned in Acts xxvii.9.

Besides the burnt offerings which served to purge the guilt of the community, the individual could also make a guilt-offering for a sin committed unintentionally. We are told of a pious man in the New Testament period who made a guilt-offering on his own behalf every day because he had *possibly* committed a sin without knowing it.[24] Furthermore, there were also votive offerings before, say, the start of a hazardous journey and thank-offerings after deliverance from danger, offerings which had to be made in fulfilment of a vow (Acts xviii.18–22, xxi.23–26), and others besides.

The temple cult unfolded with particular brilliance at the main festivals. In addition to the feast of the Passover, to be further discussed below, the "Feast of Weeks" or *Pentecost* and the *Feast of Tabernacles* deserve special mention.[25] The former was a festival of thanksgiving for the conclusion of the grain harvest; the latter, which took place five days after the great Day of Atonement, was the most popular festival. It derived its name from the fact that, according to Leviticus xxiii.42, it was commanded that for the seven days of this feast the people should live and sleep in booths erected in the open and covered with foliage. In accordance with Leviticus xxiii.40, the people in Jerusalem carried a festive nosegay for the duration of the festival, those outside Jerusalem only on the first day, and this was "swung" at the morning "Tamid-offering" while the Levites sang the great "Hallel" (Pss. cxiii–cxviii). Many other customs were connected with this feast, including a great festival of joy and illumination in one of the temple forecourts. The final day brought the climax in the form of a priestly

[23] Strack-Billerbeck, vol. iii, pp. 165–185.
[24] *Ker.*, vi.3 (Moore, *Judaism*, vol. i, p. 499).
[25] Strack-Billerbeck, vol. ii, pp. 774–812.

procession seven times round the altar, which was intended as a prayer for rain. In the account of Jesus' appearance in Jerusalem at a Feast of Tabernacles (Jn. VII and VIII) many references to the rites of this festival can be detected. Thus Jesus calls upon the Jews to seek the quenching of their thirst in Him. After the destruction of the temple a number of the customs connected with the temple were taken up into the festival celebrations of the synagogue.

The essential part of the Feast of the Passover,[26] on the other hand, the killing and eating of the Passover lamb, fell into disuse with the destruction of the temple, for the Passover lambs had to be slaughtered in Jerusalem in the temple, their blood had to be poured out at the base of the altar, and the lamb had to be eaten within the city.

The Samaritans observed the Passover differently, for to this very day they kill and eat the Passover lamb without a temple.[27]

The actual Passover celebration took place in the homes. Anything from ten to twenty persons comprised a table-fellowship, which remained together even after the eating of the Passover lamb and could not leave the precincts of Jerusalem during the night. It was for that reason that Jesus did not go to Bethany with His disciples on the night He was betrayed, but remained at the Mount of Olives, in the vicinity of Jerusalem (Mk. XIV.26). Before the Feast of the Passover all bread baked with leaven had to be removed from the very corners of the houses, and for the following seven days only unleavened bread might be eaten.[28]

The fact that this *Feast of Unleavened Bread* was originally a festival for the beginning of the harvest had at that time vanished from remembrance. The unleavened bread was intended to recall the haste of the exodus from Egypt, and the Feast of the Passover was likewise carried through in commemoration of the rescue from Egypt. The rescue from Egypt

[26] G. Dalman, *Jesus-Jeschua: Studies in the Gospels*, tr. P. P. Levertoff, London 1929, pp. 86ff.; J. Jeremias, *The Eucharistic Words of Jesus*, tr. A. Ehrhardt, Oxford 1955.

[27] J. Jeremias, *Die Passahfeier der Samaritaner*, Giessen 1932.

[28] Paul refers to this in 1 Cor. v.6–8: he uses leaven as a metaphor for the old, evil nature as did the scribes and even Jesus when in Mt. XVI.6 He warns the disciples to beware of the "leaven" of the Pharisees. In Paul's mind Christ, the sacrificial Passover Lamb, is the basis and motive for the warning to purge away the leaven of the old nature.

was in its turn a symbol and indication of the coming salvation from the misery of the world into the kingdom of God. The Passover meal thus combined a looking back upon the Exodus with a looking forward to the day of salvation. Part of the celebration were the interpretations which the father of the house or the head of the table-fellowship gave when, with reference to the unleavened bread, he said such words as: "Behold, this is the 'bread of affliction' (Deut. XVI.3) that our fathers ate when they came out of Egypt." It was in this connexion that Jesus, with reference to the bread and to the third cup, the so-called "cup of blessing" (cf. 1 Cor. X.16), added the words which interpret them and at the same time made them an imperishable gift to His disciples: "This is my body," "This is my blood of the new covenant, which is poured out for many" (Mk. XIV.22, 24).[29]

Prayer[30]

In the appendix (p. 228) is reproduced what is presumably the oldest wording of the so-called "Eighteen Benedictions." This prayer has, it is true, been preserved for us only in the form which the Pharisees gave it after the destruction of Jerusalem; the wording of it has never been entirely fixed. But it does give us a picture of the things that were precious to all Jews in Jesus' day. The first three "petitions" are praises of God. Foremost stands the fact that God is the God of the fathers; that is the unrelinquishable presupposition of faith. Then comes the fact that God is the Creator and Preserver of the world. The reference to the resurrection of the dead in the second petition shows the influence of Pharisaism. The third petition acknowledges the uniqueness of God. On these matters the whole of Jewry was united; they formed the basis of its faith. The first three of the actual petitions are the prayer for knowledge and insight, namely insight into the will of God,

[29] On account of the variations between the Synoptic accounts and that of St John's Gospel, it is of course debatable, whether Jesus' last meal with His disciples was a Passover meal. On the extensive literature see the work by Jeremias quoted in footnote 26. Interpretative words on the cup do not appear in the Jewish Passover liturgy.

[30] P. Billerbeck, "Aus dem Gebetsleben der alten Synagoge," in *Nathanael* 1912 and 1913; Moore, *Judaism*, VOL. II, pp. 212–238; N. B. Johnson, *Prayer in Apocrypha and Pseudepigrapha* (*J.B.L.*, Monograph Series 2), Philadelphia 1928.

the prayer for "turning again" (= repentance) and the prayer for the forgiveness of sins. Here again three points are mentioned which were important to all Jews, for they all desired to know God's will and continually to "turn back" to Him, and they were all conscious of God's mercy. Apart from the prayer for a good year all the other petitions revolve around redemption: redemption from the yoke of the Gentiles, redemption, i.e. return, of the scattered, redemption from foreign potentates and judges, the redemption of Jerusalem and the bringing in of the Messiah. These petitions do not go beyond an alteration of the present world-situation. No mention is made of a new covenant, a new heart, a new heaven and a new earth, of Satan and his destruction, nor is anything said about the great last judgment. This means that the new ideas which had entered into Judaism through the Hasidic movement and been developed there are lacking here; to this limit the "Eighteen Benedictions" are a prayer that *all* Jews could pray at that time. If there is no prayer for the repentance of the "apostates" and no mention of the Gentiles turning one day to the God of Israel, it is because the attitude manifest in this fact was common to most Jews at that time. It was along these lines that subsequently, after A.D. 70, the prayer against the Christians and heretics was inserted after the eleventh petition:

"Let the Nazarenes and the heretics perish as in a moment, let them be blotted out of the book of the living and let them not be written with the righteous."

A similar tendency is displayed in the collection of prayers, known by the title of "The Psalms of Solomon" (see p. 73f.). The "pious" and the "ungodly" have both sinned, but there is nevertheless a distinction between them: the one sins with intent, the other without; the one sits loosely to God, the other cleaves to Him nonetheless; the one resists God's discipline, the other accepts it; the one remains righteous even when he sins, the other is ungodly. The following verses are to be understood in this sense:

"Unto whom art Thou good, O God, except to them that call
upon the Lord?

He cleanseth from sins a soul when it maketh confession,
when it maketh acknowledgment;
For shame is upon us and upon our faces on account of all
these things.
And to whom doth He forgive sins, except to them that have
sinned?
Thou blessest the righteous, and dost not reprove them for
the sins they have committed;
And Thy goodness is upon them that sin, when they
repent."[31]

The pious will destruction upon the sinners who oppress them:

"Let the sinners perish together at the presence of the Lord;
But let the Lord's pious ones inherit the promises of the
Lord."[32]

This attitude towards the "ungodly," which appears in the New Testament in the fact that the Pharisees attack Jesus on account of his association with sinners, is expressed also in the prayer that might be quoted here as the loveliest summary of the piety of these Psalms:

"I will give thanks unto Thee, O God, for Thou hast helped
me to my salvation;
And hast not counted me with the sinners to my destruction.
Remove not Thy mercy from me, O God,
Nor Thy memorial from my heart until I die.
Rule me, O God, (keeping me back) from wicked sin,
And from every wicked woman that causeth the simple to
stumble.
And let not the beauty of a lawless woman beguile me,
Nor any one that is subject to unprofitable sin.

Establish the works of my hands before Thee,
And preserve my goings in the remembrance of Thee.
Protect my tongue and my lips with words of truth;
Anger and unreasoning wrath put far from me,
When, if I sin, Thou chastenest me that I may return (unto
Thee).

[31] Ps. Sol., IX.6f.
[32] Ps. Sol., XII.6.

But with goodwill and cheerfulness support my soul;
When Thou strengthenest my soul, what is given (to me) will be sufficient for me.
For if *Thou* givest not strength,
Who can endure chastisement with poverty?"[33]

The messianic hope is clearly expressed in the Psalms of Solomon. In the longest of the Psalms, the 17th, the writer beseeches God for a description of the mournful future:

"Behold, O Lord, and raise up unto them their king, the son of David.
At the time in the which Thou seest, O God, that he may reign over Israel Thy servant."[34]

May God, so he prays, gird the son of David with strength, so that he may destroy the wicked ruler and the Romans who have set foot in Jerusalem, and remove the sinners from amongst the Jewish people, in order that only children of Israel, divided into tribes, may live in the holy land, knowing nothing of wickedness:

"And gird him (i.e. the Messiah) with strength, that he may shatter unrighteous rulers,
And that he may purge Jerusalem from nations that trample (her) down to destruction.
Wisely, righteously he shall thrust out sinners from (the) inheritance,
He shall destroy the pride of the sinner as a potter's vessel.
With a rod of iron he shall break in pieces all their substance,
He shall destroy the godless nations with the word of his mouth. . . .

And he shall gather together a holy people, whom he shall lead in righteousness,
And he shall judge the tribes of the people that has been sanctified by the Lord his God.
And he shall not suffer unrighteousness to lodge any more in their midst,
Nor shall there dwell with them any man that knoweth wickedness,

[33] Ps. Sol., XVI.5–13.

[34] Ps. Sol., XVII.21.

For he shall know them, that they are all sons of their
God."[35]

The son of David will reign over all nations and glorify the Lord in the sight of the whole world, so that Gentiles will come to Jerusalem to see God's glory:

"He shall judge peoples and nations in the wisdom of his
righteousness.
And he shall have the heathen nations to serve him under his
yoke;
And he shall glorify the Lord in a place to be seen of all the
earth;
And he shall purge Jerusalem, making it holy as of old:
So that nations shall come from the ends of the earth to
see his glory. . . ."[36]

Of David's son, the Messiah, we then hear further:

"All nations (shall be) in fear before him,
For he will smite the earth with the word of his mouth for
ever. . . .
And he himself (will be) pure from sin, so that he may rule
a great people,
He will rebuke rulers, and remove sinners by the might of his
word;
And (relying) upon his God, throughout his days he will not
stumble;
For God will make him mighty by means of (His) holy spirit,
And wise by means of the spirit of understanding, with
strength and righteousness.
And the blessing of the Lord (will be) with him; he will be
strong and stumble not;
His hope (will be) in the Lord: who then can prevail
against him?
(He will be) mighty in his works, and strong in the fear of
God,
(He will be) shepherding the flock of the Lord faithfully and
righteously,
And will suffer none among them to stumble in their
pasture. . . .

[35] Ps. Sol., XVII.22–24, 26f.

[36] Ps. Sol. XVII.29–31a.

This (will be) the majesty of the king of Israel whom God knoweth;
He will raise him up over the house of Israel to correct him.
His words shall be more refined than costly gold, the choicest;
In the assemblies he will judge the peoples, the tribes of the sanctified,
His words (shall be) like the words of the holy ones (i.e. angels) in the midst of sanctified peoples.
Blessed be they that shall be in those days.
In that they shall see the good fortune of Israel which God shall bring to pass in the gathering together of the tribes.
May the Lord hasten His mercy upon Israel!
May He deliver us from the uncleanness of unholy enemies!
The Lord Himself is our king for ever and ever."[37]

So ends this Psalm, which manifests the messianic hopes in a form that all Jews at that time could approve.

[37] *Ps. Sol.* XVII.34b, 39; 36–40; 42f. Cf. H. Braun, "Vom Erbarmen Gottes über den Gerechten: zur Theologie der Psalmen Salomos" in *Z.N.W.*, XLIII (1950–51), pp. 1–50.

CHAPTER 14

THE NON-PHARISAIC GROUPS

WITHIN the limits set by the factors common to all Jews, we see a multiplicity of groups with more or less clearly perceptible characteristics. In the New Testament the Pharisees, Sadducees, Zealots (Lk. VI.15 = Acts I.13: "Simon the Zealot") and Herodians are named, and from Josephus and the Qumran discoveries we know also of the Essenes. We hear of further rather nebulous groups from the Church Fathers and from hints in the rabbinic writings.[1]

Of the Herodians (Mk. III.6; XII.13; Mt. XXII.16) it can only be said that they approved of the policy of Herod and his sons, either because they belonged to the princely court or because they regarded the policy of the princes as correct in principle.

The Sadducees

The Sadducees formed no party in the sense of a closed and organised community. They consisted of the leading strata of the priesthood and the influential families insofar as they had not joined the Hasidic movement for repentance and renewal. They derived their title from a man Zadok, possibly to be thought of as Zadok the high priest in David's time (II Sam. XX.25). A difficulty that still has not been resolved for certain lies in the fact that the "Sons of Zadok" play a special rôle in Essenism also.

In the rabbinic writings a series of separate points are mentioned in which the Sadducean interpretation of the Law differed from that of the Pharisees.[2] More important than

[1] M. Friedländer, *Die religiösen Bewegungen innerhalb des Judentums im Zeitalter Jesu*, Berlin 1906; Schlatter, *Geschichte Israels*, pp. 170–173; 313–316; J. Thomas, *Le Mouvement baptiste en Palestine et en Syrie 150 av. J.-Chr.*, Louvain 1935.

[2] Collected together in Strack-Billerbeck, VOL. IV, pp. 344–352.

these details is the fact that the Sadducees did not associate themselves with the "transcendentalising" of the Jewish climate of ideas (see p. 41ff.). Thus in the New Testament their particular hallmark appears to be that they did not believe in angels and spirits nor in the resurrection of the dead (Acts xxiii.8).

The Sadducees, moreover, regarded only the Pentateuch, the "Torah," as normative.[3] For this reason Jesus, in Mark xii.26, takes His evidence for the resurrection of the dead from Genesis. As the Hasidic "fence around the Law" represented an expansion beyond the limits of the Old Testament, the Sadducees demanded that the new law should be founded upon the Law itself. The Pharisees gave way to this demand in the course of time.

As a further characteristic distinction between Sadducees and Pharisees tradition has it that the former were supposed to be strict in their judgments at judicial proceedings while the latter were inclined towards leniency. The pharisaic attitude is to be understood as deriving from their earnest intention of avoiding every possibility of committing a sin; they preferred to leave the verdict to God rather than expose themselves to the risk of possibly pronouncing a wrong verdict unawares. An obvious example of this attitude is the advice given by Gamaliel (Acts v.38f.). Gamaliel, one of the leading Pharisees of his day, gave food for thought at the Sanhedrin in respect of the Sadducean proposal that the apostles should be sentenced to death, as follows: "If this plan or this undertaking is of men, it will fail; but if it is of God, you will not be able to overthrow them. You might even be found opposing God!" He did not say this because he was siding partially with the apostles, but because of his pharisaic fear of sinning. With the Sadducees, on the other hand, rational grounds of expediency dictated a heavy punishment.

Thus political considerations played a greater rôle for the Sadducees generally. The Fourth Gospel has Caiaphas the high priest pleading political reasons for the condemnation of Jesus (Jn. xi.48). Similarly, the sentencing to death of James,

[3] Although we learn this only from the Church Fathers, Schürer, *Geschichte des jüdischen Volkes*, vol. ii, pp. 480f., it tallies with the Sadducean rejection of innovations. The Sadducees were certainly also familiar with the Prophets and the "Writings," but these had only a subordinate authority for them.

the Lord's brother, by Ananias the high priest and the scruples of the Pharisees over it shows the varying attitude of both groups (see p. 105).

The Sadducean rejection of the movement of renewal in the Maccabean period left room for a weakening of the idea of God which rendered it a prey to exotic Greek ideas; thus the Sadducees used the instrument of scorn against Jesus, in order to ridicule the belief in the resurrection (Mk. XII.18ff.).[4] When Josephus mentions as a Sadducean characteristic that in their view man is autocratically the author of his own destiny,[5] that is equally a sign of the weakness of their faith in God. Yet one must not represent them as being freethinkers and infidels; the Law was sacred to them also.

During the first century the influence of the Sadducees was on the wane, so that Josephus could say that acts of divine worship took place according to the Pharisaic norm.[6]

The Zealots

The Zealots also, and indeed especially, desired to keep the Law faithfully and minutely, and again the fear of possibly committing a sin was not so characteristic of them as it was of the Pharisees, but for reasons which differed from those of the Sadducees. This fear was too passive a thing for them; according to them God demanded unconditional action. They therefore refused to pay taxes to Caesar; they did not stop at murder in order to rid Israel of the "ungodly;" they waged a forlorn struggle against Rome in, as they believed, unconditional obedience to God, and they regarded themselves as for that reason entitled to prophesy the coming of the time of salvation. After the fall of Jerusalem Zealots who fled to Egypt refused even at the price of martyrdom to call Caesar "Lord."[7]

The Essenes

We have attempted already (see pp. 49ff.; 74ff.), by means of the writings found in the caves at Qumran, to furnish ourselves

[4] A Schlatter, *Der Evangelist Matthäus*, Stuttgart 1929, on Mt. XXII.25.
[5] *War*, II.8, 14 (§§ 164f.); *Antiquities*, XIII.5, 9 (§ 173).
[6] Schlatter, *Theologie des Judentums*, p. 131, note 2; Josephus, *Antiquities*, XVIII.1, 4 (§ 17).
[7] Josephus, *War*, VII.10, 1 (§§ 418f.).

with a picture of the beginnings and later history of the Essene movement. How did this look at the time of the New Testament? We have no writings connected with them which can be ascribed with certainty to the middle of the first century A.D. Our point of departure must therefore be the extensive account of the Essenes given by Josephus some little time after the destruction of Jerusalem.[8] Although Josephus certainly, on his own admission, experimented with the Essenes in his youth, he probably did not enter upon a novitiate with them.[9] On the whole, however, his picture of the order is reliable and only imprecise to the extent that, in his formulations, he adapted himself to the understanding of his Greek readers.

From the Jewish historian we hear of an oath which the novice had to render at his eventual initiation into the order:

"But, before he may touch the common food, he is made to swear tremendous oaths: first that he will practise piety towards the Deity, next that he will observe justice towards men: that he will wrong none whether of his own mind or under another's orders; that he will for ever hate the unjust and fight the battle of the just; that he will for ever keep faith with all men, especially with the powers that be, since no ruler attains his office save by the will of God; that, should he himself bear rule, he will never abuse his authority nor, either in dress or by other outward marks of superiority, outshine his subjects; to be for ever a lover of the truth and to expose liars; to keep his hands from stealing and his soul pure from unholy gain; to conceal nothing from the members of the sect and to report none of their secrets to others even though tortured to death. He swears, moreover, to transmit their rules exactly as he himself received them; to abstain from robbery: and in like manner carefully to preserve the books of the sect and the names of the angels."[10]

In this and in what Josephus says elsewhere we perceive that the principles of the Essene order had remained the same as at the beginning: a two-year novitiate, initiation upon oath,

[8] *War*, II.8, 2–13 (§§ 119–161).

[9] Between the ages of 16 and 19 Josephus claims to have had practical acquaintance with the three groups of the Pharisees, Sadducees and Essenes, and subsequently to have lived for three years with a hermit called Bannus; this does not leave much time for getting to know the Essenes; *Life*, II (§§ 10–12).

[10] Josephus, *War*, II.8, 7 (§§ 139–142).

common meals under the presidency of a priest, together with counsellings and study of the scriptures as the peculiar functions of the Essene community; order, subordination and set penalties; a simple corporate life together with manual labour, celibacy (in the main branch), pooling of possessions and rejection of unlawful gains in the sense that nothing in the way of presents could be accepted from non-members.[11] Even the figure of ten as the quorum for the community life appears in Josephus, as well as the particularly strict observance of the sabbath and readiness to remain faithful to the Law to the death.

The doctrine of predestination apparent in the earlier Qumran writings recurs in Josephus when he ascribes to the Essenes the view that fate determines everything;[12] the consequence of this doctrine, namely hatred towards the unrighteous regarded as a duty, is mentioned in the oath. But, notwithstanding, we glimpse in Josephus the development of the Essene ideas found in the apocalyptic literature: he mentions that the Essenes had complete freedom in two respects: in the rendering of assistance and the showing of mercy; each man was permitted to help the "worthy." By the "worthy" were meant not so much members of the order as the outsiders: the early belief that outside the order there were only the ungodly had faded; the obligation to love extended beyond the order without, of course, cancelling the obligation to hate the unrighteous.

Josephus tells of remarkable Essene customs which were connected with a cult of the sun and probably betray exotic influences;[13] the north-south arrangement of the graves in the great cemetery at Qumran is probably bound up with this. The duty of keeping secret the names of the angels and the preoccupation with the powers of the plants and stones point to the apocalyptic writings.[14]

Of the eschatological conceptions held by the Essenes Josephus tells us only of what relates to individuals and drapes the con-

[11] This alone explains the fact that an Essene punished by expulsion ran the risk of starving to death; Josephus, *War*, II.8, 8 (§§ 143f.).

[12] *Antiquities*, XIII.5, 9 (§ 172).

[13] *War*, II.8, 5, 9 (§§ 128, 147–149).

[14] Josephus, *War*, II.8, 6 (§ 136). This is paralleled in *Jub.* x.12f., but differs, on the other hand, from *Enoch* VII.1 and elsewhere.

ceptions of the order in the garment of the doctrine (intelligible to the Greeks) of an immortality of the soul: to the souls of the good was assigned an existence in Elysian fields, to the souls of the wicked was assigned an existence of eternal torture in a dark cavern. This matches well with the picture of the time of salvation sketched for us in the Book of Jubilees (see p. 79), no real development of the hope of a return of paradise upon this earth appears to have ensued in Essenism.

About the messianic hopes of the Essenes we learn nothing from Josephus—probably intentionally. We hear, certainly, of John, an Essene, who became the leader of a district at the beginning of the Jewish War,[15] but as Josephus says nothing about a general participation of the Essenes in the war, we must assume that they did not view this war as the final struggle between the Sons of Light and the Sons of Darkness. If the attitude mentioned in the oath above towards those in authority related to the political rulers, then the passiveness of the resistance of the "Teacher" to the "Wicked Priest" as well as the abstention of the order in the Jewish War might be regarded as a matter of principle.

On the whole the order would have developed away from the principles of the Teacher only in the direction indicated in the apocalyptic literature; it would certainly not have developed its legal casuistry any further; the ethical impulses of the "Teacher" would have continued to exercise their influence. On the other hand, the Teacher's expectation that the messianic age was imminent would have been postponed; the order would have laid emphasis upon a pure community-life, and upon preoccupation with the scriptures and apocalypticism.

[15] Josephus *War*, II.20, 4 (§ 567); cf. *War*, III.2, 1 (§ 11).

CHAPTER 15

PHARISAISM

THE greatest influence upon the life of the people in New Testament times was exerted by the Pharisees. After the fall of the temple it was they who preserved the essential nature of Judaism. Despite their relatively small numbers their prestige was so great that if a man wanted to be pious he had, in the general view, to proceed along their lines.

From this we can understand many a story in the Gospels. In Mark II.18 the query as to why Jesus' disciples do not fast when the Pharisees themselves do so, as also the mention of fasting in the parable in Luke XVIII.12, presupposes that if a man wanted to be pious he had to behave and fast in exact accordance with the pharisaic usage.[1] In Mark VII.5 the fact that the disciples do not live according to the pharisaic tradition and wash their hands before meals is made a reproach. In each case it has to do with specifically pharisaic regulations which it is simply taken for granted any pious man will observe.

The reason why, of all the various groups in Judaism, Pharisaism alone was preserved, lies in the fact that it was the logical continuation and fulfilment of the line that had begun with Ezra and Nehemiah. Sadduceism, for all the zeal it could muster on behalf of the Law, had become spiritually enervated. It had lost sight of the goal of capturing the whole nation and contented itself with the old *status quo*. The Essene groups had withdrawn from the life of the people; it is no coincidence that the New Testament does not mention them. Only the Zealots could pit against Pharisaism a will that was directed

[1] The intention behind fasting is not asceticism, but rather a representative and atoning act of repentance, Strack-Billerbeck, VOL. II, pp. 242–244.

towards vindicating the Law amongst the total population. They too determined the course of events in the final period before the fall of Jerusalem. But they were broken by those events. The Pharisees, however, logically and persistently pursued the *one* aim of fulfilling the whole life of the nation with a decisive "Yes" towards the Law, and thus became the typical expression of Judaism in its religious aspect.

Pharisaism attempted to control the whole of life by seeking to determine what God's will might be in relation to every life-situation. As life is forever creating new situations, this gave rise to a never ending task. This task found a certain fulfilment in the Mishnah, in the Talmud and in an *ethos* whose influence has survived in part until today. At the time of Jesus the development of the whole system was still in full swing, and those who developed it were the scribes. The other groups also had their scribes, but Pharisaism developed scribal thought most extensively and logically and placed it at the centre of its existence

In the process the original stipulation, "Make a fence around the Torah" (see p. 36) soon receded into the background. This fence was still basic, of course, and was drawn ever more tightly as time passed. But at the same time the fear of committing a possible sin which typified the whole of Pharisaism resulted in the long run in a fear of innovation and a desire to cultivate only what was given. So the principle of the "fence" was gradually replaced by that of the Tradition. A good part of the scribes' efforts were devoted to committing to memory and reproducing what the teachers had said. It was high praise indeed when Johanan ben Zakkai compared one of his disciples with a plastered cistern which lost not a drop of water; in other words he was praising him because he retained every word of his teacher and forgot nothing.[2]

These decisions of the fathers, the "tradition of the elders" (Mk. VII.3) were then applied by means of analogies and ingenious speculations to new cases as they arose. The fresh decision achieved in this way then formed in its turn an item that was handed down and later became, for its part, the starting-point for new decisions. Thus, day by day, there soon accumulated a body of tradition that could hardly be taken in

² *M. Ab.*, II.8.

at a glance; the sum of what man had to know in order to live by the Law became ever greater.

The story of Akiba's enrolment as a scribe makes this clear: "R. Akiba said: my association with the scribes began thus. One day as I was on a journey I found a corpse with which no one would bother. I carried it for four miles until I brought it to the cemetery and buried it myself. (He thought that he had thus done a good deed, cf. Tob. II.2ff.) When I told this to R. Eleazar and R. Joshua, they said to me: 'Every step that you took (with the corpse) must be treated as though you had shed blood.' Then I replied. 'If even my intention to do good (by burying the corpse) is declared guilty, how much more so if I had lacked such an intention.' " Whereupon Akiba, who was already married, sat down upon the school bench, learnt to read and became a scribe. Ignorance of the Law and its exegesis had allowed a well-intentioned deed to become a transgression.[3]

In the long run the exegesis of scripture took up an increasingly important place alongside the application of the traditions of the fathers. Attempts to quote a reason for everything from a passage of scripture were redoubled.

Naturally this did not happen without violence. The basis of this exegesis was the belief that the scriptures were God's Word right down to the individual word and even to the individual letters. This being so, one could sit down and brood over every preposition and "if" and "and," even, indeed, over the liberties and peculiarities of Hebrew spelling, and draw broad conclusions from them.

One of the men who developed this minute and arbitrary exegesis—not, it must be said, without arousing controversy—was again Akiba. A Jewish legend expresses this perfectly. When Moses, so it runs, ascended Sinai he found God occupied in making the coronets, (the "tittles" of Matthew v.18 [A.V.], i.e. the embellishments on the Hebrew letters) for the letters of the Law (which was regarded as written by God Himself):

"Said Moses, 'Lord of the Universe, Who stays Thy hand?' He answered, 'There will arise a man, at the end of many generations, Akiba b. Joseph by name, who will expound upon each tittle heaps and heaps of laws.' "[4]

[3] *J.T.Naz.*, 35b; cf. Schlatter, *Geschichte Israels*, pp. 357f.
[4] *B.T.Men.*, 29b, quoted Strack-Billerbeck, VOL. I, p. 248.

An example of such arbitrary exegesis, although in another cause, is Paul's argument in Galatians III.15–18 which he explicitly designates in verse 15 as "human." In the Old Testament we read, in connexion with the promises to Abraham, "To thee and to thy seed" (A.V.) will I give this land. It is clear that "seed" in the singular is intended to refer to the descendants of Abraham, i.e. to a great number of people, as we read in Genesis xv.5, where it says that "Abraham's seed" (sing. A.V.) will be as innumerable as the stars in the heavens. But Paul here presses the word "seed" in the singular to the point of declaring that with it the scriptures mean only one person, namely the one Christ.

Any attempt to establish what is "right," i.e. what is God's will, in every individual case, leads to deductions which immediately contradict the essence of morality. Thus the effort to establish exactly when an oath was valid led to such nice and unethical, even though legally hardly avoidable decisions, as Jesus castigated in Matthew XXIII.16ff. Again the more precisely, i.e. the more violently, one tried to squeeze out of the scriptures what was to be done, the greater was the arbitrariness with which one in reality rose above them.

In its development of casuistry, i.e. the establishment of what action was to be in every case, Pharisaism was confronted with a factor which conflicted with its avowed object of fulfilling the Law with the greatest possible exactitude, namely that of practicability. In the very effort to capture the people as a whole, the Pharisees had to beware of demanding impossibilities. Alongside the earnest striving to do God's will and to make every sacrifice for this cause, there stood considerations of practicability, and in pursuit of this the pharisaic scribes applied their exegetical skill to relaxing the Law.

For example, one of the "works" prohibited on the Sabbath was the carrying of a burden from one "domain" to another. Not only did the scribes lay down that eatables the size of a dried fig could be "carried" without objection, but they also defined the concept of the "domain." In general, a house formed a "domain" in itself. But when several houses surrounded a courtyard, the occupants—and all of them had definitely to participate in this—could deposit some food in the courtyard before the onset of the Sabbath; by this symbolic action they made all the houses surrounding the courtyard into *one* house, *one* "domain;" and thus any number of objects could be carried over the courtyard on the Sabbath. By means of other actions a whole alleyway could be made into a "domain."[5]

As one could attach varying importance to the question of the Law's practicability, many differences of opinion arose between the pharisaic scribes in New Testament times centring in the two most prominent scribes of the Herodian period, Hillel and Shammai. The former laid more stress upon practicability than his colleague.

Here we might consider the narratives which tell of Jesus' clashes with the Pharisees.

First and foremost there was the question of the *sabbath.* According to Matthew xii.1f. the disciples were attacked because they plucked ears of corn on the sabbath as they were walking through the fields and ate the grain. This action was viewed by the Pharisees as a sub-category of reaping, and reaping was one of the works which were forbidden on the sabbath. Jesus' question in Luke xiv.3 whether it was lawful to heal on the sabbath received assent from the pharisaic scribes only in the case of a grave threat to life. Thus the ruler of the synagogue says quite logically in Luke xiii.14: "There are six days on which work ought to be done; come on those days and be healed, and not on the sabbath day."

In the effort to make clear to all the things that fell under the concept of "works" forbidden on the sabbath, the rabbis enumerated thirty-nine chief categories of work, *inter alia,* sowing, ploughing, reaping, threshing, winnowing, slaughtering, writing, tilling. Other occupations were forbidden on the sabbath, not, of course, because they were gainful activities or "works" but because they ran counter to the rest which had to be observed on the sabbath, namely, riding, swimming, dancing, sitting in judgment, *inter alia.* When Jesus asks in Luke xiv.5 whether a man, say, would let his son (R.S.V. mg.) or ox fall into a well and would not immediately pull him out on the sabbath day, the answer to His question was not one upon which Judaism had a common mind at all times and in

[5] Schürer, *Geschichte des jüdischen Volkes,* vol. ii, pp. 555, 574f.

all groups. At the beginning of the Maccabean period the pious, as we saw (see p. 37), allowed themselves to be massacred unresistingly on the sabbath, and the Zadokite Fragments expressly lay down that no one is to lift a beast out of a cistern or pit on the sabbath day.

Again, the question of purity and impurity was important for daily life. The Pharisees had introduced the custom of washing their hands before meals. That was only a part of the regulations that were laid down in this sphere; Mark vii.3f. enumerates others. The Pharisees developed a complicated system in respect of the purity of the inside and outside of vessels (Mt. xxiii.25), the purity of the space inside a hollow vessel and the means for removing any kind of defilement.

A question that was especially important in the Diaspora concerned the attitude towards idol-worship. The Pharisees proceeded on the assumption that a Jew must not lift a hand even indirectly to anything that would cause an infringement of the Law of the Old Testament. For this reason a Jew could not help with the construction of a law-court or an arena, as the court that would be held in the former would not take place according to the "Law," and animal fights in the arena were wholly a Gentile abomination. A Jew could not even sell to a Gentile animals which might be used for sacrifices or animal-baiting. For many a Jewish Christian in Corinth it was a question of conscience whether they might buy the meat that was offered for sale in the market, for it frequently came from animals that were slaughtered as sacrifices for Gentile gods (1 Cor. viii–x; Rom. xivf.).

The fact already mentioned above, that all casuistry leads to conclusions that violate the essence of morality, can be well illustrated at this point. It is actually laid down in the Mishnah, the oldest part of the Talmud, that a Jewish woman must render no assistance in childbirth to a non-Jewish woman, although she might *vice versa* accept such help from a Gentile woman.[6] This terrible stipulation is only a logical consequence of the system: the Jewish woman would in fact be helping a little Gentile to see the light of day, and thus be furthering the Gentile race while, on the other hand, no scruples were attached to a Gentile woman assisting a Jewess in childbirth.

[6] *M.A.Zar.*, ii.1; cf. Strack-Billerbeck, vol. i, pp. 547f.

The very logicality of this shows that the definition by casuistic means of what was to be done led in the wrong direction when carried to its limit. It shows, secondly, the corrupting power of the Jewish doctrine of election, for the stipulation mentioned is based on the assumption that a Jew, even before he is born, is a superior being precisely because he is a member of the chosen people, who have accepted the Torah, while the Gentile is regarded as ungodly from the very hour of his birth.

Another example of rabbinic exegesis may be quoted. On one occasion the 14th Nisan, on which the Passover lambs were to be slain, fell on a sabbath. The question arose amongst the pharisaic scribes as to whether the sabbath commandment or the commandment to slay the Passover lambs on the 14th Nisan took precedence. The Samaritans even today postpone the slaughter in such an event. At that time Hillel taught thus: In Numbers IX.2 it states that the children of Israel must keep the Passover "at its appointed time;" regarding the daily offering, the Tamid (see p. 153), it is stated in Numbers XXVIII.2 that it should be offered "in its due season."[7] This Tamid-offering was also slain on the sabbath. The same expression, "at its appointed time" or "in its due season," in both verses now proved, according to Hillel, that the Passover lamb had also to be slain on the sabbath when occasion arose. Even before Hillel's day the 14th Nisan had, of course, frequently taken precedence over the sabbath. We see here how Pharisaism eventually felt the necessity to find in the Law a reason for the established practice by means of precise attention to every word of the Bible.[8]

Along with this more theoretical work on the Law it was a part of the Pharisee's practical educative function continually to set a public example of correct behaviour and to condemn its opposite. This gave rise to the ostentatious piety that Jesus castigates in the Sermon on the Mount (Mt. VI.1f.).

As those who knew the Law and were concerned with its development, as those, therefore, who performed an essential task for the community, the scribes received homage from men as if it were theirs by right. They accepted the chief places in

[7] The text of the Luther version as quoted in the original contains the same phrase, "zu seiner Zeit" ("in its season"), in both verses. (Tr.)

[8] *J.T.Pes.*, 33a, quoted Strack-Billerbeck, VOL. II, p. 819, note 2; Schlatter, *Geschichte Israels*, p. 249.

the synagogues and at banquets and allowed themselves to be addressed by the respectful title of "Rabbi" (Mt. xxiii.6f.).

In conclusion we may quote an ancient prayer that offers a good parallel to the prayer of the Pharisee in the parable:

"I give thanks to Thee, O Lord my God, that Thou hast set my portion with those who sit in the Beth-ha-Midrash and Thou hast not set my portion with those who sit in [street] corners, for I rise early and they rise early, but I rise early for words of Torah and they rise early for frivolous talk; I labour and they labour, but I labour and receive a reward and they labour and do not receive a reward; I run and they run, but I run to the life of the future world and they run to the pit of destruction (i.e. hell)."[9]

This illustrated Paul's words regarding the Jews generally and applicable to the Pharisees in particular: "I bear them witness that they have a zeal for God, but it is not enlightened. For, being ignorant of the righteousness that comes from God, and seeking to establish their own, they did not submit to God's righteousness." (Rom. x.2f.).

Conclusion: The Groups Together

The Law both united and separated the Jews. First it united them: this became obvious, for example, when Pilate wanted to bring images of Caesar, or Caligula his own effigy, into Jerusalem, as well as in many other situations. Josephus frequently states that the Jews would rather forfeit their lives than give up their customs, sacrifices and feasts; Philo, the Alexandrian Jew, expressed himself similarly.[10]

Prominent amongst the host of the law-abiding were those to whom God had perceptibly given acknowledgement: John ascribes the gift of prophecy to the high priest (Jn. xi.51) and Josephus recounts similar examples. Many Essenes, in particular, were held to be in possession of this gift, and at the height of his power Herod himself asked an Essene how long he still had to reign.[11] We frequently hear of famous intercessors amongst the Pharisees. It is related of Onias the "Circle-maker" that once in a time of drought he drew a circle around

[9] *B.T.Ber.*, 28b, quoted Strack-Billerbeck, vol. ii, p. 240.
[10] Josephus, *Against Apion*, ii.32 (§§ 232ff.); Philo, *Embassy to Gaius*, xxxi (§ 209).
[11] Josephus, *Antiquities*, xv.10, 5 (§§ 373ff.).

himself and prayed for rain. Little rain fell at first, but redoubled prayer produced a torrential downpour; again he prayed until it rained normally, and when it became excessive he prayed again and the sun broke through the clouds. Then Simon ben Shetach the scribe sent a message to him:

"Hadst thou not been Onias (i.e. this noted suppliant) I had pronounced a ban against thee! But what shall I do to thee?—thou importunest God and He performeth thy will."[12] Even the leading Pharisee did not dare to lift a hand against him.

But, secondly, the Law separated the Jews from each other. This is clearest amongst the Essenes, who held aloof from the life of the people because it did not square with their conception of the Law. The Pharisees likewise regarded it as their duty to make explicit their condemnation of those who did not live according to the Law as they thought fit. The Jewish nation was shot through with the mutual "judging" against which Jesus warned in Matthew VII.1ff. The "weak" members of Corinthian and Roman Christian communities, who felt themselves bound to the Law, also judged, i.e. condemned the "strong" who did not feel themselves so bound (I Cor. X.29; Rom. XIV.3ff.).

We saw from the Jewish War what embittered forms this struggle for the Law could assume (see p. 109). The epithets "pious" and "sinner," involving as they did a judgment upon whether one observed the Law according to the precise interpretation of a group or not, divided the community; each group thought itself obliged to give visible expression to its condemnation of the other.

Besides the antithesis of the pious and the sinners Pharisaism also gave rise to the antithesis of the children of the world and those instructed in the Law; thus the Pharisees say in John VII.49; "This crowd, who do not know the law, are accursed."[13]

As the pious condemned the sinner and the scribe the worldling, so the Zealot condemned the Pharisee and the Essene the

[12] *M.Taan.*, III.8, quoted Strack-Billerbeck, VOL. IV, pp. 109f. Cf. Schlatter, *Geschichte Israels*, p. 157.

[13] Strack-Billerbeck, VOL. II, pp. 494ff.; A. Büchler, *Der galiläische 'Am-hā'āres des 2. Jahrhunderts*, Wien 1906; S. Zucrow, *Women, Slaves and the Ignorant in Rabbinic Literature*, Boston 1932; R. Meyer, "Der 'Am-hā'āres", in *Judaica*, III (1947), pp. 169–199.

Zealot. The Jewish people at the time of Jesus were "harassed and helpless, like sheep without a shepherd" (Mt. IX.36).

Akiba's saying is revealing:

"When I was an 'am ha-arez' (i.e. ignoramus) I said: I would that I had a scholar [before me], and I would maul him like an ass."[14]

[14] *B.T.Pes.*, 49b, quoted Strack-Billerbeck, VOL. I, p. 366.

Chapter 16

THE CONVICTIONS DETERMINING PHARISAISM

Introduction

Judaism at the time of Jesus, split as it was into groups of many kinds, had no universally agreed dogmatics. The belief in the one God was professed daily in the Shema, and the story, recorded in the Bible, of God's dealings with the people of Israel and His will as laid down in the Torah together with the promises attested in it were the bond which united all Jews; but neither the individual groups in Judaism at the time of Jesus, let alone the whole of Jewry at that time, managed to summarise the convictions which were binding either upon the groups or upon the whole nation. Judaism had no binding "dogmatics." But just as every man and every movement have a series of related convictions which sustain their action and thought, even though unawares, so every group in Judaism was sustained by definite convictions which find expression in their writings and are capable of description.

By far the most comprehensive body of Jewish writings in the centuries before and after the birth of Jesus originated in pharisaic circles, and thus one can only attempt to summarise the leading convictions which are found there. But even so the attempt to do this is beset by considerable obstacles. In the Talmud, which sprang out of Pharisaism, and in the whole corpus of rabbinic writings is stipulated what is regarded as the will of God in relation to such questions as when the sabbath begins, when the Shema is to be recited, what quantity and what kind of water suffices to remove this or that kind of defilement, how a valid bill of divorce should look, what formula the father of the house should use to summon to prayer at table, what wine one is permitted to drink for pleasure, how evidence is to be heard at trials and innumerable other matters. But as regards a unanimous pronouncement upon whether Israel was chosen unconditionally by God's grace out of all "nations" or rightly became, because of its own and the patriarchs' piety, the recipients of the Law and the promises, whether there are sinless men or even men with a superfluity of merit through good works, or whether all men stand in need of the unqualified grace of God, whether, too, the intention to do an evil deed or only the accomplished deed counted, and whether the "fear of God" was the essential prerequisite of every so-called good deed—upon such and similar questions we can with little effort collect contradictory answers from the rabbinic writings. These variations set their seal on the fact that Judaism did not entirely fall prey to casuistic legalism, but that in it the impulses deriving from the scriptures have remained permanently alive up to the present day. In the New Testament period itself we can trace a struggle between these two forces of scripture and casuistic legalism.

A second difficulty in the way of isolating from the rabbinic writings the convictions which guided Judaism in the New Testament period lies in the fact that after A.D. 70 and 135, i.e. after the destruction of the temple, Pharisaism concentrated explicitly upon the "Law" and pushed wholly into the background the lines of thought that we were able to trace out in Essenism and the apocalyptic writings. Thus the picture of Pharisaism in the New Testament period is necessarily blurred.

It is a mistake therefore to rely upon individual rabbinic writings without paying regard to their value in the appropriate context and in the sum total of pharisaic ideas; we must also not forget those other groups and movements in the Judaism of the New Testament period whose views we have already portrayed.

God the Lord and His Rule

The thing that separates the God of the Jews from all other gods is that He is the *Lord of history* and, indeed, of a history moving towards a definite goal. As such He is a "Person," i.e. conscious will. This starting-point of the Jewish faith flowed from the Old Testament, where God is primarily the One who acts in history.

From this follow the "attributes of God." For history develops in the sphere allotted to us by nature; whoever is Lord of history must also of necessity be the Lord of nature. The Lord of history and therefore of nature and the world is all-powerful and all-knowing. His lordship is most clearly manifest in the fact that He is the *Creator* of the world. By His word He has called it into existence out of nothing; it is He "who spoke and the world became," as the rabbis frequently refer to Him.[1] This all-powerful creative activity means sovereignty, giving history its beginning and its end. God confronts the world and everything in it as Creator and Lord and owes nothing to anyone, but everything and everyone owe their existence to Him. The relationship of creator and creature is personal; the creatures "respond to" His will. When God receives in Judaism titles such as "King of kings," or is called "Lord of the universe, seated on high, Thou who rulest over the world," these are images of personal power taken from earthly potentates, and express the certainty that God is not impersonal, blind nature, but powerful will asserting Himself in history and nature.

This forms the foundation of genuine religious life; for only in relation to a God who acts personally are responsibility, trust and prayer possible; only He can be the ground of hope. Without a faith that aroused the will, awakened trust and quickened hope, the Maccabean wars would have been impossible, and the story of Judaism would have come to an end with the destruction of Jerusalem. Genuine religious life becomes apparent in prayer and in Judaism prayer was customary even in Jesus' day. The Hymns of Qumran and the Psalms of Solomon (see pp. 48, 73) are collections of prayerful songs; the whole of IV Ezra (see p. 114) is an agonised prayer revolving round the destruction of Jerusalem; the Eighteen Benedictions (see p. 156f.) go back in their basic form at least as far as the New Testament period; with these we must often include detached prayers, of which many are still extant.[2]

The decisive factors are now the point at which God's will, as personally addressed to man, becomes so visible in history

[1] A. Marmorstein, *The Old Rabbinic Doctrine of God*, London 1927, VOL. I, p. 89.
[2] Strack-Billerbeck, VOL. I, pp. 406f.; *B.T.Ber.*, 16b–17a.

that men can be immediately caught up by it, and what the goal of world-history is.

Before we discuss the basis and goal of history, something must be said about *cosmology*. The Jewish cosmology of the New Testament period differed basically from the current Greek cosmology. The latter proceeded from the spirit-matter antithesis, and ordered the world in an ascending series from the earth to beyond the ethereal regions, to the limpid sphere of the sun and stars, above which, as the purest manifestations of the divine, lay the sphere of fire. Like the Old and New Testaments Judaism knows nothing of this conception of the divine as a quintessence of nature and of nature as a manifestation of the divine. God confronts every created thing as personal will; the whole of nature is conceived to a certain extent in personal terms, as having been "called" into existence by Him. In Psalm XIX the heavens "tell" the glory of God; according to Isaiah XL.26 God "calls" the starry hosts by name; in Psalm CXLVIII.3f. the sun, moon and stars, the heavens and the waters above the heavens are summoned to praise God: they are "beings" who obey a will and command. James is thinking in the same terms when he calls God the "Father of lights" (Jas. I.17).

The Pharisees, like the pseudepigrapha, speak, too, of angels who are set over the stars and over nature and its processes, and have their abode in "the heavens."[3] Thus the Book of Revelation mentions an angel who has power over fire, and an angel of water (Rev. XIV.18; XVI.5). The plural "heavens" derives from the fact that Judaism distinguished between a series of "heavens;" even Paul speaks in II Cor. XII.2 of the "third heaven," and the apocalyptic writings tend to transfer paradise to it.[4] To the individual heavens are assigned the things that nature gives to man in the way of good and evil: rain and snow, hail and tempest, storm and wind, sun, moon and stars; but then also paradise and the tree of life and the angel of the judgment tribunal on the Last Day. The decisive thing in this series of concepts, the details of which are developed most heterogeneously, is the un-Hellenistic

[3] H. Bietenhard, *Die himmlische Welt im Urchristentum und Spätjudentum*, Tübingen 1951.

[4] Strack-Billerbeck, VOL. III, pp. 533ff.

conception of nature as an order of powers, dominated by one Will and responsive to one Will. Thus God is not even He who once, at the beginning, wound up the clockwork of nature and is now letting it run down; He "clothes" the grass of the field (Mt. VI.30) (not "*once* clothed it"), and the rabbis speak of God every day "making new the works of creation."[5]

According to the account of creation in Genesis I, a "firmament" divides the upper waters in heaven, from which the rain comes, from the earthly waters. This firmament therefore separates heaven and earth from one another. This is what is meant in Revelation IV.6 by the "sea of glass." With it is linked the echo in Revelation XV.2–4 of the passage through the Red Sea. According to the conception evident in the Jewish Passover, the exodus from Egypt points towards the day of salvation. Therefore, just as the Israelites struck up a hymn of praise (Ex. XV) after the gracious deliverance from all the tribulations of Egypt and the passage through the Red Sea, when the entrance to the Promised Land stood open for them, so the victors of the New Covenant strike up a hymn of praise in Revelation XV.3f. when, delivered from all the tribulations of earth, they stand at the heavenly firmament of the sea of glass before entering into the heavenly kingdom of God.

Despite these echoes of the Jewish cosmology, the multiple heavens are missing in Revelation. It is noticeable in the New Testament generally how the "principalities, thrones, dominions and authorities" are separated, as belonging to the fallen creation, from heaven as the unalloyed world of God.

The fundamental point of departure for thought and belief that God is the personal Lord of history finds its characteristic expression in a phrase often used by Jesus: "kingdom of heaven."

Two things are noteworthy about this expression. First, it has nothing to do with a localised kingdom that has its abode somewhere in heaven. The phrase "to enter into the kingdom of heaven" does not mean "to arrive in heaven." Instead of "kingdom" it can be more accurately translated: "dominion."

[5] Benediction before the Morning Shema I.1, W. Staerk, *Altjüdische liturgische Gebete*, 2nd edn., Berlin 1930, p. 4; Moore, *Judaism*, VOL. I, p. 384.

In Psalm CIII.19, instead of "his kingdom rules over all," as the R.S.V. renders it, Moffatt translates it more clearly as "his dominion covers all the world." "To enter into the kingdom of heaven" therefore means to come under the rule of heaven.

Secondly, "heaven" in the expression "kingdom of heaven" is only a Judeo-Palestinian circumlocution for "God." Thus "kingdom of heaven" is found almost exclusively in the Matthean Gospel written for Jewish Christians, while the other Gospels, and Paul, speak of the "kingdom of God." The title "God," written in the old Testament YHWH and probably pronounced "Yahweh" ("Jehovah" is a distortion) was, in New Testament times, used only in the temple cult. At the reading of the Old Testament, in quotations, etc., the word "Lord" (Heb. *Adonai*) was used in place of it, just as the Septuagint puts *kurios*, i.e. Lord, in place of YHWH. In daily life, however, other circumlocutions were used, among them "Heaven" (cf. 1 Macc. III.19; IV.10, 40, etc.). The New Testament frequently reflects this awe of the name of God, indeed of any direct mention of God at all. The prodigal son in the parable says: I have sinned "against heaven," i.e. against God; the Pharisee asks Jesus: was the baptism of John "from heaven," i.e. from God, or from men (Mt. XXI.25). The naming of God is often completely avoided, either by the little word "men" (e.g. Lk. VI.38 A.V.) or by the use of the passive.

The "kingdom of heaven" means then the dominion, the realm of God. God's dominion exists where His will is done in a personal and responsible fashion. To recite the confession of the one God, the Shema, is called by the rabbis "taking upon oneself the yoke of the kingdom of heaven."[6]

The Torah as the Eternal Will of God and the Meaning of World-History

Now where in history does God's dominion draw near to men? What is this will of God that must be done? To this question Judaism, and indeed the whole of Judaism of every type and generation, replies: in the "Torah." This answer distinguishes Jews and Christians from each other. In the dialogue with

[6] *M.Ber.*, II.2, 5, quoted Strack-Billerbeck, VOL. I, p. 177 under m.

Christianity Judaism has always held firmly as a matter of principle and of fact that the "Torah" is the unique and fully adequate expression of the will of God.

"Torah" is the Hebrew name for that which the LXX and Paul render with the Greek word *nomos*, and the EVV translate as "Law." It is, first, the comprehensive title of the Pentateuch, and we saw that in the total canon these books have a paramount significance in relation to all other writings. For the rabbis even the prophetic writings are merely elucidation of the Torah; they add nothing new to it, and they take nothing away from it.[7] The Pentateuch, illustrated by the Prophets and the "Writings," interpreted in various ways by the Sadducees, Pharisees, Zealots, Essenes and other groups, and rendered profitable for daily life—that is the will of God.

The unanimous conviction of Judaism is that the Torah is from all eternity and for all eternity the valid will of God: in the Book of Jubilees the laws of the Torah are eternal; they are kept in heaven and inscribed upon heavenly tables; the apocryphal book of Baruch speaks of the "law that endures for ever" (Bar. IV.1); Josephus speaks of "our immortal law"; Philo, the Alexandrian, who was widely influenced by Hellenism, says nonetheless:

"But Moses is alone in this, that his laws, firm, unshaken, immovable, stamped, as it were, with the seals of nature herself, remain secure from the day when they were first enacted to now, and we may hope that they will remain for all future ages as though immortal, so long as the sun and moon and the whole heaven and universe exist."[8]

Towards the end of the first century A.D. the rabbis were already calling the Torah "the instrument with which this world and the world to come were created,"[9] and about fifty years later we hear: "Solomon and a thousand of his peers will pass away, but a word of Thine (= the Torah) will not pass away."[10]

[7] *B.T.Meg.*, 14a, quoted Strack-Billerbeck, VOL. IV, p. 446; *Sifre Lev.*, XXVII.34; Strack-Billerbeck, VOL. IV, p. 448 under b.

[8] *Moses*, II.3 (§ 14); Jub. II.18 and elsewhere; Josephus, *Against Apion*, II.38 (§ 277).

[9] R. Eleazar b. Zadok, *Sifre Deut.*, XI.22 (§ 48), quoted Strack-Billerbeck, VOL. I, p. 917.

[10] R. Simeon b. Jochai, *J.T.Sanh.*, II.20c, quoted Strack-Billerbeck, VOL. I, p. 244.

Later, in clear antithesis to the New Testament, Deuteronomy xxx.12 is paraphrased thus:

"Do not say: 'Another Moses will arise and bring us another Torah from heaven'; I therefore warn you, IT IS NOT IN HEAVEN, that is to say, no part of it has remained in heaven."[11]

Thus the Torah is the primary foundation of the world. This finds clearest expression in a relatively ancient rabbinic speculation regarding that which preceded the creation of the world, to which we shall have occasion to refer frequently:

"Six things preceded the creation of the world; some of them were actually created, while the creation of the others was already contemplated (by God). The Torah and the Throne of Glory were created. The creation of the Patriarchs . . . Israel . . . the Temple . . . and the name of the Messiah were contemplated (by God)."[12]

The throne of glory is the abode of the world-ruling activity of God; the world and its history are the product of this activity. The Torah, however, is the purport of the entire world and its history. *The creation of the world is intended to provide a sphere in which God's will (= Torah) will be done.* Therefore the throne of glory and the Torah were actually created before the world. The things, however, that were merely contemplated by God are the decisive nodal points of world-history, which were equally determined beforehand, because the meaning of world-history, i.e. the doing of the Torah, would be actualised in them. Thus the patriarchs are those who are to do God's will first; Israel is the nation to whom the Torah could be entrusted and who would be the bearers and doers of God's will in world-history. The temple has been chosen as the shrine of God's presence in the world and amongst His people, and the title "Messiah" is the title of him who will bring about the situation in which the whole world fulfils God's will. Thus world-history is orientated in its decisive nodal points upon the Torah. Only because God foresaw in His mind's eye that men would exist who would perform the Torah, and only because He conceived the goal of world-history as being

[11] *Deut. R.*, VIII.6 on Deut. XXX.11f.

[12] *Gen. R.*, I.4 on Gen. I.1, quoted Strack-Billerbeck, VOL. I, 974.

the absolute fulfilment of His will, could He create the world.[13]

The supreme event and the real cornerstone of world-history is accordingly the handing over of the Law to Israel on Mount Sinai; this event has been depicted with manifold lustre and a wealth of speculation. The first tables of the Law, for example. are supposed to have been created on the eve of the creation-sabbath, to have consisted of sapphire stones, and to have been written by God's own finger. If the children of Israel had not, so it was conceived, accepted the Law at that time, the world would have lost its meaning and God would have annihilated it again.[14] But when Israel accepted the Law with the words: "All that the Lord has spoken we will do, and we will be obedient" (Ex. XXIV.7) the age of paradise dawned again for this people. There were at Mount Sinai, it is said, no blind, dumb, lame, deaf, imbeciles or lepers, the angel of death lost his authority over them and the evil impulse its power.[15] Although the sin with the golden calf did, it is true, put an end to this period, the significance of the Law-giving remained, namely, that through it Israel and only Israel was integrated into the purpose of world-history and thus world-history received its meaning. As the nation which has "shouldered the yoke of the kingdom of heaven" Israel is now the nation which matters in world-history.

To have received the Torah and thus to have been integrated into the purpose of world-history means life to Israel, for God is life itself; to be separated from His will means to be separated from life; to know His will and to do it means to have life.

Jewish men have affirmed in words that are often moving that the Torah signifies life: from the first Psalm, which compares the man who meditates day and night upon the Law with a tree planted by the water yielding its fruit in due season to the martyrs of the Maccabean period and their

[13] *Gen.R.*, I.6 on Gen. I.1, "The world and the fullness thereof were created only for the sake of the Torah" (R. Banayah), quoted Strack-Billerbeck, VOL. III, p. 580.

[14] *B.T.Shab.*, 88a, R. Resh Lakish, quoted Strack-Billerbeck, VOL. III, p. 33.

[15] R. Eliezer (*circa* A.D. 90), *Mekilta Ex.*, XX.18, quoted Strack-Billerbeck, VOL. I, p. 594 under c, where see further references; *Lev. R.*, XVIII (tradition of *circa* A.D. 150), quoted Strack-Billerbeck, VOL. I, p. 596; *Midr. Song of Sol.*, I.2 (tradition of *circa* A.D. 150), quoted Strack-Billerbeck, VOL. IV, p. 482 under 5a.

successors three hundred years later. When, after the Bar-Cocheba revolt, the possession and study of the Torah were punishable with death, we hear of a rabbi who was burnt alive wrapped up in the Torah-roll that was found on him. When at that time Rabbi Akiba, who subsequently also died as a martyr, busied himself with the Torah despite the ban and taught from it publicly, he was asked if he did not fear the Roman authorities. He replied with a parable: A fox advised the fish who were fleeing from the fisherman's nets to escape to the dry land. Whereupon the fish told him that if they were not safe even in the water that was their life's element, then to go on to the dry land would mean certain death for them. So it was also with Israel: if the preoccupation with the Torah, which after all was for Israel life, was dangerous in itself, then to abandon it would be certain death.[16]

Despite all the burdens and tribulations that the Torah involved for the man who shouldered it earnestly, it was nonetheless the cause of great joy, gratitude and pride to Israel. The Gentiles who have not received it are "declared to be nothing and . . . like unto spittle."[17]

Thus we understand the depths of the apostle Paul's words: "But whatever gain I had" (namely, in receiving the Torah), "I counted as loss for the sake of Christ" (Phil. III.7); hence it becomes clear what a powerful breakdown Paul's conversion signified when he declared that the Law, which was for the Jews the centre of world-history, had "come in, to increase the trespass" (Rom. V.20).

Israel the People of the Torah

The history of salvation begins in the Old Testament with the fact that God called Abraham out from his land and people and made him a promise that pointed far beyond his own life and embraced all nations upon earth. No indication is given why God called precisely him: His action is unconditional; it is "election." So it is in the narrative of the exodus of the children of Israel out of Egypt: "I have seen the affliction of my people who are in Egypt . . . and I have come down to

[16] *B.T.Ber.*, 61b, quoted Strack-Billerbeck, VOL. III, p. 131.
[17] IV Ezra, VI.56.

deliver them" (Ex. III.7f.); and in Deuteronomy we read: "It was not because you were more in number than any other people that the Lord set his love upon you and chose you, for you were the fewest of all peoples; but it is because the Lord loves you, and is keeping the oath which he swore to your fathers" (Deut. VII.7f.). God has bound Himself to Israel of His own free-will, but His action pledges the nation to trust and obedience; God remains the Lord who can visit His people once more with punishment. The prophets waged a stern struggle against the view that God's election bound Him to save His people in any event. Amos puts it clearly and distinctly: "You only have I known of all the families of the earth; therefore I will punish you for all your iniquities" (Am. III.2).

This struggle between two different conceptions of election continued in Judaism, although with the result that in increasing measure the conception that the prophets of the Old Covenant fought for gained the upper hand.

According to the one conception God chose the patriarchs because He loved them and gave the Law out of love for Israel.

One of the oldest prayers surrounding the Shema goes back probably to the New Testament period and runs:

"With great love Thou hast loved us, O Lord, our God; with great and abundant compassion Thou hast dealt leniently with us. . . . Thou hast chosen us out of all peoples and tongues and hast brought us near to Thy great Name."[18]

R. Akiba, who has already been mentioned frequently, said once:

"Beloved are Israel, for to them was given the precious instrument by which the world was created (= the Torah)."[19] Even a single commandment is regarded as the gift of God's love: "Of Thy love, O Lord our God, with which Thou hast loved Israel Thy people and of Thy compassion on the sons of Thy covenant, Thou hast given to us, O Lord our God, this great and holy seventh day in love."[20]

Because of this attitude on God's part towards the fathers

[18] Staerk, *Altjüdische liturgische Gebete*, p. 6.

[19] *M.Ab.*, III.14.

[20] *Tos.Ber.*, III.7, trans. A. Lukyn Williams, London 1921.

and the whole people, He is their Father and Israel His son. The fatherhood of God is not a matter of natural affinity but a matter of historical action on the part of God and not of men; it involves therefore the summons to trust and obedience. The title "Father" was given to God by the Judaism of that time on account of His relationship to the whole people. The linked phrase "Our Father, our King" occurs frequently.[21] Even the "Eighteen Benedictions" only invoke God's relationship to His people, without alluding to any particular worthiness on Israel's part.

Alongside this, however, stands the other conception which signifies precisely the abrogation of any "election." In its extreme, post-New Testament form, it maintains that at Sinai the Law was in fact offered in miraculous fashion to all nations, but that only Israel was willing to accept it, the others having rejected it as they did not wish to desist from their sins.[22] According to this conception God gave all nations the same possibility of becoming the people of the Torah; it was of the nations' free-will that they did not so become; it was of Israel's free-will that they seized the opportunity offered. It was out of love for God's will that Israel accepted the Law; it was out of love for sin that the Gentiles rejected it. It is men's will that divides humanity.

This conception of "election" was also transferred to the patriarchs; this is shown, for example, by the portrayal of Abraham's call in the Book of Jubilees and in Josephus: before his call Abraham perceived the stupidity of idol-worship and turned to the one God.[23] Abraham and the people of Abraham "are" something different from the "nations;" thus IV Ezra can say:

"And I said: O Lord my Lord, out of all the woods of the earth and all the trees thereof Thou hast chosen Thee one

[21] Marmorstein, *The Old Rabbinic Doctrine of God*, VOL. I, pp. 56–61.

[22] *Mekilta Ex.*, XX.2, quoted Strack-Billerbeck, VOL. III, pp. 38–40, where see the other passages and related speculations also quoted. This conception is certainly no later than the middle of the second century A.D.

[23] *Jub.*, XII.1ff.; Josephus, *Antiquities*, I.7, 1 (§§ 154–157); cf. the summing up of Abraham's character in *Antiquities*, I.17 (§ 256): "A man in every virtue supreme, who received from God the due meed of honour for his zeal in His service." Cf. on this point O. Schmitz, "Abraham im Spätjudentum und im Urchristentum" in *Aus Schrift und Geschichte, Theologische Abhandlungen Adolf Schlatter zu seinem 70 Geburtstag*, Stuttgart 1922, pp. 99–123; J. Jeremias, *Th.W.*, VOL. I, pp. 7–9.

vine; out of all the lands of the world Thou hast chosen Thee one planting-ground; out of all the flowers of the world Thou hast chosen Thee one lily; out of all the depths of the sea Thou hast replenished for Thyself one river; out of all the cities that have been built Thou hast sanctified Sion unto Thyself; out of all birds that have been created Thou hast called for Thyself one dove; out of all the cattle that have been formed Thou hast provided Thee one sheep; and out of all the peoples who have become so numerous Thou hast gotten Thee one people. . . ."[24]

This conception of Israel's and the patriarchs' worth sounds throughout the whole of rabbinic literature: the world was created for the sake of Abraham, of the patriarchs, of Moses and of Israel. Thus in one instance God is compared with a king who wished to build a city, but the waters prevented him from finding any foundations, until he discovered a great rock, on which He was able to found it; likewise God was unable to found the world on account of the transgressors and the wickedness of men, until He thought of the fathers; then He said: "Upon these will I found the world."[25]

The change in the concept of election that occurred in the process is shown by two rabbinic parables. The one is supposed to have been told by a scribe to a matron in answer to the assertion that God had proceeded arbitrarily in His election. The rabbi offered her a basket of figs, and she selected the best for eating. Thereupon he said to her: "You know how to select the good figs; should not God know how to do the same? Him in whom He sees good works He chooses." The election therefore has its ultimate basis in the quality of Israel and the patriarchs. Israel was worthy of being chosen, the Gentiles were not. The other parable goes somewhat further: Between Israel and God matters stand as between a king and his spouse. The king wanted to divorce her. Then she pulled a haughty face. He replied that he had scorned other women for her sake and that she was therefore in his debt. She countered by saying that no other woman had wanted him apart from her. In the same way God did not scorn other nations for Israel's sake; no other nation had wanted Him except Israel.[26] God is likewise

[24] IV Ezra, V.23–27.

[25] *Ex.R.*, XV.7 on Ex. XII.1f.

[26] *Num.R.*, III.2 on Num. III.16; *Midr.Lam.*, III.1.

in Israel's debt, not *vice versa*. These parables are not, of course, binding dogmatic pronouncements, but they do show the direction in which the thoughts and feelings of many were tending: the belief, inspired by the Old Testament, that God chose Israel out of unconditional love is overlaid and rendered ineffective by the other view that Israel was chosen because it "is" better than the other nations.

Now it is not the case that these two conceptions of the "election" of Israel would have been recognised with conscious clarity as contradicting one another and mutually exclusive; the decisive thing is precisely that they were held together in a unity full of contradictions. This is clearly shown by the passage from IV Ezra quoted above where in the most varied phraseology it is said that God "chose," "called," "provided," "gotten," but whom?—precisely the nation that contains greater worth than the other nations: the one vine, the one lily, the one dove, the one sheep, the one people. If ever the thought had come alive that Israel had been chosen because of its acceptance of the Torah, then the belief in election would have foundered on the fact of Israel's sin. "We indeed are not worthy to obtain mercy," says IV Ezra in one place, but the writer continues: "but what will He do for His own name whereby we are called?"[27] The idea that God would punish Israel with full severity is inconceivable. Even as a sinful people Israel remains separated from the Gentiles. In one place IV Ezra goes as far as challenging God to weigh the sins of Israel and those of the world's inhabitants against each other.[28] Therefore the judgment upon Israel in the fall of Jerusalem in the year 70 can only be a judgment of purgation; upon the Gentiles, however, a judgment of punishment and destruction will be passed. But the implication here is that Judaism views its own sin differently from that of the nations. This has the effect of rupturing the belief in God; God becomes a partisan of the Jews: "He judges Israel standing; He shortens the trial and makes concessions," but in relation to the Gentiles "He judges sitting, for He prolongs the trial and is rigorous in judgment."[29] II Maccabees puts it in almost classical terms:

"Now I urge those who read this book not to be depressed

[27] IV Ezra, IV.25f. [28] IV Ezra, III.34.
[29] *Gen.R.*, LXXXII.8, quoted Strack-Billerbeck, VOL. I, pp. 288f.

by such calamities, but to recognise that these punishments were designed not to destroy but to discipline our people. In fact, not to let the impious alone for long, but to punish them immediately, is a sign of great kindness. For in the case of the other nations the Lord waits patiently to punish them until they have reached the full measure of their sins; but he does not deal in this way with us, in order that he may not take vengeance on us afterward when our sins have reached their height. Therefore he never withdraws his mercy from us. Though he disciplines us with calamities, he does not forsake his own people." (II Macc. VI.12–16.)

The pronouncements of the prophets to the effect that God remains sovereign in His election and reprobation are unable to exert their full influence. The words of Amos IX.7, "Are you not like the Ethiopians to me, O people of Israel," is interpreted in one instance thus: "The truth is that as the Cushite (i.e. the Ethiopian) is distinguished by his skin, so are Israel distinguished by their ways from all other nations;"[30] the meaning is completely reversed.

It was to this situation that John the Baptist spoke the words:

"Do not presume to say to yourselves, 'We have Abraham as our father;' for I tell you, God is able from these stones to raise up children to Abraham" (Mt. III.9). And in Romans IX.11f. Paul portrays with fundamental clarity the unconditional freedom of God's election: "Though they (i.e. Jacob and Esau) were not yet born and had done nothing either good or bad, in order that God's purpose of election might continue, not because of works but because of his call, she (i.e. Rebecca) was told, 'The elder will serve the younger.' "—Even the very different predestinarian concept of election in the earlier Qumran writings was unable to develop its real potential, as it included hatred towards the non-elect.

World-History and its Goal

The theme of world-history is the antithesis between Israel and the nations. The ungodly nations, whose godlessness is manifest in the non-acceptance of the Torah, oppress and attack the nation which has accepted it. But the world is

[30] *B.T.M.Kat.*, 16b, quoted Strack-Billerbeck, VOL. III, p. 127.

created to be a place where God's will shall be done. The fact that only *one* nation on earth has accepted the Torah signifies that the world and its history only fulfil imperfectly the purpose implicit in them. The fact also that Israel, because it has erred against God's will, has been chastened through subjugation to the "nations," signifies an additional burden. It would be intolerable if it remained thus, for then world-history would ultimately become meaningless. Everything leads one to look for a time when God's will shall be perfectly obeyed and fulfilled throughout the whole world. This is the messianic age.

The Messianic Age [31]

The meaning and content of the messianic age are summed up for the whole of Jewry in the fact that world-history will move on into a period in which evil will be annihilated and God's will shall be fully acknowledged throughout the world.[32] This comprises three things: first, that within the people of God a process of separation will begin, the ungodly will disappear and perish and thus, for a start, God's will shall rule in Israel in justice and purity. The rabbis held that Elijah's task on his return would be to purge the nation of the ungodly and to remove obscurities regarding the proper exegesis of the Law and also regarding the purity of the national character. Secondly, the messianic age would mean that the dispersion of Israel amongst the Gentiles would come to an end, that all twelve tribes would be assembled in Palestine around Jerusalem and, finally, that the people of the Law would no longer be enslaved by the nations who despise God's will, but that they would pay homage to Israel and its God.[33]

Although the general features remain fixed, the conceptions vary greatly in their details. Sometimes the figure of a Messiah is totally lacking, elsewhere the Messiah is One who will vindicate God's rule on this earth with power, and yet other

[31] Cf. on this subject P. Volz, *Die Eschatologie der jüdischen Gemeinde im neutestamentlichen Zeitalter*, henceforth cited as *Eschatologie*, Tübingen 1934; Strack-Billerbeck, VOL. IV, pp. 799–976; H. Gressmann, *Der Messias*, Göttingen 1929.

[32] Sibyll., III.757–761 says of the messianic age: "A common law for men throughout all the earth shall the Eternal perfect in the starry heaven . . . . For He above is God and there is none else. He too shall burn with fire the race of stubborn men."

[33] IV Ezra, XIII.39ff.; *Eighteen Benedictions*, Article 10 (see Appendix); Strack-Billerbeck, VOL. IV, pp. 881f., 902–910; VOL. III, pp. 144ff.

sources have Him as Ruler over mankind at the end of history, after God has Himself destroyed His enemies.

Besides the three things already mentioned: the purging of the wicked in Israel, the return of the Diaspora and the end of the Gentile domination of Israel, it will be a feature of the messianic age that the "evil impulse," the tendency to evil, will be destroyed, the devil and the wicked spirits will lose their power, a new heart of flesh will be given to the people of Israel in line with Ezekiel XXXVI.26 and the Holy Spirit will be poured out; death will be abolished (totally or in part), the curse imposed upon the earth after the Fall will be lifted and the age of paradise will return.[34] Although feelings of revenge, joy in the destruction of the Gentile nations and the ungodly in Israel and national egotism are often enough blended into the pictures of the messianic age, the decisive thing about this period is that it will bring the "rule of God" upon this earth, and that now God's will can and will be done.

Although the conceptions just mentioned remain wholly in the context of this world, the Pseudepigrapha refer in places to a "new world," a new heaven and a new earth, where transience itself will pass away. The Ethiopic Book of Enoch speaks, too, of a "son of man" in terms of a heavenly figure who will be a staff to the pious and a judge of the ungodly (see pp. 80f.).

These two series of pronouncements, the one concerning a messianic kingdom on this curse-free earth and the other concerning a time of salvation in a new order of things, were subsequently linked together, as is first clearly evident in IV Ezra, in such a way that the earthly messianic kingdom is (certainly for those who will experience it) separated as a kingdom of limited duration from a new state of the cosmos after the general resurrection and the great world-judgment.[35] The pharisaic tradition, on the whole, moves in this direction and distinguishes between the "days of the Messiah" and the "world to come." Thus the book of Revelation itself separates the "millennium," in which Christ will reign with His own,

[34] References in Strack-Billerbeck, VOL. IV, pp. 886ff.

[35] *Ps. Sol.*, XVII.44, "Blessed be they that shall be in those days" (i.e. of the Messiah); likewise *Ps. Sol.* XVIII.6. This differs from Paul in I Thess. IV.13ff. and Rev. XX.4; those who have fallen asleep in Christ will be wakened at the coming of Christ.

from the consummation, although it does not give any further details regarding this "reign." Paul's statements in I Thessalonians IV.13ff. and I Corinthians XV.23ff. are identical with Revelation in this respect.[36]

In the earliest picture of the messianic age (Dan. VII) the kingdoms of the world are depicted in terms of beasts of prey and the kingdom of the people of God as a "man" (expressed in Aramaic fashion as a "son of man"). God judges the predatory world-kingdoms and brings to pass the kingdom "of the people of the saints of the Most High" (Dan. VII.27). The power-struggle of world-history ends with this people being given "dominion and glory and kingdom" and "all peoples, nations and languages" serving it; "his dominion is an everlasting dominion, which shall not pass away, and his kingdom one that shall not be destroyed" (Dan. VII.14). In the more or less contemporary vision of animals in the Ethiopic Book of Enoch (see pp. 42f.) the people of God themselves bring about the messianic age with God's help, in that they conquer the alien peoples with the edge of the sword. Subsequently a divine judgment upon men and angels, but especially upon the ungodly in Israel, is awaited and a new temple looms up before the seer's gaze; finally even the Gentiles who experience that age are converted into men who do God's will. The Messiah will be King over the then united humanity, who will no longer know sin.[37] Elsewhere, in writings from the first century B.C. (Psalms of Solomon, Parables of Enoch), it is the Messiah Himself who vanquishes His enemies and rids Israel of the ungodly (see pp. 80f., pp. 159ff.). In IV Ezra reference is made to a messianic dominion lasting four hundred years. After it the world shall be "turned into the primeval silence seven days. . . . And it shall be after seven days that the age which is not yet awake shall be roused, and that which is corruptible shall perish."[38] The day of salvation is described thus: "For to you (i.e. the pious) is opened Paradise, planted the Tree of life, the future Age prepared, plenteousness made ready; a City (i.e. Jerusalem) builded, a Rest appointed; Good works established, wisdom preconstituted; The (evil) root is sealed

[36] Cf. W. Foerster, "Die Bilder in Offenbarung XIIf. und XVIIf." in *Theologische Studien und Kritiken*, CIV (1932), p. 302.

[37] *Enoch*, XC.18–38.

[38] IV Ezra, VII.28f.

up from you, infirmity (i.e. of sin) from your path extinguished; And Death is hidden, Hades fled away; Corruption forgotten, sorrows passed away; and in the end the treasures of immortality are made manifest."[39]

The figure of the Messiah is sometimes missing completely, as for example in the Book of Jubilees, but the Pharisees did not follow this trend; for them a messianic age without a Messiah was unthinkable.

The Date of the Messianic Age[40]

While Jesus said that no one knew of the day and the hour, not even the son (Mk. XIII.32), Judaism at that time tried to calculate the date of the arrival of the messianic age. Even in times prior to the New Testament, two opinions prevailed concurrently, the one that the date was fixed and could be found, the other that it depended upon Israel's attitude to the Law.

Jesus refers to date-calculations in Luke XVII.20: "Being asked by the Pharisees when the kingdom of God was coming, he answered them, 'The kingdom of God is not coming with signs to be observed.'"

The Pseudepigrapha and rabbinic literature both give us a vivid picture of the efforts expended on calculating the date. The earliest ascertainable attempt at such a calculation is Daniel IX.22ff. Jeremiah had spoken of the Babylonian captivity lasting seventy years (Jer. XXV.11; XXIX.10). This prophecy was made to refer to the whole period of Israel's "Dispersion," which would only come to an end in the messianic age. With it a period—seventy years after the destruction of Jerusalem by Nebuchadnezzar—was quoted, at the end of which the time of salvation would begin. Daniel IX, written in about 164 B.C., interprets these seventy years as "weeks of years," consequently as 490 years, and thus entertains the possibility of a reference to its own time. Others proceeded on other assumptions, for example, that the world would last for 6,000 years, corresponding to the six days of God's creation, each of which was like a thousand human years, and this period was divided into two thousand years prior to the

[39] IV Ezra, VIII.52–54.
[40] Strack-Billerbeck, VOL. IV, pp. 977–1015.

Law-giving, two thousand years after it and two thousand years of the messianic age.

Common to these speculations is the fact that the messianic age will be preceded by a period of special trials, the so-called "pangs of the Messiah" (Mk. XIII.8).[41]

The other view was that the coming of the messianic age depended upon the exact fulfilment of the Law on the part of Israel. For servitude to the Gentiles had come upon Israel because it had sinned; desisting from sin would therefore turn away God's wrath. We have seen how the various movements of renewal in Judaism were movements of repentance with the object of uniting the whole nation in conscientious fulfilment of the Law in order that the time of salvation could come. Right into the New Testament period and increasingly so, in fact, as more and more "dates" elapsed without the messianic age arriving, we hear in the most varied phraseology:

"All the predestined dates [for redemption] have passed, and the matter [now] depends only on repentance and good deeds."[42]

A few similar sayings selected at random:

"If Israel repent, they will be redeemed; if not, they will not be redeemed."[43]

"If Israel were to keep two Sabbaths according to the laws thereof, they would be redeemed immediately."[44]

"The Son of David will not come until there are no conceited men in Israel."[45] "Great is repentance, because it brings about redemption."[46] "Great is charity in that it brings the redemption nearer."[47] Paul was right when he spoke of the "hope in the promise made by God to our fathers, to which our twelve tribes hope to attain, as they earnestly worship night and day" (Acts XXVI.6f.).

These conceptions of the onset of the time of salvation can even be conjoined, as in the moving statement that "through our many iniquities all these years (of the messianic era) have been lost."[48] The calculation of the date is correct in itself, but it is Israel's fault if the Messiah is unable to come at the predicted time.

[41] Strack-Billerbeck, VOL. I, p. 950.
[42] *B.T.Sanh.*, 97b.
[43] *B.T.Sanh.*, 97b.
[44] *B.T.Shab.*, 118b.
[45] *B.T.Sanh.*, 98a.
[46] *B.T.Yom*, 86b.
[47] *B.T.B.B.*, 10a.
[48] *B.T.Sanh.*, 97b. (beginning); B.T.A.Zar., 9a.

There are differing views, too, regarding the *duration* of the messianic age. The conjectures vary from forty to two thousand years and more.[49] The Book of Revelation speaks of a kingdom lasting a thousand years (Rev. xx.1–6), but this figure has more of a symbolic meaning, like the figures in it generally.

There is little mention in Jewish writings of an *Antichrist*, a personal, demonic opponent of Christ who will usurp to himself the glory that is due to Christ.[50]

The Messiah

"Messiah" means "The Anointed," and describes the anointed King of the people of God. Besides this frequently used title there was the familiar "Son of David" that goes back to II Samuel VII.12–16. Both titles express the fact that the essential task of the Messiah is to be the King of Israel appointed by God.

The title "Son of God" does not exactly appear to have been given frequently to the Messiah in New Testament times, even though Psalm II, the main Old Testament passage, was at that time understood messianically.[51] Israel means, as we saw above, "God's son," because it has entered into a relationship to God akin to that of the child to its father. Similarly, "Son of God" means for the Messiah just such a relationship to God as should exist between father and son. Although the expression "Son of God" does not occur, Psalm of Solomon XVII.33–37 unfolds what a Jew read out of this expression: "For he shall not put his trust in horse and rider and bow. . . . The Lord Himself is his king, the hope of him that is mighty through (his) hope in God. . . . And he himself (will be) pure from sin, so that he may rule a great people. . . . And (relying) upon his God, throughout his days he will not stumble, for God will make him mighty by means of (His) holy Spirit" (see pp. 142ff.).

That the Messiah would go before His people in justice and holiness, in unwavering trust in God and in mercy: such was the messianic hope of the best men at that time.

[49] Strack-Billerbeck, VOL. III, pp. 823–827.

[50] Cf. W. Bousset, *Der Antichrist*, Göttingen 1895; Strack-Billerbeck, VOL. III, pp. 637–640; Volz, *Eschatologie* (see footnote 31), p. 282; Bousset-Gressmann, *Die Religion des Judentums* (see ch. IV footnote 8), pp. 254–256.

[51] Strack-Billerbeck, VOL. III, pp. 15ff.

Although it is said that the "name of the Messiah" preceded the creation of the world (see p. 185) this does not mean that a real "*pre-existence*" was ascribed to the Messiah; it means rather that, like the patriarchs and Israel, so also the Messiah was conceived in God's mind before the creation of the world. Not to the Messiah but only to the Torah did the rabbis ascribe a rôle in the creation of the world; they would relate John I.3 to the Torah, not to the Messiah.

The fact that the conception of the Messiah's birth in Bethlehem is now only to be found in a few, somewhat late passages in rabbinic literature is connected with the suppression of messianic sayings in the dispute with Christianity.[52]

It is significant that the picture in Daniel of the "son of man" was soon no longer interpreted with reference to the whole people but to the one Messiah. Only a century after Daniel "son of man" was a messianic title. As it is said of him in Daniel VII.13 that he would come with the clouds of heaven, this title lent itself as a means of describing the Messiah not as the earthly king of the time of salvation but as the judge of all nations equipped with supra-mundane power. A heavenly "son of man" was only a late phenomenon in the rabbinic writings, but was then assumed to be familiar.[53] But already in the Parables of Enoch (see pp. 80f.) the "Chosen One of God," the "son of Man," is a heavenly figure who is supposed to judge the nations and to be a "staff for the righteous," a "light of the Gentiles and the hope of those who are troubled of heart"; He is chosen for this end and sojourns, still hidden, with God. It is noteworthy that here phrases from the "Servant Songs" in Deutero-Isaiah are applied to him. To what extent was the language that was used there of the divine servant, in particular Isaiah LIII, interpreted of the Messiah? How far did Judaism at that time expect a suffering Messiah? It has been recently considered probable[54] that Isaiah XLII.1ff. and LII.13ff. were already related to the Messiah in pre-New Testament times, that mention was made of suffering on the part of the Messiah before the final vindication of His rule and

[52] Strack-Billerbeck, VOL. I, pp. 82f.

[53] *B.T.Sanh.*, 98a; cf. Moore, *Judaism*, VOL. II, pp. 334f. and Justin, *Dialogue with Trypho*, XXXII.2.

[54] J. Jeremias in *Th.W.*, VOL. V, pp. 680ff.; cf. also G. Dalman, *Jesaja LIII, das Prophetenwort vom Sühneleiden des Gottesknechtes*, 2nd edn., Leipzig 1914.

that this suffering was thought of as happening for the atonement of Israel's sins. The fact that only traces of these ideas are to be found is connected for one thing with the fact that in its struggle with the growing Christian Church Judaism passed over in silence or interpreted in a non-Christian sense all the passages that could be interpreted with reference to Jesus Christ. Furthermore, however, a suffering Messiah had at that time a place in the circle of Jewish ideas only insofar as, by means of special fidelity to the Law, which also involved the voluntary suffering of "chastisements," he achieved so much atonement or merit that the time of salvation could be delayed no longer. Thus in II Maccabees VII.38 the last of the brothers martyred for his fidelity to the Law says: "[I appeal to God] through me and my brothers to bring to an end the wrath of the Almighty which has justly fallen on our whole nation." And the "Assumption of Moses," written in the New Testament period, hopes fervently for the great turning-point in the time of direst distress as a result of a voluntary death assumed for the sake of the Law by a man from the tribe of Levi named Taxo (= "the one who will set to rights?") and his three sons[55] (see p. 91).

But the hope of a suffering Redeemer did not belong to the conceptions which determined the actions and deeds of the Jewish nation in New Testament times. The idea that the Messiah would be rejected by His own people was entirely unthought of at that time.

In the Judaism of the time the Messiah had significance only for the nation as a whole; He had significance only for world-history and its outcome, rather than for the life-story of the individual.

The Consummation

The earlier Pseudepigrapha had decked out the messianic age, the time of the final consummation, with supra-mundane characteristics; the later Pseudepigrapha, on the other hand—and the rabbis followed them in this respect—separated the "days of the Messiah" from the "world to come" (see p. 37) and ascribed a provisional character to the former. The

[55] *Ass. Mos.*, IX.

pronouncements regarding the time of the consummation are therefore full of contradictions, as earlier and later views clash. On the other hand it is said that the "days of the Messiah" are distinguished from this world only in the fact that Israel's slavery to the Gentiles has ceased.[56] Rabbi Shemuel, the author of this statement accordingly transferred the destruction of the "evil impulse" and the like to the time of the consummation. On the other hand, however, Rabbi Johanan said: "All the prophets prophesied [all the good things] only in respect of the Messianic era; but as for the world to come, 'the eye hath not seen, O Lord, beside thee, what he hath prepared for him that waiteth for him.'" (Is. LXIV.3.)[57]

He therefore expected the destruction of evil and the gift of the Holy Spirit in the messianic age and regarded the state of consummation as beyond the reach of our thought.

For the rabbis, however, the decisive hall-mark of "the world to come" remained always the general resurrection of the dead and the great world-judgment, in which the final, conclusive verdict would be pronounced upon all nations in history and upon all men. Something will be said later regarding the resurrection of the dead; in any event, the time of the consummation is eternal and imperishable. We quote just one expression of the manifold ideas of the rabbis regarding existence in that new world:

"In the future world there is no eating nor drinking nor propagation nor business nor jealousy nor hatred nor competition, but the righteous sit with their crowns on their heads, feasting on the brightness of the divine presence."[58]

For others, the consummation is comprised of preoccupation with the Torah, which God will then teach Himself, and a heavenly banquet. However variously and, as is often the case, in whatever earthly and human terms this age is depicted, the decisive thing is nevertheless the fulfilment of the ancient promise, "they will see God" and "God will dwell with them."

[56] *B.T.Shab.*, 63a; B.T.Pes. 68a.

[57] *B.T.Sanh.*, 99a; Moore, *Judaism*, VOL. II, pp. 378f. On a kind of purgatory see Strack-Billerbeck, VOL. IV, pp. 1043ff.

[58] *B.T.Ber.*, 17a, quoted Strack-Billerbeck, VOL. I, p. 890; more detailed information in Strack-Billerbeck, VOL. IV, Exkurs., 29 and 31.

The Torah and Human Righteousness in the Judgment

Introduction: The Medley of Jewish Statements

As long as we were dealing with Israel and the Gentiles there was no need to enquire more deeply regarding what in fact constituted the Torah and what was the detailed will of God which gave world-history its meaning. For the fact that the possession of the scriptures separated Israel from the Gentiles was plain for all to see. But if we now enquire not after the end of world-history but after the outcome of the life of the individual, and if we think about the great world-judgment which initiates the consummation, then we must enquire about the content of the Torah and the criteria of judgment.

If we do this, we constantly hear antithetical statements which can all be verified in the Judaism of that time. In the midst of all this coming and going stands the figure of Jesus, in danger of being dragged into the whirlpool of contradictory opinions.

In one instance it is said that the content of the Torah, and especially what the scribes have made of it, is a medley of innumerable separate and external commandments and prohibitions, and Jesus is celebrated as a Liberator from the yoke of these dead laws, having singled out as the decisive thing the dual commandment of love for God and love for one's neighbour. But then our attention is drawn to the fact that neither the isolating of this dual commandment nor a single word of, say, the Sermon on the Mount was without its counterpart in contemporary Judaism.

Again, it is said that the Jew at that time strove to pile up for himself a treasury of good works, as he knew nothing of the forgiveness of sins, and as God was for him only the remote and exacting Judge, while Jesus demonstrated the merciful Father-God:—the answer to this is, again, that Judaism was very well acquainted with the forgiveness of sins and God's merciful nature.

Again, it is said that for Judaism only the completed action counted, that in Judaism the intention that produces every action receded entirely into the background and that Jesus was the first to produce a pure ethic of intention:—this is again contradicted, however, by rabbinic sayings, declaring that every action that was not performed "for God's sake" was valueless.

Finally, evidence is adduced for saying that there were scribes who believed themselves to have piled up such a treasury of merits that there was enough left to stand many others in good stead, and it is said that Jesus was the first to make clear the lost state of every man before God, even in the best of lives; but this idea compares with many similar-sounding rabbinic sayings.

In what follows we must illustrate these antithetical views by means of some characteristic *dicta*, remembering that Jesus and the primitive Church lived in fact in the midst of this babel of voices; it is also possible to say to a certain extent where the chief emphasis in the Jewish pronouncements lies. But we must attempt to press forward to a point from which all voices in the Judaism of that time join together into a unity and stand in antithesis to the message of Jesus and the primitive Church.

The Content of the Torah

We shall begin our enquiry into the content of the Torah by casting a glance at the contents of the Talmud.[59]

The Talmud consists of two parts, the earlier part being the so-called Mishnah, and the later part the Gemara. The former received its final shape in about A.D. 200, and the latter three hundred years later. The Gemara is a kind of continuous commentary on the Mishnah. The Talmud is concerned with the exposition of the "Law," and offers the discussions and decisions of the scribes regarding the many problems of expounding and applying the Old Testament precepts, and of their extension by means of the "fence around the Law;" it is sometimes more like a journal of case law than a collection of laws: the most contradictory opinions are often delivered without a decision one way or the other.

The Mishnah, or Talmud, is divided into six orders, and each order into "Tractates," of which there are sixty-three in all. The *first order*, "Seeds," contains the Tractate regarding

[59] Cf. H. L. Strack, *Introduction to Talmud and Midrash*, Philadelphia 1945, translation of *Einleituing im Talmud und Midrasch*, 5th edn. München 1930.

the corner of the field which, according to Leviticus xix.9f., xxiii.22 and Deuteronomy xxiv.19ff., must be left standing for the poor, the Tractates regarding the heave-offering, the first and second tithes, the heave of leaven, etc., and the "minglings" forbidden in Leviticus xix.19 and Deuteronomy xxii.9ff. The *second order*, "Festivals," deals with the sabbath, the Passover, the great Day of Atonement, etc. and also the method of alleviating or even evading the sabbath-commandment in certain cases (cf. p. 172f.). The *third order*, "Women," contains the Tractates regarding levirate marriage (Deut. xxv.5ff.; cf. Mt. xxii.24), betrothal, marriage and divorce (only regarding the bill of divorce and not the grounds for divorce), adultery and the Nazirite and other vows, in accordance with Numbers vi and xxx (cf. Acts xviii.18; xxi.23–27). The *fourth order*, "Injuries," covers the treatment of cases where damage is caused to property (Ex. xxi.18ff.; xxii.5), and deals with things found, buying and selling, loans and the conduct of trials, and especially with the interrogation of witnesses, the death-penalty and flogging, and the avoidance of idolatry; this order also contains the important Tractate "Ethics of the Fathers" which exhibits propositions of well-known scribes. The Tractates of the *fifth order* deal with everything connected with the temple, with sacrificial victims, food-offerings, first-born and offerings for first-born, the daily sacrifice and the dimensions of the temple. Finally, the *sixth order* deals in twelve Tractates with the various questions of purity and impurity. The whole Mishnah is headed by the Tractate *Berakoth*, "Benedictions." It deals, first, with the Shema, the periods, morning and evening, during which it should be recited, the point at which, if one is reciting it while travelling, one may greet others, how the building artisan should say it when at work, and who is exempt from the duty of reciting it (e.g. the next of kin in the few hours between death and burial). The "Eighteen Benedictions" are treated in similar fashion, as well as grace before meat and its form, the question of who is to say it, what is the minimum amount of food over which one is obliged to say it, and other prayers of thanksgiving.

This brief survey of the contents suffices to give a general impression of the departments of life for which the Pharisees attempted unequivocally to determine just how a faithful observer of the Law should behave, by consideration and establishment of every possible case.

Some details which illuminate the content and spirit of the Talmud have been mentioned above (see p. 72), and the evil consequences of all casuistry have already been indicated (see p. 171f.).

Another example may be quoted. We hear of a lament by R. Johanan ben Zakkai (see p. 112f.). It concerns the problem of how far lengths of wood which have been hollowed out are pure or impure: for example, a hollow beam on a pair of scales which has been filled with metal in order to give short weight, or a hollowed-out stick filled with pearls and used for smuggling. R. Johanan complains that this puts him in a predicament; if he refuses to make a decision he is leaving the question of purity and impurity unanswered at one point. He knows and sees that anyone could enquire about purity and impurity with the intention at the same time of using this decision for deceitful ends. It is astonishing that R. Johanan ben Zakkai finds no comfort in the one fact made evident by his and his colleagues' training in the Law, namely that all enquiries regarding purity and impurity are meaningless in respect of instruments used to deceive and of men who wish to deceive.[60]

But now we also find expressions of a high-minded ethic. We saw how the Wisdom Literature attempted, without the aid of separate legal precepts, to permeate daily life with the "fear of the Lord" as the beginning of wisdom. Amongst the Essenes we observed a direct struggle for the *fulfilment of the commandment of love.* And if Jesus equated the lustful glance with adultery, we have already mentioned a similar statement from the Book of Jubilees (see p. 77), and this can be compared with many a statement of the rabbis (see p. 72), e.g., "You must not suppose that only he who has committed the crime with his body is called an adulterer. If he commits adultery with his eyes, he is also called an adulterer,"[61] and "Unchaste imagination is more injurious than the sin itself."[62]

And when the pharisaic scribes asked themselves what the *greatest commandment* was, they certainly named the prohibition

[60] *Tos.B.M.*, VII. 9; Schlatter, *Jochanan ben Zakkai*, p. 30.
[61] *Lev.R.*, XXIII, quoted Strack-Billerbeck, VOL. I, p. 299.
[62] *B.T.Yom.*, 29a, quoted Strack-Billerbeck, VOL. III, p. 373.

of idolatry, meaning—positively speaking—the commandment to worship God alone, as the one thing that outweighed everything else; matters singled out elsewhere as being primary commandments are the honouring of parents, the practice of charity, peacemaking between a man and his friend (cf. Mt. v.9) and the study of the Torah.[63]

At this point we might quote some more rabbinic sayings which give an answer to the query regarding the greatest commandment. A Gentile came on one occasion to Hillel and said he would become a Jew if he could teach him the whole Torah standing on one foot. Hillel said: "What is hateful to you, do not to your neighbour: that is the whole Torah, while the rest is the commentary thereof; go and learn it."[64] One must not overlook two things in this saying which is often quoted as a parallel to Matthew VII.12: first, the negative formulation which marks it off very clearly from Jesus' saying, and, secondly, the fact that the "rest" that is said to be the "commentary" of this chief commandment is not an organic development of the essence of the chief commandment but, in reality, a superimposition of innumerable inorganically juxtaposed commandments which must indeed be "learned" as Hillel says.

A different answer is given by Akiba when he says regarding the commandment to love one's neighbour in Leviticus XIX.18, that it is a great and comprehensive principle of the Torah. Here the "neighbour" means the compatriot, for Ben Assai, a contemporary of Akiba, remarked on his colleague's statement, that there was a greater and more comprehensive principle in Genesis V.1 where the rabbis translate: "When God created man, he made him in the likeness of God." Ben Assai means to say by this that the likeness to God of *all* men, as proclaimed by scripture, is the most comprehensive norm for the attitude of men towards one another.[65]

From a later period (*circa* A.D. 200) two further sayings along these lines have been handed down, one of which declares of

[63] *B.T.Hor.*, 8a, end; B.T.Peah, I.I.

[64] *B.T.Shab.*, 31a, quoted Strack-Billerbeck, VOL. I, p. 357.

[65] *Sifre. Lev.*, XIX.18, quoted Strack-Billerbeck, VOL. I, pp. 357f. Cf. the discussion of the rôle of neighbourly love in the Talmud in *Judaica*, IV (1948), pp. 247ff.; V (1949), pp. 203ff., 241ff.; VI (1950), pp. 290ff. and *Th.W.*, VOL. VI, pp. 310–314 (J. Fichtner); pp. 314–316 (H. Greeven).

Proverbs III.6 ("In all your ways acknowledge him, and he will make straight your paths") that it is the verse on which "hang" all the decisive stipulations of the Torah (cf. Mt. XXII.40: "On these two commandments 'hang' all the law and the prophets" A.V.). The other saying maintains that David brought the 613 commandments and prohibitions of the Law down to eleven (Ps. XV.2–5), Isaiah down to six (Is. XXXIII.15), Micah down to three (Mic. VI.8, justice, love, humility), and Amos down to two (Am. V.4: seek God and live); finally Habakkuk summarised the whole Torah in one commandment: "The righteous shall live by his faithfulness" (Hab. II.4 mg.).[66]

Something more can and must be said. Pharisaism also spoke of demands that were not laid down legalistically, but, as the lovely expression has it, are "known to the heart."

In the Mishnah it is said: "Like as the law against defrauding applies to buying and selling, so does it apply to spoken words. . . . If a man had repented they may not say to him, 'Remember thy former deeds'; if a man was descended from proselytes they may not say to him, 'Remember the deeds of thy fathers'; for it is written, *And a stranger thou shalt not wrong nor shalt thou oppress him*."[67] Commenting on these words, the Gemara says after an explanation: "This is known to the heart only, and of everything known only to the heart it is written, *and thou shalt fear thy God*."[68] The fear of God shows the right way, even when no express law is given.

Furthermore, warnings are often given against putting one's neighbour to shame publicly. Much is said also of the "charitable actions" which, though they are not commanded in the Torah, are highly cherished. Along with the giving of alms mention is also made of showing hospitality (which also plays a great part in the New Testament), visiting the sick and comforting the mourners (cf. Mt. XXV.31–46). Special importance is laid upon not standing upon one's rights towards others and peacemaking between men. There is also the familiar saying of Hillel's: "Be of the disciples of Aaron, loving

[66] *B.T.Ber.*, 63a; *Tanh B. Shophetim* (§ 10), quoted Strack-Billerbeck, VOL. I, p. 907.

[67] *M.B.M.*, IV.10.

[68] *B.T.B.M.*, 58b.

peace and pursuing peace, loving mankind and bringing them nigh to the Torah."[69]

What, then, are we to make of this juxtaposition of two series of pronouncements? We saw that the Hasidim heightened their exegesis of the Law by drawing a fence around it. In the various movements for repentance and reform from Ezra onwards there was a far-reaching preoccupation with individual legal precepts. No fence can be drawn round the commandment: "You shall love the Lord your God . . . and your neighbour as yourself," as it has to do with a whole, and not with a more or less. On the other hand, a fence can be drawn round the command to tithe the fruits of the field, by extending the range of the fruits concerned or the circle of those who are obliged to tithe; a fence can be drawn round the sabbath-commandment by having the sabbath begin *before* sunset or laying down more precisely what falls into the category of "work" forbidden on the sabbath. Thus from the earliest days of the Hasidim stress was laid as a matter of principle upon things that could be regulated externally by means of adding to or subtracting from individual precepts. Moreover it must be said that the only things that grew in importance for the Hasidim were the things that had gained special weight since the Babylonian captivity as being outward marks of distinction from the Gentiles.

The Essene movement attempted to permeate legalistic with moral considerations. With Pharisaism, however, so far as we can see from the slender evidence of its beginnings, a stronger emphasis was laid from the very first upon the "legalistic," which led to the Talmud. But it remains symptomatic not merely of the New Testament period that although Jesus, it is true, singled out the illogicalities of pharisaic casuistry (Mt. xxIII.16–22), we also hear of the scribe for whom the fulfilment of the double commandment to love God and one's neighbour is more than all sacrifices, and to whom Jesus replies: "You are not far from the kingdom of God" (Mk. xII.33f.).

The Jewish scholar, J. Klausner, writes in his book "Jesus of Nazareth":

"The Pharisees and the *Tannaim*—even the earliest of them—did, indeed, 'pile up the measure' of the ceremonial laws, and

[69] *B.T.Shab.*, 127a; *B.T.R.Sh.*, 17a, end; *B.T.B.M.*, 88a, end; *M.Ab.*, I.12.

they so overlaid the inner nucleus with a multiplicity of detail and minutiae as unwittingly to obscure the divine purpose of these laws. This habit Jesus rightly opposes."[70]

Klausner continues: "Thus, his ethical teaching apparently goes far beyond that of *Pirqe Aboth*[71] and of other *Talmudic* and *Midrashic*[72] literature. It is not lost in a sea of legal prescriptions[73] and items of secular information. From among the overwhelming mass accumulated by the Scribes and Pharisees Jesus sought out for himself the 'one pearl.' "[74]

When Klausner nevertheless judges that Jesus' teaching was unacceptable to Judaism, it is because Jesus "fails to see the *national* aspect of the ceremonial laws." "Judaism is not only religion and it is not only ethics: it is the sum-total of all the needs of the nation, placed on a religious basis. It is a national world-outlook with an ethico-religious basis."[75]

The important thing was to allow the Torah to penetrate every area of the nation's life in order to "save the tiny nation, the guardian of great ideals, from sinking into the broad sea of heathen culture and enable it, slowly and gradually, to realise the moral teaching of the Prophets in *civil life* and in the *present world* of the Jewish state and nation."[76]

In many of his utterances Jesus had been more Jewish than the Jews, "yet nothing is more dangerous to national Judaism than this *exaggerated* Judaism . . . Where there is no call for the enactment of laws, for justice, for national statecraft, where belief in God and the practice of an extreme and one-sided ethic is in itself enough—there we have the negation of national life and of the national state."[77]

But however good a nation's legislation may be, it is always somewhat provisional and somewhat fragmentary. No judge can condemn the evil glance as adultery. Likewise every good and pious custom is always external and a hazard—even in the Christian Church! Jesus certainly did not wish to be a "judge or divider" (Lk. XII.14), but He did not say that judges

[70] Klausner, *Jesus of Nazareth*, p. 371.

[71] *Pirqe Aboth* = Sayings of the Fathers, a tractate of the Talmud, see p. 204.

[72] Midrashim are commentaries on the Old Testament.

[73] The German translation used by the author reads "halakhic prescriptions," these being prescriptions regarding correct conduct in different situations.

[74] Klausner, *op. cit.*, p. 390.

[75] Klausner, *op. cit.*, p. 390.

[76] Klausner, *op. cit.*, p. 376.

[77] Klausner, *op. cit.*, p. 374.

should stop their activity. He did not concern Himself with the regulations regarding the tithing of mint and dill and cummin, but did say that one ought to practise justice, mercy and faith, without neglecting the other things, namely tithing (Mt. XXIII.23). He came to "fulfil;" He conveyed the unadulterated will of God not as the sum total of individual demands but by plumbing the depths of his final position in each single point as it arose. He did not set up an ideal: all nations have ideals and they bear a wide similarity to one another. It does not matter whether "in his ethical code there is a sublimity, distinctiveness and originality in form unparalleled in any other Hebrew code," nor whether "the Book of the Ethics of Jesus will be one of the choicest treasures in the literature of Israel for all time,"[78] but whether he had the commission, the authority from God to proclaim the pure, unbroken will of God as the fulfilment of the Law.

In Mark VII.15 Jesus may well have declared all foods "clean," but He would nevertheless have kept the Law and not eaten pork. And the primitive Palestinian Church were certainly conscious of standing in the "law of liberty" (Jas. I.25) but nevertheless preserved their national identity by observing the Law in common with their compatriots.

The motives for Action

The decisive element in every act is the source from which it flows. Jesus did not merely pursue hatred back to the evil word and adultery back to the lustful glance but also expressed the unity of individual acts with the innermost tendency of a man's life by means of the metaphor of the tree and its fruits (Mt. VII.16–19; XII.33). As far as I can see, the metaphor of "fruits" was never employed in this way either in ancient Judaism, nor even in the Qumran writings. What, in the judgment of the rabbis, was the connexion between individual acts and the "being" of man, between the external action and its inner motives?

Already in the first century A.D. the disciples of Shammai and Hillel were arguing whether the evil intention alone rendered man guilty or only the performance of the deed; the disciples of Shammai asserted the first view, the disciples of Hillel the

[78] Klausner, *op. cit.*, p. 414.

second. It was even said later that God counted a good intention for the (completed) action, but not so a wicked intention and it went on in fact to be said that this applied only to Israel and that as far as the Gentiles were concerned God, on the contrary, counted only the completed good actions on the one hand, along with the evil intention on the other;[79] this statement is indicative of how easily God at that time could become a partisan of the Jews. But these statements, which can be compared with many similar ones, are not binding and can be contrasted with others of the opposite kind.

We shall come across a passage later (see pp. 220f.) according to which God, through the redemption of Israel from Egypt, has a claim upon the total obedience of the nation: the Old Testament story involves a *spiritual obligation* to fulfil God's will. Johanan ben Zakkai said that man was created to fulfil God's will, and ought not to claim credit for obeying the Torah. But even in the second century B.C. we hear: "Be not like slaves that minister to the master for the sake of receiving a bounty; but be like slaves that minister to the master not for the sake of receiving a bounty,"[80] and it was later said with reference to Deuteronomy XI.13, "to love the Lord your God," that these words were there in order that "you should not say: See, I will study the Torah in order that I may become rich and be called 'Rabbi' (cf. Mt. XXIII.8) and receive a reward; therefore Scripture instructs us 'to love the Lord your God.' Everything that you do should be done only for love."[81]

By New Testament times the pharisaic scribes were already drawing a distinction between the deeds done from fear (of God) and from love (to God),[82] and the aged Akiba rejoices that with his martyr's death for the sake of the Law he can fulfil the injunction "You shall *love* the Lord your God with all your heart." Mentioned amongst the various and mainly unattractive types of Pharisees that are listed here and there are the Pharisees from fear and from love, and the latter is

[79] *Mekilta Ex.*, XXII.8; *J.T.Peah*, I.16a, 5, quoted Strack-Billerbeck, VOL. I, p. 206.

[80] *P.Ab.*, II.8, I.3

[81] *Sifre Deut.*, § 41 on Deut., XI.13, quoted Strack-Billerbeck, VOL. I, p. 918 top; similarly *Sifre Deut.*, § 48 on Deut., XI.22, and *B.T.Ned.*, 62a. quoted Strack-Billerbeck, VOL. I, 917f.

[82] R. Sander, *Furcht und Liebe im palästinischen Judentum*, Stuttgart 1935.

depicted either as of the highest rank of Pharisaism or as the only genuine Pharisee, beloved of God.[83]

But a determining motive for all action is also presented when, instead of the fear of God being contrasted with love to God, it is mentioned as the only factor which imparts to all actions their genuine worth. "It is all one whether a man offers much or little (in sacrificial offerings to the temple), if only he directs his mind towards Heaven."[84] And a later statement runs:

"When a man is led (i.e. by God, see p. 183) for judgment (in the next world) he is asked, Did you deal faithfully (i.e. with integrity), did you fix times for learning?. . . Yet even so, if '*the fear of the Lord is his treasure*,' it is well: if not, [it is] not [well]," i.e. without the fear of God all good deeds are worthless.[85]

Alongside the fear of God and love towards Him other motives are mentioned which have the effect of excluding the thought of reward. In this respect the phrase, to do the commandments "for heaven's sake" (i.e. for God's sake; see p. 183) or "for the sake of the Torah" ought to be mentioned. II Corinthians II.15f. is recalled in the saying:

"Whosoever occupies himself with the Torah for its own sake his learning becomes an elixir of life to him. . . . But, whosoever occupies himself with the Torah not for its own sake, it becomes to him a deadly poison."[86] There is also the ancient saying: "Let all thy deeds be done for the sake of heaven."[87]

Another motive that is even more likely to lead to a deepened conception of conduct arises when one asks whether an action serves to "hallow the Name" (i.e. of God) or not. There can be a genuine enquiry after God's will which is not restricted to learning what is written in the Law but seeks to clarify God's will independently. It mainly concerns consideration for the judgment of non-Jews who draw conclusions from the conduct

[83] *J.T.Sot.*, v.20d, Sander, *op. cit.*, p. 78; A. Büchler, *Studies in Sin and Atonement in the Rabbinic Literature of the First Century*, henceforth cited as *Studies in Sin and Atonement*, (Jewish College Publications, Nos. 7 and 11), Oxford/London 1928, p. 148, notes 1 and 2.

[84] *M.Men.*, XIII.11, quoted Strack-Billerbeck, VOL. II, p. 46 top.

[85] *B.T.Shab.*, 31a, towards the end, quoted Strack-Billerbeck, VOL. I, p. 235.

[86] *B.T.Taan.*, 7a, quoted Strack-Billerbeck, VOL. III, p. 498 top.

[87] *M.Ab.*, II.12.

of a Jew regarding his God. In this way the moral judgment can be sharpened, but is in fact often bound up with bad casuistry.

We have already come across an example of this above (p. 73). Yet another might be mentioned: Rabbi Ishmael, a contemporary of Akiba, was accustomed, whenever a Gentile and a Jew had a dispute and appealed to him for arbitration, to decide on one occasion according to Gentile, on another occasion according to Jewish law, depending upon whichever was more favourable to the Jewish party. Akiba condemned this behaviour of his colleague, because the "Name" (of God) would be profaned in the process.[88] Does that imply, however, that Rabbi Ishmael's action was condemned as being wrong in itself or only on account of its consequences?

The hallowing of the Name played a part in connexion with yet another serious event. After the terrible war of A.D. 132–135 the practice of the Jewish religion was forbidden. The question then arose for the scribes as pastors and leaders of the people whether one must observe *all* parts of the Torah under all circumstances, even under pain of death. The martyrs of the Maccabean period laid down their lives for refusing to eat pork; now, however, Rabbi Ishmael (just mentioned) put forward the view that a Jew might even practise idolatry, if by so doing he could save his life, though only as long as the public learned nothing about it; if they did actually hear of it, then the Name was profaned. The other rabbis decided that if a Jew was compelled, under pain of death, to do any act forbidden by the Law, then he could do it with the exception of idolatry, unchastity and murder. Others later opined that one must observe even the least commandment at the risk of one's life, and there were yet others who distinguished between public and secret actions.[89] There are, of course, "ethical" commandments which should be observed in all circumstances, but why is the commandment "You shall not lie" not amongst them?

This point of view regarding the "hallowing of the Name" sheds no unequivocal light upon the goal of behaviour.

Finally we can also mention as a deeply penetrating motive

[88] *B.T.B.K.*, 113a.

[89] *B.T.Sanh.*, 74a, quoted Strack-Billerbeck, VOL. I, pp. 221f.; Schlatter, *Geschichte Israels*, p. 379 and note 384; Strack-Billerbeck, VOL. I, pp. 222f.

the imitation of God: "Just as God is called the Merciful and Gracious One, so you must also be merciful and gracious."[90]

If we put alongside it the phrase mentioned earlier regarding the things "known to the heart" (see p. 207), we see that Pharisaism was striving at that time to avoid becoming swamped in the requirements of a plethora of external commandments in order to assert motives of a profoundly penetrating character. Yet we have also seen that these had no power to act as the leaven of all behaviour in penetrating, moulding and organising the multiplicity of commandments and prohibitions.

The rabbis did at any rate distinguish between legal statutes which, if they had not been written in the Pentateuch, would have had to be written there—referring to the commandments regarding idolatry, fornication, the shedding of blood, robbery and blasphemy of the Name—and "decrees," to which the Gentiles could make objection, such as the prohibition of pork-eating, etc.[91] Johanan ben Zakkai once said that neither did a dead body make a man "unclean" nor did water used to complete "purification" make a man clean, but God had given a commandment and man was not competent to overstep it.[92] This implies that the laws of purity and impurity had no discernible meaning in themselves; one could only take cognisance of them and keep them. The *content* of the commandment did not speak to the heart and did not attest itself there as God's commandment; the intellect laid down in smallest detail what was commanded and memory firmly retained it—that was the task of the "scribes"—and the will of man said its "yea" to this commandment which not only came from without but also *remained* alien to the heart.

With His words, "he who is forgiven little loves little" (Lk. VII.47) Jesus hinted that the deepest spring from which the fulfilment of the central commandment of love flows is the forgiveness of sins. Paul appeals to the Christians in Rome: "Be transformed by the renewal of your mind, that you may prove what is the will of God, what is good and acceptable and perfect" (Rom. XII.2; c Phil. I.9–11). Here one cannot

[90] *Sifre Deut.* §49 on Deut. XI.22, quoted Strack-Billerbeck, VOL. I, p. 372, where see further references.

[91] *Sifre Lev.*, XVIII.4, quoted Strack-Billerbeck, VOL. III, pp. 36f.

[92] *Pes. K.*, 40a; Schlatter, *Jochanan ben Zakkai*, p. 42.

learn by heart what God's will is, but the renewed mind can reach a verdict upon it and love can test it.

The Practicability of God's Will

Can man fulfil God's will? We intend to answer this question by proceeding from the difference that was made to humanity and the world by Adam's fall according to the Judaism of that time. According to one speculation, akin to the tradition of the six pre-existent things described above (see p. 185), the following *seven things* were created or conceived before the creation of the world: the Throne of Glory, the Torah, repentance, the Garden of Eden, Gehenna, the Temple and the name of the Messiah.[93] If the statement quoted earlier regarding the pre-existent things was orientated upon the course of world-history, this other speculation is directed towards the fate of the individual, towards paradise and hell as the eternal destinations of the righteous and of sinners. It is remarkable, however, that in this connexion even repentance is mentioned as being conceived before the creation of the world. Whether or not God created the world with the two dimensions of judgment and of mercy, or prepared the means of repentance for men even before the creation of the world, they both signify the same thing, namely, that sin was written into the course of world-history from the very beginning. Instead of being the great disturber, an actuality that in every single case is incomprehensible and enigmatic to its very core, the final reason, in fact, why the shape of the world is not as it should be, sin is now something unavoidable, for which a means of salvation has been created from the very beginning.

Repentance means the condemnation of a wrong action and the resolve of the will henceforth to avoid the sin committed. Correspondingly atonement must be rendered in full by everyone; even this depends upon the free decision of man.[94]

A further conception points in the same direction, that of the two "impulses" in man.[95] There are two impulses in man, the

[93] *B.T.Pes.*, 54a; *B.T.Ned.*, 39b, Tannaitic tradition.

[94] Cf. E. K. Dietrich, *Die Umkehr* (*Bekehrung und Busse*) *im Alten Testament und im Judentum*, Stuttgart 1936; E. Sjöberg, *Gott und die Sünder im palästinischen Judentum*, Stuttgart 1938, pp. 9–11, and ch. 14.

[95] F. C. Porter, "The Yecer Hara" in *Biblical and Semitic Studies* (Yale Bicentennial Publications 16), New York 1901; Strack-Billerbeck, VOL. IV, pp. 466–483.

good and the evil. By the latter is meant the natural striving for survival and for activity in the widest sense of the word, a striving which, if unbridled and uncontrolled, becomes sin. Now it was already declared in pre-New Testament times that man *was created with both impulses*.[96] It follows from this, therefore, that although Adam's fall certainly caused his expulsion from paradise and brought death upon him and his posterity, Adam before his fall was fundamentally no different from his posterity after the fall.[97] Man had free-will both before and after. The "evil impulse" was, it is true, strengthened by the fall, but the Law and the possibility of repentance were available to man. Akiba's aphorism that "freedom," the free choice between good and evil, was given to humanity,[98] was a principle that Pharisaism never surrendered.

We are here confronted with a simple, transparent and rounded picture of the world: God created humanity with its sinfulness and provided it from the very beginning with the Torah and "repentance" as the means of salvation for the totally inevitable fall. Paradise is destined as of right for the nation which has accepted the Torah and for the man who shoulders it and "turns again" to it after every fall, while hell is destined equally as of right for the nations which have rejected the Torah and for the Israelites who cast off its yoke. Adam's fall was not something fundamental: he transgressed "one only observance,"[99] one that was in no way different from a hundred other possible commandments.

This total conception is also matched by the picture of *Satan's power and activity* that we gain from the rabbinic writings.[100] There he sometimes personifies the seductive power of the evil impulse, with which he is occasionally identified, sometimes he is the prosecutor, before God's throne (cf. Rev. XII.10) and the angel of death.[101] No comprehensive and

[96] *Test Asher*, I.3; Sir. XV.14 (cf. in addition, Moore, *Judaism*, VOL. I, p. 481, note 5) and *Sifre Deut.*, § 45 on Deut. XI.18, "My sons, I created for you the evil impulse; I created for you the Law as an antiseptic"—translation by Moore, *op. cit.*, VOL. I, p. 481.

[97] Moore, *op. cit.*, VOL. I, p. 479, "[Adam] was not conceived (by Judaism) as being mentally and morally otherwise constituted than his posterity."

[98] *M.Ab.*, III.15.

[99] IV Ezra, III.7.

[100] W. Foerster in *Th.W.*, VOL. II, pp. 74–78, VOL. VII, pp. 151–156.

[101] *B.T.B.B.*, 16a, quoted Strack-Billerbeck, VOL. I, p. 139, under No. 3.

fundamental significance is ascribed to him, however; he is as it were a symbol for various factual insights.

This series of conceptions is now cut across by other ideas, which are expressed mainly in the pseudepigrapha, but find an echo in the rabbinic writings. According to these ideas, the time of consummation is separated from the present age by a gulf. Mention is made, although rarely amongst the rabbis, of a new heaven and a new earth; we hear that the evil impulse will then be destroyed and the devil will meet his end.[102] This implies that Adam was not immediately created with the "evil impulse" and that Satan had first gained an effective position in creation which was all-embracing, inimical to God, and seductive of men. The pseudepigrapha especially deal fully with the story of the fall and see in it, and even more in the fall of the "sons of God" (Gen. VI. 1ff.) the invasion into human history of forces inimical to God (see pp. 43; 76f.). IV Ezra movingly voices the complaint:

"O thou Adam, what hast thou done! For though it was thou that sinned, the fall was not thine alone, but ours also who are thy descendants! For how does it profit us that the eternal age is promised to us, whereas we have done the works that bring death?"[103] and:

"When Adam transgressed my statutes, then that which had been made was judged, and then the ways of this world became narrow and sorrowful and painful, and full of perils coupled with great toils. But the ways of the future world are broad and safe, and yield the fruit of immortality."[104] But the basic assumption that man, with perhaps the co-operation of divine grace, creates good or evil of his own free-will, is not overturned. The angel replies to the complaint in IV Ezra:

"This is the condition of the contest which (every) man who is born upon earth must wage; that, if he be overcome, he shall suffer as thou hast said: but if he be victorious, he shall receive what I have said. For this is the way of which Moses, while he was alive, spoke unto the people, saying: 'Choose thee life, that thou mayst live!' Nevertheless they believed not him, nor the prophets after him, not yet me who have spoken unto them.

[102] IV Ezra, VII. 30: After the days of the Messiah the world shall be "turned into the primeval silence seven days, like as at the first beginnings"; further references in Strack-Billerbeck, VOL. III, pp. 840ff.; VOL. IV, p. 882.

[103] IV Ezra, VII. 118f.

[104] IV Ezra, VII. 11f.

Therefore shall there be not such grief at their perdition, as there shall be joy over the salvation of those who have believed."[105]

In the New Testament period itself we can see a deep-going struggle around the question of the Law's practicability; although rabbinism gradually overlaid these questionings more and more and allowed them to recede into the background, they never completely died out.

Merit and Forgiveness: God's Justice and His Mercy

Who is righteous? The man who does what the Torah demands. It is at once clear that the various conceptions of the will of God also determine the righteousness of man. In the earlier writings the difference between the righteous and the sinner lay not in the fact that the former was sinless and wholly fulfilled what the Law prescribed but in the fact that he constantly returned to it in penitence (see p. 158).

But by the New Testament period Judaism had taken a further step and the man was declared "righteous" in whom the fulfilments of the commandment outweighed the transgressions. In a conversation between Rabbi Akiba and Rabbi Gamaliel II the former developed this view:

"When Rabbi Gamaliel read this verse (Ezek. XVIII.5–9) he wept, saying, 'Only he who does all these things shall live, but not merely one of them!' Thereupon Rabbi Akiba said to him, '*If* so, *Defile not yourselves in all these things* (Lev. XVIII.24)—is the prohibition against *all* [combined] only, but not against one?' [Surely not!] But it means, *in one* of these things; so here too, for doing one of these things [shall he live]."[106] A later account of this conversation adds: "A man who does any of the good things of which it is written *He that doeth these things shall never be moved*, yea, does any one at all of them—it is as though he had done all of them. Thereupon Rabban Gamaliel said to R. Akiba: 'Thou hast comforted me, Akiba, thou hast comforted me.'"[107]

Just as *one* transgression renders a man "unclean," so *one* fulfilment of the commandment makes him righteous. The

[105] IV Ezra, VII.127ff.

[106] *B.T.Sanh.*, 81a.

[107] *Midr. Ps.*, XV, § 7, trans. W. G. Braude, 2 vols., New Haven 1959, VOL. I, p. 195; quoted Strack-Billerbeck, VOL. IV, p. 22.

latter must therefore be a source of merit. We are here confronted with what is basically a system of accounts, in which the fulfilments of the commandment are written on the credit side and the transgressions on the debit side. Even the schools of Hillel and Shammai argued over the eternal destiny of the "intermediates;"[108] by the "intermediates" were meant the men in whom the merits and the faults were equally balanced. In quiet contradiction to the whole conception James says: "For whoever keeps the whole law but fails in *one point* has become guilty of all of it" (Jas. II.10).

We do not here need to portray the whole system in detail according to which, so it was believed, the human account was conducted. Briefly, it can be said that on the "credit side" was entered the keeping of the commandments,[109] "acts of charity" and similar works of supererogation, the study of the Torah, etc.; on the debit side were entered the transgressions of the commandments which had actually occurred. Now there were various means of reducing the debit account, viz. the sacrificial cult in the temple, above all the great Day of Atonement (see p. 154), sufferings and particularly "repentance." Many held that the merits of the fathers were also written on the credit side, and occasionally even those of righteous men alive at the time. Frequent mention is made of sufferings and "chastisements"; the ancient problem of why it often fares so well with the ungodly upon earth and so badly with the righteous is frequently answered in these terms: God punishes the righteous for their few sins while they are still here on earth, in order subsequently, in the world beyond, to pay them their reward for innumerable good deeds without deduction; He rewards the ungodly, on the other hand, for their few good deeds here, in order one day to cast them utterly into hell.[110] This doctrine of retribution taught

[108] *B.T.R.Sh.*, 16b, quoted Strack-Billerbeck, VOL. IV, p. 1024f.; *Tos. Sanh.*, XIII.3, quoted Strack-Billerbeck, VOL. IV, p. 1178

[109] *M.Makk.*, III.16, quoted Strack-Billerbeck, VOL. IV, p. 6 under c, "The Holy One . . . was minded to grant merit to Israel; therefore hath he multiplied for them the Law and commandments."

[110] In *B. T. Kidd.*, 40b, R. Eleazar ben Zadok (*ca* A.D. 100) explains with a parable how God "brings suffering upon the righteous in this world in order that they may inherit the future world," and "makes (the wicked) prosper in this world, in order to destroy and consign them to the nethermost rung." Further examples in W. Wichmann, *Die Leidenstheologie*, Stuttgart 1930, pp. 51ff.

the pious in times of need and persecution to shoulder all sufferings, even death, joyfully as evidence of the gracious visitation of God, but it also shows how far-reachingly the deeds of men were viewed only in their isolation.

When two rabbis were being led to execution during the great period of persecution under Hadrian, one of them was grieved because he did not know why he had deserved this death. The other asked him whether, in his life as a scribe, when approached on any question for advice and decision, he had not refrained from answering until he had drained his goblet, put on his sandals or wrapped himself in his mantle. If such had been the case, then he had "afflicted" his questioner and Exodus XXII.22f. applied to him. Then the other answered: "Thou hast comforted me."[111]

But this whole series of views is not the only thing that must be mentioned in this connexion. At no point do the Eighteen Benedictions speak of the merits of Israel or of the supplicant, but appeal to God's forgiveness. The relationship between Israel and God is conceived of in terms of Luke XVII.10.

"Why, at every performance of a Commandment, must we have *the Exodus* in our thoughts? (e.g. Num. XV.37–41).[112] Here is a parable: It can be likened unto a king whose friend's son was taken prisoner. The king redeemed him, but expressly on the understanding that he should become his slave, so that at any time, if he should disobey the king, the latter could say: 'Thou art my slave!'. . . . So when the Holy one (blessed be His Name) redeemed the descendants (the seed) of Abraham, his beloved (friend), he did not redeem them with the view that they should be [His] sons, but [His] slaves, in order that when He commands and they do not obey, He could say to them: 'Ye are my slaves!'"[113] This means that God, through His saving deeds towards Israel, has an unconditional claim upon the obedience of the nation. There is no question of merit in this connexion. From Johanan ben Zakkai comes the saying: "If thou hast wrought much in the Law, claim not merit for thyself, for to this end wast thou created."[114]

[111] *Mekilta Ex.*, XXII.22.

[112] In Mk. IV.30 a parable is introduced with a similar rhetorical question.

[113] *Sifre Num.*, XV.41, § 115, quoted Strack-Billerbeck, VOL. IV, p. 488 under c.

[114] *M.Ab.*, II.8. Cf. the following passage from *Sifre Deut.*, § 26 on Deut. III.23: "Israel had two good leaders, Moses and David: they could have had their own

Man is committed in obedience to his Creator, and Israel to its Redeemer; this is expressed with the same clarity as the statement that fulfilments of the commandment are the basis of merit.

This quality is matched by a similar one in the conception of God: God has two "measures" with which He "measures"[115] the world, the measure of judgment and the measure of mercy. It is absolutely decisive for an understanding of Judaism that it cannot let go of the divine compassion.[116] The Eighteen Benedictions appeal only to God's mercy. The love of God applies especially to His people, and His mercy is evident in the fact that He does not impute sins to the man who "repents" but forgives them. Exodus xxxiv.6f is quoted in the ancient Jewish commentaries and prayers with the omission of the continuation: "[He] will by no means clear the guilty, visiting the iniquity of the fathers. . . ," so that only God's mercy is mentioned.[117] The "measure of grace" that comes from God is greater than the "measure of retribution."[118]

Akiba once said: "The world is judged by grace, yet all is according to the excess of works [that be good or evil]."[119] There the two "measures" are linked together. But how are they related? In the fact that they limit one another. This is clear from a parable intended to explain how God could have created the world:

"This may be compared to a king who had some empty glasses. Said the king: 'If I pour hot water into them, they will burst; if cold, they will contract [and snap]!' What then did the king do? He mixed hot and cold water and poured it into

---

sins cancelled through their good deeds, but they asked God that He should give them [forgiveness] only by grace gratuitously. One conclusion can be drawn from this: if even these, who could have counterbalanced their transgressions with their good works, could ask God to forgive them by grace gratuitously, how much more so should he who is not even one of the least disciples"—translation based upon C. G. Montefiore and H. Loewe, *A Rabbinic Anthology*, London 1938, p. 234 [620]. On the whole question cf. A. Marmorstein, *The Doctrine of Merits in Old Rabbinical Literature*, London 1920, and Büchler, *Studies in Sin and Atonement* (see footnote 83).

115 Cf. Mt. vii.2; "measure" = judge.

116 E. Sjöberg, *Gott und die Sünder im Palästinischen Judentum* (see footnote 94), makes this point emphatically.

117 G. Kittel, *Sifre* (see ch. iii, footnote 12), p. 130, note 1.

118 Sjöberg, *op. cit.*, pp. 10f.

119 *M.Ab.*, iii.16.

them, and so they remained [unbroken]. Even so, said the Holy one, blessed be He: 'If I create the world on the basis of mercy alone, its sins will be great; on the basis of judgment alone, the world cannot exist. Hence I will create it on the basis of judgment and of mercy, and may it then stand.'"[120]

Just as hot and cold mixed together produce something tolerable, so God's grace and righteousness together result in something on which the world and men can survive. But the mixing of righteousness and mercy does not give rise to a unified whole. The question remains as to *when* God goes over from the "measure of judgment" to the "measure of mercy." "For we know not how we are to meet our Maker, whether He be wroth with us, or be merciful and intend to pity and receive us."[121] Thus a great uncertainty remains; from the assumption that all Israelites will be saved with the exception of a few utterly great sinners from whom Abraham removes the sign of circumcision before letting them go to hell,[122] to the lament of IV Ezra that the future world has been created only for the few,[123] we hear every note ranging from arrogant pride to deepest despair.

"When Rabbi Johanan ben Zakkai fell ill, his disciples went in to visit him. When he saw them he began to weep. His disciples said to him: Lamp of Israel, pillar of the right hand,[124] mighty hammer! Wherefore weepest thou? He replied: If I were being taken today before a human king who is here today and tomorrow in the grave, whose anger if he is angry with me does not last for ever, who if he imprisons me does not imprison me for ever and who if he puts me to death does not put me to everlasting death, and whom I can persuade with words and bribe with money, even so I would weep. Now that I am being taken before the supreme King of kings, the Holy One, blessed be He, who lives and endures for ever and ever, whose anger, if He is angry with me, is an everlasting anger, who if He imprisons me imprisons me for ever, who if He puts me to death puts me to death for ever, and whom I

[120] *Gen.R.*, XII.15, on Gen.II.4.

[121] *The Books of Adam and Eve*, Apocalypsis Mosis, XXXI.

[122] *Gen.R.*, XLVIII, quoted Strack-Billerbeck, VOL. IV, p. 1066 under c; Justin Martyr, *Dialogue with Trypho*, CXL.2.

[123] IV Ezra, VIII.1.

[124] Cf. Gal. II.9; "James and Cephas and John, who were reputed to be pillars."

cannot persuade with words or bribe with money—nay more, when there are two ways before me, one leading to Paradise and the other to Gehinnom, and I do not know by which I shall be taken, shall I not weep?"[125]

On the other hand Simeon ben Jochai said of himself towards the middle of the second century A.D.:

"I am able to exempt the whole world from judgment from the day that I was born until now (through my merits), and were Eliezer, my son, to be with me [we could exempt it] from the day of the creation of the world to the present time, and were Jotham the son of Uzziah with us (II Chron. XXVII.1–6), [we could exempt it] from the creation of the world to its final end."[126]

Any survey of the Judaism of those days, in its struggle for the Law and for its understanding and fulfilment, ought not to be based upon isolated pronouncements. Even if it is clear that the emphasis lies upon an external conception of the Law, upon an idea of election that acts as a dangerous soporific, upon a rounded view of all that happens in the world that looks for salvation from the pious man's achievements, it is nevertheless characteristic that this range of ideas is just as little able to win unequivocal acceptance as the other which sees as the distinguishing mark of world-history and the history of the individual a breach that only God can heal. Rather did Judaism vacillate between these two general outlooks without committing itself consistently to either.

Conclusion: Judaism and the New Testament

Jesus appeared on the scene with the message: "Repent, for the kingdom of heaven is at hand" (Mt. IV.17). Measured against the ideas of contemporary Judaism regarding the coming of the messianic age, and even against most of the Old Testament sayings, this message offered no clue to what its basis might be. Jesus may well have seen in John the Baptist the returning Elijah promised in Malachi IV.5f. (Mt. XI.10), but one cannot say that he turned "the hearts of fathers to their children and the hearts of children to their fathers,"

[125] *B.T.Ber.*, 28b, quoted Strack-Billerbeck, VOL. IV, p. 1034 under e.

[126] *B.T.Sukk.*, 45b; parallels in Büchler, *Studies in Sin and Atonement*, p. 187, footnote 3.

as it says there, let alone that he purged the nation of the ungodly or removed obscurities regarding the blood-purity of certain families, as the Jews anticipated (see p. 193). And Jesus' own appearance was different from the picture that the nation had formed of the coming of the Messiah, even from the Old Testament; He came neither to save Israel from the hand of its enemies (Lk. I.71ff.), nor in order to destroy the ungodly in Israel, nor even as a king over Israel. "Flesh and blood," i.e. human philosophising, could not have taught Peter to see the Messiah in Rabbi Jesus of Nazareth, and hardly had the secret of His Person been revealed to him than Peter's flesh and blood opposed the way of suffering that lay before this Messiah. Jesus' confession before the Sanhedrin led to His condemnation as a blasphemer against God. And after the first Easter Day His Church appeared on the scene with the message that now were the last times of which the prophets had spoken and to the present day it must put up with the reproach already implicit in II Peter III.4 and expressed more recently in the following words: "The Jews cannot concede that the prophetic promises regarding the character of the final age have been fulfilled—neither in the literal nor in the metaphorical sense . . . they sense at bottom the irredeemability of the world."[127]

Let us set the appearance of Jesus of Nazareth and the activity of the primitive Church in the light of what we have been saying about contemporary Judaism. Throughout the whole of the New Testament God is the God of the Old Testament, the "Lord of heaven and earth" (Mt. XI.25), the "God of Abraham, and the God of Isaac, and the God of Jacob" (Mk. XII.26). It is the promise to Abraham, embracing the Gentile world, whose fulfilment Jesus sees drawing near in the centurion at Capernaum (Mt. VIII.11); Paul is able to do his work amongst the Gentiles only in order that through it the Gentiles will, in the faith of Abraham, become sons of Abraham (Gal. III.6f.) and be grafted as wild olive branches into the noble olive tree of Israel (Rom. XI.17). Jesus repulses the tempter with words from the Book of Deuteronomy (Mt. IV.4, 7, 10); He sees His own path traced out in the scriptures (Mt. XXVI.54); He prays on the Cross in the words of Psalm

[127] H. J. Schoeps in *Th.L.Z.*, LXXIX (1954), p. 74.

XXII; Paul, Peter, James and John were steeped in the writings of the Old Testament.

But Jesus heard God's voice out of the Old Testament differently from the scribes who sought painfully and with exegetical ingenuity to excogitate answers to their questions from the Old Testament. He lived in the world of the Old Testament like a son in his father's house. John records Him as saying sternly that all who came before Him were thieves and robbers (Jn. x.8). He alone is the true Guide, even for an understanding of the Old Testament. Thus He pits His "but I say to you" against the Old Testament commandment, not in order to abrogate the Law, but to fulfil it, and Paul says expressly that his Gospel "upholds" the Law (Rom. III.31). Jesus in no way taught the nation to throw overboard the Law that separated it from the Gentiles, although He did show them what the pure will of God was. The primitive Jewish-Christian Church did not feel itself authorised to put away the Law of their nation, although it felt obliged to speak of the law of liberty, the royal law of love (Jas. I.25; II.8).

Similar to His attitude to the Old Testament was the attitude that Jesus adopted to the development of the Old Testament ideas that we pursued in Part I. He affirms the resurrection of the dead, but for Him it is a new state in which there is no marriage nor giving in marriage (Mk. XII.25); for Him also the reign of God is the final goal of all history, but its content is not idle enjoyment but fresh service of God (Mt. XXV.21, 23) and complete fellowship with Him; like the rabbis and the Pseudepigrapha He speaks of Satan and his activity as prosecutor, seducer and destroyer of life, but for Him Satan is the strong man whom only the stronger One can conquer, and whose accusations before God are ended by his fall from heaven (Mk. III.27; Lk. x.18; Jn. XII.31; Rev. XII.7ff.). The fundamental concepts of Judaism receive a new significance from Him.

Jesus puts an end to all questions regarding the motives for action and their value through the metaphor of the tree and its fruits (Mt. VII.16ff.; XII.33ff.). Along the same lines Paul says that God judges the hidden purposes of the heart (I Cor. IV.5), and James says that fresh water and brackish cannot flow from the *same* spring at the same time (Jas. III.11f.).

Can man fulfil God's will? "You, who are evil. . . ." says Jesus without any reservation (Mt. VII.11), and Paul sees the goal of the Law as understood by Christ in the fact that "every mouth may be stopped, and the whole world may be held accountable to God" (Rom. III.19). The source, the motive from which the action flows, is destroyed.

Yet although all men, Pharisees and "sinners," stand before God equally as debtors who cannot pay their debt, however much it may vary in amount (Lk. VII.41f.), the Father goes out to meet His lost sons (both of them!—Lk. XV.20, 28) in Jesus Christ. Thus the kingdom of God is brought near.

"Repentance," one of the central concepts in Judaism, is not, as it is there, the human ability, conceived at the creation of the world, to turn away, in face of the weakness of the human race, from individual wicked actions which have overtaken man; it is rather the fundamental turning away from one's own ways to salvation in Christ. When the Holy Spirit was poured out at Pentecost, so that men proclaimed this salvation, the period characterised by the absence of prophecy and the emphasis on scribal learning came to an end and the last times, heralding the full manifestation of God's reign, dawned.

God's righteousness is wielded without partiality over Jews and Gentiles alike. The whole world, with or without the Law (Rom. II.12), is equally guilty before God. But God fulfils the promise made to Abraham in a wonderful fashion by offering salvation first to the physical sons of Abraham through the mission, the Cross and the Resurrection of His Son in such a way that, while every human claim on the part of Israel is destroyed, they are able to grasp the salvation in faith. The same salvation in the same faith is also offered to the Gentiles so that Abraham's blessing is bestowed upon them, and Jews and Gentiles are welded into *one* community in thankful praise of the grace of God (Rom. XV.8–12). Thus the joy over the judgment upon Gentiles and ungodly men which we found so widespread in Judaism falls away of its own accord; but Judaism's final object of hope—that God would dwell amongst His community—now emerges with undiminished brilliance as the object of God's ways with mankind.

No exposition of the Old Testament ever discovered this

way of God with Israel and the Gentiles; but the Son heard the voice of His Father in the Old Testament pointing out the way he was to tread to the Cross itself, and His disciples learnt after the first Easter Day to interpret the Old Testament as directed towards Jesus Christ and alluding to him as its fulfilment.

The New Testament and coeval Judaism are not separated from each other by individual ideas in the former, of which there are frequent intimations and more or less close approximations in the latter; but in the last analysis quite simply by the attitude towards Jesus himself, the King of the people of God.

APPENDIX

The Eighteen Benedictions

Note: The version which follows is the so-called Palestinian Recension based upon the original text as reconstructed by G. Dalman in *Messianische Texte*, published as an Appendix to *Die Worte Jesu*, Leipzig 1898. The prayer against the Nazarenes (see p. 114), which was only inserted *circa* A.D. 80, is therefore missing. The translation is based upon that by C. W. Dugmore in *The Influence of the Synagogue upon the Divine Office*, Oxford 1944, pp. 115–124.

1. Blessed art Thou, O Lord, God of Abraham, God of Isaac and God of Jacob, God Most High, who art the Possessor (Creator) of heaven and earth, our Shield and the Shield of our fathers. Blessed art Thou, O Lord, the Shield of Abraham!

2. Thou art mighty, strong, that livest for ever, that raisest the dead, that sustainest the living, that quickenest the dead. Blessed art Thou, O Lord, who quickenest the dead!

3. Holy art Thou and Thy Name is to be feared, and there is no God beside Thee. Blessed art Thou, O Lord, the holy God!

4. O favour us, our Father, with knowledge from Thyself and understanding and discernment from Thy Torah. Blessed art Thou, O Lord, who vouchsafest knowledge!

5. Cause us to return, O Lord, unto Thee, and let us return anew (in repentance) in our days as in the former time. Blessed art Thou, O Lord, who delightest in repentance!

6. Forgive us, our Father, for we have sinned against Thee; blot out and cause our transgressions to pass from before Thine eyes. Blessed art Thou, O Lord, who dost abundantly forgive!

7. Look upon our afflictions and plead our cause, and redeem us for the sake of Thy Name. Blessed art Thou, O Lord, the Redeemer of Israel!

8. Heal us, O Lord our God, from the pain of our heart, and cause Thou to rise up healing for our wounds. Blessed art

Thou, O Lord, who healest the sick of Thy (His) people Israel!

9. Bless for us, O Lord our God, this year and satisfy the world from the treasuries of Thy goodness. Blessed art Thou, O Lord, who blessest the years!

10. Blow the great horn for our liberation and lift a banner to gather our exiles. Blessed art Thou, O Lord, who gatherest the dispersed of Thy (His) people Israel!

11. Restore our judges as at the first, and our counsellors as at the beginning; and reign Thou over us, Thou alone. Blessed art Thou, O Lord, who lovest judgment!

12. For apostates let there be no hope, and the dominion of arrogance (= Rome) do Thou speedily root out. Blessed art Thou, O Lord, who humblest the arrogant!

13. Towards the righteous proselytes may Thy tender mercies be stirred, and bestow a good reward upon us together with those that do Thy will. Blessed art Thou, O Lord, the trust of the righteous!

14. Be merciful, O Lord our God, towards Jerusalem, Thy City, and towards Zion, the abiding place of Thy glory, and towards the kingdom of the house of David, Thy righteous anointed one. Blessed art Thou, O Lord, God of David, the Builder of Jerusalem!

15. Hear, O Lord our God, the sound of our prayer, for a God gracious and merciful art Thou. Blessed art Thou, O Lord, who hearest prayer!

16. Accept (us), O Lord our God, and dwell in Zion; and may Thy servants serve Thee in Jerusalem. Blessed art Thou, O Lord, whom in reverent fear we serve!

17. We give thanks to Thee, who art the Lord our God, for all the good things, the steadfast love which Thou hast shown to us. Blessed art Thou, O Lord, unto whom it is good to give thanks!

18. Bestow Thy peace upon Israel Thy people and bless us, all of us together. Blessed art Thou, O Lord, who makest peace!

BIBLIOGRAPHY

A. English Translations of Sources Quoted

Note: Where no English translation of any source quoted exists, e.g. The Jerusalem Talmud, translations have as far as possible been made from or checked against the original text.

Apocrypha, The: Revised Standard Version.

Dead Sea Scriptures:

Complete Translations:

T. H. Gaster, *The Scriptures of the Dead Sea Sect*, London 1957.

A. Dupont-Sommer, *The Essene Writings from Qumran*, trans. G. Vermes, Oxford 1961.

Selections:

M. Burrows, *The Dead Sea Scrolls*, London 1956.

—— *More Light on the Dead Sea Scrolls*, London 1958 (includes important fragments from Caves I and IV).

Josephus, *Works*, tr. H. St. J. Thackeray, Loeb Classical Library, 9 vols., London 1926 *et seq.* (only 7 vols. have so far been published; accordingly from *Jewish Antiquities*, XV, onwards the translation of W. Whiston, London n.d. has been quoted). The paragraph references in brackets are those of the Greek text, ed. B. Niese (see Bibliography under B).

Midrash Rabbah, edd. H. Freedman and M. Simon, Soncino edn., 10 vols. London 1939.

Mishnah, trans. H. Danby, Oxford 1933.

Philo of Alexandria, *Works*, trans. F. H. Colson and G. H. Whitaker, Loeb Classical Library, 10 vols., London 1939. (vol. 10 containing the *Embassy to Gaius* [*Legatio ad Gaium*] has not yet been published; accordingly, the quotations from this work have been translated directly from the Greek text [see Bibliography under B]).

Pseudepigrapha, The: English translation ed. R. H. Charles. *Apocrypha and Pseudepigrapha of the Old Testament*, vol. II. Oxford 1913. Reprint, 1963. *A Rabbinic Anthology*, edd. C. G. Montefiore and H. Loewe, London 1938.

Talmud, The Babylonian, ed. I. Epstein. Soncino edn. 34 vols. plus index vol., London 1935–52.

B. Original Texts

The Apocrypha of the Old Testament are contained in the edition of the LXX by A. Rahlfs, 3rd edn., Stuttgart 1949. As well as the traditional Apocrypha it includes the text of III and IV Maccabees and the Psalms of Solomon.

Texts of the so-called "Pseudepigrapha" (so far as they have been preserved in Hebrew, Greek or Latin versions) as follows:—

Letter of Aristeas: *Aristeae ad Philocratum epistula*, ed. P. Wendland, Leipzig 1900.

Sybilline Oracles: *Die Oracula Sibyllina*, ed. J. Geffken, Leipzig 1902.

Book of Enoch: the extant Greek fragments in J. Fleming and L. Radermacher, *Das Buch Henoch*, Leipzig 1901; more recently discovered fragments in C. Bonner, *The Last Chapters of Enoch in Greek* (Studies and Documents, VIII), London 1937, pp. 32–106.

Assumption of Moses: *Die Himmelfahrt des Mose*, ed. C. Clemen (Kleine Texte für theologische und philologische Vorlesungen und Übungen 10), Bonn 1904, reprinted 1924.

IV Ezra: *Die Esra-Apokalypse* I, ed. B. Violet, Leipzig 1910; also the Latin version, ed. R. L. Bensley (Texts and Studies, III.2), Cambridge 1895.

III Baruch: "Apocalypsis Baruchi tertia graece" in *Apocrypha Anecdota*, Second Series, ed. M. R. James (Texts and Studies, V.1), Cambridge 1897.

Testaments of the Twelve Patriarchs: *The Greek Versions of the Testaments of the Twelve Patriarchs*, ed. R. H. Charles, Oxford 1908.

Books of Adam and Eve: Greek version in C. Tischendorf, *Apocalypses Apocryphae*, Leipzig 1866, under the title "Apocalypsis Mosis"; Latin version ed. W. Meyer in *Abhandlungen der Münchner Akademie der Wissenschaften*, philos.-philol. Kl., XIV, 1878.

Damascus Document: *Die Damaskusschrift* revised edn. by L. Rost (Kleine Texte für theologische und philologische Vorlesungen und Übungen 167), Berlin 1933; C. Rabin, *The Zadokite Documents*, 2nd edn., Oxford 1958.

III Enoch: *III Enoch; or, the Hebrew Book of Enoch*, ed. and tr. by H. Odeberg, Cambridge 1928.

Dead Sea Texts: M. Burrows, *The Dead Sea Scrolls of St. Mark's Monastery*, New Haven, VOL. I, 1950, VOL. II, 1951; E. L. Sukenik, *The Dead Sea Scrolls of the Hebrew University*, Jerusalem 1955; D. Barthélémy and J. T. Milik, Qumran Cave I, Oxford 1955.

Rabbinic Writings: for text editions, translations and other matters see H. L. Strack, *Introduction to Talmud and Midrash*, Philadelphia 1945.

Josephus: *Flavii Josephi Opera*, ed. B. Niese, 6 vols., Berlin 1888–95.

Philo of Alexandria: *Philonis Alexandrini Opera*, edd. L. Cohn and P. Wendland, 6 vols., Berlin 1896–1906.

C. Works of Reference and Modern Literature

1. *On the history of the New Testament times generally*

BULTMANN, R. *Primitive Christianity in its Contemporary Setting*. Trans. R. H. Fuller, London 1956.

FELTEN, I. *Neutestamentliche Zeitgeschichte*, 2 vols, 2nd. edn., Regensburg 1925.

PFEIFFER, R. H. *History of New Testament Times*, New York 1949.

PREISKER, H. *Neutestamentliche Zeitgeschichte*, Berlin 1937.

SCHNEIDER, C. *Einführung in die Neutestamentliche Zeitgeschichte*, Leipzig 1934.

STAERK, W. *Neutestamentliche Zeitgeschichte*, 2 vols. 2nd. edn., Berlin 1912 (Sammlung Göschen 325, 326).

WENDLAND, P. *Die hellenistisch-römische Kultur*, 2nd. and 3rd. edns., Tübingen 1912.

2. *On Palestinian Judaism at the time of Jesus and the Apostles*

BARON, S. W. *A Social and Religious History of the Jews*, VOLS. I–III, 3rd edn., New York 1958.

KITTEL, G. *Die Probleme des palästinischen Spätjudentums und das Urchristentum*, Stuttgart 1926.

KLAUSNER, J. *Jesus of Nazareth: His Life, Times and Teaching*. Trans. from Hebrew by H. Danby, London 1925. Book II, "The Period", pp. 129–228.

LAGRANGE, M.-J. *Le Judaisme avant Jésus Christ*, Paris 1931.

LEVISON, N. *The Jewish Background of Christianity*, Edinburgh 1932.

SCHÜRER, E. *Geschichte des jüdischen Volkes im Zeitalter Jesu Christi*. 3rd and 4th edns. 3 Vols. and Index, Leipzig 1901–11 (dated but indispensable). [English translation of 2nd German edn., *History of the Jewish People in the Time of Jesus Christ*. Trans. J. Macpherson, S. Taylor and P. Christie. Edinburgh 1900–01 (out of date and therefore not quoted in the text)].

3. *On the Sources*

BENTZEN, A. *Introduction to the Old Testament*, 2nd edn., 5th reprint, Copenhagen 1959.

CHARLES, R. H. *Apocrypha and Pseudepigrapha of the Old Testament*, 2 vols., Oxford 1913 (Introductions to the several books).

EISSFELDT, O. *Einleitung in das Alte Testament*, 2nd edn., Tübingen 1956.

HEMPEL, J. *Die althebräische Literatur und ihr hellenistisch-jüdisches Nachleben*, Potsdam 1930.

KAUTZSCH, E. *Die Apokryphen und Pseudepigraphen des Alten Testaments*. 2 Vols., Tübingen 1900, reprinted 1921 (Introductions to the several books).

PFEIFFER, R. H. *History of New Testament Times. With an Introduction to the Apocrypha*, New York 1949.

SELLIN, E., & ROST, L. *Einleitung in das Alte Testament*, 8th edn., Heidelberg 1950. [English Translation, *Introduction to the Old Testament*. Trans. W. Montgomery. London 1923.]

STÄHLIN, O. "Die hellenistisch-jüdische Literatur" (Off-print from W. von Christ [ed]. *Geschichte der griechischen Literatur*, VOL. II, Part I, pp. 535-656), München 1920.

VOLZ, P. *Die Eschatologie der jüdischen Gemeinde im neutestamentlichen Zeitalter*, Tübingen 1934 (Introductory section).

WIESER, A. *Einleitung in das Alte Testament*, 4th edn., Göttingen 1957.

(Cf., in addition, the introductory sections in the works by W. Bousset and H. Gressmann, and G. F. Moore cited in 6 below. For literature on the Dead Sea Texts see ch. IV, footnote 10).

4. *On Part I: The Historical Situation*

ABEL, F.-M. *Histoire de la Palestine depuis la conquête d'Alexandre jusqu'à l'invasion arabe*, 2 Vols., Paris 1952. VOL. I, "De la conquête d'Alexandre jusqu'à la guerre juive."

EHRLICH, L. *Geschichte Israels*, Berlin 1958 (continues up to A.D. 70).

KITTEL, R. *Geschichte des Volkes Israel*, 3 Vols., Stuttgart 1923–29. VOL. III 1–2 (continues up to the end of the Persian period).

MEYER, E. *Ursprung und Anfänge des Christentums*, 3 Vols., Stuttgart and Berlin 1921–23. VOL. II, "Die Entwicklung des Judentums und Jesus von Nazareth."

NOTH, M. *The History of Israel*. Revised translation by P. R. Ackroyd of 2nd edn. of *Geschichte Israels*, London 1960 (continues up to A.D. 70).

OESTERLEY, W. O. E., & ROBINSON, T. H. *A History of Israel*, 2 Vols., Oxford 1932. VOL. II, "From the Fall of Jerusalem, 586 B.C., to the Bar-Kokhba Revolt, A.D. 135."

SCHLATTER, A. *Geschichte Israels von Alexander dem Grossen bis Hadrian*. 3rd edn., Stuttgart 1925.

SELLIN, E. *Geschichte des israelitisch-jüdischen Volkes*. VOL. II, Leipzig 1932 (continues up to the end of the Persian period).

WELLHAUSEN, J. *Israelitische und jüdische Geschichte*. 8th edn., Berlin and Leipzig 1921 (continues up to A.D. 70).

5. *On Part II: Palestine at the Time of Jesus*

ABEL, F.-M. *Géographie de la Palestine*, Paris, VOL. I, 1933, VOL. II, 1938.

DALMAN, G. *Arbeit und Sitte in Palästina*, 7 Vols., Gütersloh 1923–41.

GRANT, F. C. *The Economic Background of the Gospels*, Oxford 1926.

JEREMIAS, J. *Jerusalem zur Zeit Jesu*, Leipzig and Göttingen, VOL. I, 1923, VOL. IIA, 1924, VOL. IIB, 1937 (2nd edn. of VOLS. I and II, Göttingen 1958).

6. *On Part III: The Religious Situation*

BONSIRVEN, J. (S. J.). *Le judaisme palestinien aux temps de Jésus-Christ, sa théologie*, 2 Vols., Paris 1935.

BOUSSET, J. *Die Religion des Judentums im späthellenistischen Zeitalter*, 3rd edn., ed. H. Gressmann, Tübingen 1926 (gives a distorted picture of Judaism through the one-sided use of the Pseudepigrapha).

MOORE, G. F. *Judaism in the First Centuries of the Christian Era, the Age of the Tannaim*. 3 Vols., Cambridge, Mass. 1927–30. Index 1940 (very valuable).

SCHLATTER, A. *Die Theologie des Judentums nach dem Bericht des Josephus*, Gütersloh 1932.

STEWART, R. A. *Rabbinic Theology*, Edinburgh 1960.

WEBER, F. *Jüdische Theologie auf Grund des Talmud und verwandter Schriften*, 2nd edn. Leipzig 1897 (contains a great deal of material, but with no indication of its dates).

7. *Bibliographical Works*

FINKELSTEIN, L. *The Pharisees*. VOL. II, 3rd edn., Philadelphia 1946, pp. 711–751.

MARCUS, R. "A Selected Bibliography (1920–45) of the Jews in the Hellenistic-Roman Period," in *Proceedings of the American Academy for Jewish Research*, XVI (1946–47), New York 1947, pp. 97–181.

PFEIFFER, R. H. *History of New Testament Times*, New York 1949, pp. 531–541.

THOMSEN, P. *Die Palästinaliteratur*, VOLS. I–VI, Leipzig 1907–54.

(Good bibliographical data in the following two works in course of publication: *Die Religion in Geschichte und Gegenwart*, 3rd edn., Tübingen 1957, *et seq. Evangelisches Kirchenlexikon*, Göttingen 1956 *et. seq.*)

Index of Scripture Passages

A. Old Testament

B. Apocrypha *

* In agreement with the original, see general index for references to inter-testamental literature, other than that here listed.

C. New Testament

General Index